6

Wide Angle

KRISTIN DONNALLEY SHERMAN
FRANCES WATKINS

OXFORD
UNIVERSITY PRESS

198 Madison Avenue
New York, NY 10016 USA

Great Clarendon Street, Oxford, OX2 6DP,
United Kingdom

Oxford University Press is a department of the University of Oxford. It furthers
the University's objective of excellence in research, scholarship, and education by
publishing worldwide. Oxford is a registered trade mark of Oxford University Press
in the UK and in certain other countries

ISBN: 978 0 19 452859 7   Wide Angle American 6 SB W/OP PK
ISBN: 978 0 19 452835 1   Wide Angle American 6 SB
ISBN: 978 0 19 454668 3   Wide Angle American 6 OP & SRC

Printed in China

This book is printed on paper from certified and well-managed sources

ACKNOWLEDGEMENTS

Back cover photograph: Oxford University Press building/David Fisher

Illustrations by: 5W Infographics p. 43; A. Richard Allen/Morgan Gaynin Inc
p. 17; Stuart Bradford pp. 92; Martin Hargreaves/Illustration Web p. 126; John
Holcroft/Lindgren & Smith p.136; Sam Kalda/Folio Illustration Agency p. 68; Shaw
Nielsen pp. 13, 25, 37, 49, 61, 73, 85, 97, 109, 121, 133, 145.

Video Stills: Mannic Productions: pp. 12, 24, 36, 48, 60, 72, 84, 96, 108, 120, 132, 144.

*The Publishers would like to thank the following for their kind permission to reproduce
photographs and other copyright material:* **123rf:** pp. 55 (beard trimmer/Paul Grecaud),
122 (office colleagues/Dmitriy Shironosov), 148 (lifting weights/langstrup);
Alamy: pp. 7 (Haring shop/Matt Smith), (Keith Haring's artwork/LorenzoP),
40-41 (animal chase/Stock Connection Blue), 52 (banana fabric/Chris Willson), (Hagfish/
Brandon Cole Marine Photography), 53 (Hagfish slime/PJF Military Collection), 55 (coffee
machine/Jane Campbell), (Echo/JIRAROJ PRADITCHAROENKUL), 60 (Matisse painting/Artepics),
98 (arguement/Dmitriy Shironosov), 100 (young chess prodigy/Carolyn Jenkins), 105 (cooking
class Italy/Bruce yuanyue Bi), 107 (campers/veryan dale), 112 (tornado/Shotshop GmbH), 118
(overturned truck/Jim Nicholson), 125 (animal trainer/H. Mark Weidman Photography), 146
(students/Olena Kachmar); **Blink:** Cover, Quinn Ryan Mattingly, pp. 3 (pottery/Quinn
Ryan Mattingly), 7 (musician/Edu Bayer), 15 (man on rock/Quinn Ryan Mattingly),
21 (book store/Gianni Cipriano), 27 (woman walking field/Krisanne Johnson), 30
(barber/Edu Bayer), 39 (boy wreckage/Quinn Ryan Mattingly), 44 (man smelling
scallions/Edu Bayer), 51 (jeweler/Gianni Cipriano), 57 (man in shop/Edu Bayer), 63
(people on speakers/ Edu Bayer), 69 (man identity theft/Gianni Cipriano), 75 (man in
bath/Edu Bayer), 81 (architecture employee/Quinn Ryan Mattingly), 87 (walking up
wall/Krisanne Johnson), 95 (woman on horse/Krisanne Johnson), 99 (man in field/
Edu Bayer), 111 (sinking ship/Nadia Shira Cohen), 116 (tech conference/ Edu Bayer),
123 (boat passenger/Edu Bayer), 131 (young people/Krisanne Johnson), 135 (mother and child/
Krisanne Johnson), 143 (typewriter /Nadia Shira Cohen); **Getty:** pp. 4 (street art/Handout),
10 (woman in headphones/valentinrussanov), 14 (Biomuseum/Ixefra), 31 (expert/
Hero Images), 33 (Scottish female/Plume Creative), (teen hugging parent/Terry Vine),
35 (Cairo street/Edwin Remsberg), 40 (anmal fight/Aditya Singh), 47 (robot woman/
Bloomberg), 50 (helpful/David Leahy), (household chores/Uwe Krejci), 55 (SAD light/
Rocky89), (straightener/ImagesBazaar), 66 (man carrying wood/Tiko Aramyan),
70 (safety deposit boxes from Hatton Garden Heist/Hatton Garden Properties Limited), 76
(playing piano/MoMo Productions), 79 (Mahatma Gandhi/Dinodia Photos), (Usain Bolt/Heinz
Kluetmeier), (Wangari Maathai /Charley Gallay/Stringer), 88 (Chang Hye Jin gold medal/Quinn
Rooney), (parent pushing their child on a swing/paul mansfield photography), (woman eating
chocolate cake /Robert Daly), 93 (car being towed/Bobby Bank), 98 (sports team/NCAA Photos),
(work colleagues/Hero Images), 100 (Blake Leeper/BEN STANSALL/Stringer), (Lang lang/Lester
Cohen), 102 (Supergirl tv still/CBS Photo Archive), 105 (elephant refuge/Jenny Jones), (hikers/
Aleksander Rubtsov), (yoga/Science Photo Library), 110 (robotic rehabilitation/BSIP), (surgical
robot/3alexd), 112 (volcano/Ingólfur Bjargmundsson), 122 (doctor and patient/Hinterhaus
Productions), 138 (taking photo of baby/Alija), 140 (selfie/verity jane smith), 142 (lost job/
WillSelarep), 148 (graduation/Steve Debenport), 149 (urban street/Toshi Sasaki); **iStock:**
pp. xvi, (phone/lvcandy), (tablet/RekaReka), 38 (fun office/vgajic), 106 (Using laptop/skynesher);
OUP: pp. 16 (Night Without End/Oxford University Press), (Stories about Stories/
Oxford University Press), (The Hound of the Baskervilles/Oxford University Press),
(The Oxford Book of Science Fiction stories/Oxford University Press),
22 (Great Expectations /Oxford University Press); **REX:** pp. 79 (Malala Yousafzai/Andy Rain/
Epa/REX/Shutterstock), 102 (Spiderman movie still/Snap Stills/REX/Shutterstock);
Shutterstock: pp. 22 (reading/greenaperture), 52 (banana plant stem/Santhosh
Varghese), (coconuts/Solodovnik), (milk/PPPS), (pineapple/jipatafoto89), 55 (cake
mixer/Dmitry_Evs), 56 (food blender/gcafotografia), 58 (3d printing/guteksk7),
(prosthetic limb/Photo Oz), 62 (smartphone/Rashevskyi Viacheslav), 64 (lights of
a police car/schmidt13), 76 (engaging teacher/DGLimages), (top of moutain/Olga
Danylenko), (viewing art/WAYHOME studio), 77 (lightbulb graphic/ art4all),
82 (happy man/Ozgur Coskun), 88 (yoga/rdonar), 112 (fire/Nico Jacobs), 142 (applying
for job online/Rawpixel.com), 148 (dry lake/ssbooklet), (stubborn/Mark Umbrella),
149 (quiet urban street/Pierdelune).

Authentic Content Provided by Oxford Reference

The publisher is grateful to those who have given permission to use the following extracts and adaptations of copyright material:

p.6 adapted from "Street Art and Graffiti." In *Encyclopedia of Aesthetics*, edited by Michael Kelly. Oxford University Press, 2014. http://www.oxfordreference.com/view/10.1093/acref/9780199747108.001.0001/acref-9780199747108-e-692

p.26 adapted from "Kafka, Franz." In *The Oxford Companion to Fairy Tales*, edited by Jack Zipes. Oxford University Press, 2015. http://www.oxfordreference.com/view/10.1093/acref/9780199689828.001.0001/acref-9780199689828-e-405

p.28 adapted from "Behavioral Economics." In *The Oxford Encyclopedia of American Business, Labor, and Economic History*, edited by Melvyn Dubofsky. Oxford University Press, 2013. http://www.oxfordreference.com/view/10.1093/acref/9780199738816.001.0001/acref-9780199738816-e-43

p.46 adapted from "artificial intelligence." In *Encyclopedia of Semiotics*, edited by Paul Bouissac. Oxford University Press, 1998. http://www.oxfordreference.com/view/10.1093/acref/9780195120905.001.0001/acref-9780195120905-e-24

p.58 adapted from "3D printing." In *New Oxford American Dictionary* Oxford University Press, 2010. http://www.oxfordreference.com/view/10.1093/acref/9780195392883.001.0001/m_en_us1444263

p.62 adapted from "innovation." In *A Dictionary of Marketing*, edited by Charles Doyle. Oxford University Press, 2016. http://www.oxfordreference.com/view/10.1093/acref/9780198736424.001.0001/acref-9780198736424-e-0901

p.67 adapted from "fraud." In *A Dictionary of Law Enforcement*, edited by Graham Gooch and Michael Williams. Oxford University Press, 2015 http://www.oxfordreference.com/view/10.1093/acref/9780191758256.001.0001/acref-9780191758256-e-1350

p.67 adapted from "identity theft." In *A Dictionary of the Internet*, edited by Darrel Ince. Oxford University Press, 2013. http://www.oxfordreference.com/view/10.1093/acref/9780191744150.001.0001/acref-9780191744150-e-1592

p.80 adapted from "Carter, Jimmy." In *The Oxford Companion to United States History*, edited by Paul S. Boyer. Oxford University Press, 2001. http://www.oxfordreference.com/view/10.1093/acref/9780195082098.001.0001/acref-9780195082098-e-0251

p.88 adapted from "happiness." In *The Oxford Companion to Philosophy*, edited by Ted Honderich. Oxford University Press, 2005. http://www.oxfordreference.com/view/10.1093/acref/9780199264797.001.0001/acref-9780199264797-e-1070

p.101 adapted from "psychology of music." In *The Oxford Companion to Music*, edited by Alison Latham. Oxford University Press, 2011. http://www.oxfordreference.com/view/10.1093/acref/9780199579037.001.0001/acref-9780199579037-e-5404

p.105 adapted from "What doesn't KILL you makes you stronger." In *Oxford Dictionary of Proverbs*, edited by Jennifer Speake. Oxford University Press, 2015. http://www.oxfordreference.com/view/10.1093/acref/9780198734901.001.0001/acref-9780198734901-e-2545

p.114 adapted from "news." In *A Dictionary of Journalism*, edited by Tony Harcup. Oxford University Press, 2014. http://www.oxfordreference.com/view/10.1093/acref/9780199646241.001.0001/acref-9780199646241-e-891

p.128 adapted from "Dante Alighieri." In *Oxford Dictionary of Scientific Quotations*, edited by W. F. Bynum and Roy Porter. Oxford University Press, 2006. http://www.oxfordreference.com/view/10.1093/acref/9780198614432.001.0001/q-author-00007-00000333

p.128 adapted from "Confucius." In *Oxford Essential Quotations*, edited by Susan Ratcliffe. Oxford University Press, 2016. http://www.oxfordreference.com/view/10.1093/acref/9780191826719.001.0001/q-oro-ed4-00003204

p.128 adapted from "Mark Twain." In *Oxford Essential Quotations*, edited by Susan Ratcliffe. Oxford University Press, 2016. http://www.oxfordreference.com/view/10.1093/acref/9780191826719.001.0001/q-oro-ed4-00011053

p.128 adapted from "Hippocrates." In *Oxford Essential Quotations*, edited by Susan Ratcliffe. Oxford University Press, 2016. http://www.oxfordreference.com/view/10.1093/acref/9780191826719.001.0001/q-oro-ed4-00005454

p.128 adapted from "Colette." In *Oxford Essential Quotations*, edited by Susan Ratcliffe. Oxford University Press, 2016. http://www.oxfordreference.com/view/10.1093/acref/9780191826719.001.0001/q-oro-ed4-00003167

p.128 adapted from "Jonathan Swift." In *Oxford Essential Quotations*, edited by Susan Ratcliffe. Oxford University Press, 2016. http://www.oxfordreference.com/view/10.1093/acref/9780191826719.001.0001/q-oro-ed4-00010553

p.134 adapted from "Negotiation." In *The Oxford Companion to American Law*, edited by Kermit L. Hall. Oxford University Press, 2002. http://www.oxfordreference.com/view/10.1093/acref/9780195088786.001.0001/acref-9780195088786-e-0643

p.138 adapted from "Advertising." In *Oxford Encyclopedia of the Modern World*, edited by Peter N. Stearns. Oxford University Press, 2008. http://www.oxfordreference.com/view/10.1093/acref/9780195176322.001.0001/acref-9780195176322-e-12

p.147 adapted from "Creativity." In *Oxford Essential Quotations*, edited by Susan Ratcliffe. Oxford University Press, 2016. http://www.oxfordreference.com/view/10.1093/acref/9780191826719.001.0001/q-oro-ed4-00003345

p.148 adapted from "J. W. Eagan." In *Oxford Essential Quotations*, edited by Susan Ratcliffe. Oxford University Press, 2016. http://www.oxfordreference.com/view/10.1093/acref/9780191826719.001.0001/q-oro-ed4-00012220

p.149 adapted from "FIRST thoughts are best." In *Oxford Dictionary of Proverbs*, edited by Jennifer Speake. Oxford University Press, 2015. http://www.oxfordreference.com/view/10.1093/acref/9780198734901.001.0001/acref-9780198734901-e-799

p.149 adapted from "He who HESITATES is lost." In *Oxford Dictionary of Proverbs*, edited by Jennifer Speake. Oxford University Press, 2015. http://www.oxfordreference.com/view/10.1093/acref/9780198734901.001.0001/acref-9780198734901-e-1054

p.150 adapted from "Alvin Toffler." In *Oxford Essential Quotations*, edited by Susan Ratcliffe. Oxford University Press, 2016. http://www.oxfordreference.com/view/10.1093/acref/9780191826719.001.0001/q-oro-ed4-00010964

p.151 adapted from "John Wooden." In *Oxford Essential Quotations*, edited by Susan Ratcliffe. Oxford University Press, 2016. http://www.oxfordreference.com/view/10.1093/acref/9780191826719.001.0001/q-oro-ed4-00016691

p.152 adapted from "The LEOPARD does not change his spots." In *Oxford Dictionary of Proverbs*, edited by Jennifer Speake. Oxford University Press, 2015. http://www.oxfordreference.com/view/10.1093/acref/9780198734901.001.0001/acref-9780198734901-e-1261

p.153 adapted from "Max Weber." In *Oxford Dictionary of Scientific Quotations*, edited by W. F. Bynum, and Roy Porter. Oxford University Press, 2006. http://www.oxfordreference.com/view/10.1093/acref/9780198614432.001.0001/q-author-00007-00001282

p.154 adapted from "Eleanor Roosevelt." In *Oxford Essential Quotations*, edited by Susan Ratcliffe. Oxford University Press, 2016. http://www.oxfordreference.com/view/10.1093/acref/9780191843730.001.0001/q-oro-ed5-00008903

p.155 adapted from "Nicholas Murray Butler." In *Oxford Dictionary of Quotations*, edited by Elizabeth Knowles. Oxford University Press, 2014. http://www.oxfordreference.com/view/10.1093/acref/9780199668700.001.0001/q-author-00010-00000544

p.156 adapted from "Arthur Miller." In *The Oxford Dictionary of American Quotations*, edited by Hugh Rawson, and Margaret Miner. Oxford University Press, 2006. http://www.oxfordreference.com/view/10.1093/acref/9780195168235.001.0001/q-author-00008-00001139

p.157 adapted from "Adrienne Rich." In *The Oxford Dictionary of American Quotations*, edited by Hugh Rawson, and Margaret Miner. Oxford University Press, 2006. http://www.oxfordreference.com/view/10.1093/acref/9780195168235.001.0001/q-author-00008-00001367

p.158 adapted from "FIRST impressions are the most lasting." In *Oxford Dictionary of Proverbs*, edited by Jennifer Speake. Oxford University Press, 2015. http://www.oxfordreference.com/view/10.1093/acref/9780198734901.001.0001/acref-9780198734901-e-795

p.16 Extract from *Oxford Bookworms Night Without End* by Alistair Maclean, retold by Margaret Naudi. Original edition © Gilach A. C. 1959. First published 1959 by Williams Collins Sons & Co Ltd. This simplified edition © Oxford University Press 2008. Reproduced by permission of HarperCollins UK on behalf of the Estate of Alistair Maclean and Oxford University Press.

 Cover photo by Quinn Ryan Mattingly.
Dalat, Vietnam, December 2016.
Dang Viet Nga, owner and architect of Crazy House, an eclectic and surrealist hotel complex in Dalat, Vietnam. The daughter of a former president of Vietnam, she holds a PhD in architecture which she earned while studying in Moscow. Crazy House was first imagined and began to take shape in 1990, and is still evolving and growing.

Contents

v

Acknowledgments

AUTHOR

Kristin Donnalley Sherman holds an M.E. in TESL from the University of North Carolina, Charlotte. She has taught ESL/EFL at Central Piedmont Community College in Charlotte, North Carolina for more than fifteen years, and has taught a variety of subjects, including grammar, reading, composition, listening, and speaking. She has written several student books, teacher's editions and workbooks in the area of academic ESL/EFL. In addition, she has delivered trainings internationally in ESL methodology.

Frances Watkins has an MSc in Teaching English as a Foreign Language and has taught and trained in various countries abroad, including Singapore, Hungary and Oman. She currently lives and works in the UK, dividing her working life between teaching, training and writing. She has been involved in numerous writing projects over the years, including face-to-face and online materials for adult and teenage learners, business students, and teachers. She is particularly interested in methodology and how to activate 'learned' knowledge, students' perceptions of what constitutes 'learning', as well as the relationship between language and whole skills work.

SERIES CONSULTANTS

PRAGMATICS **Carsten Roever** is Associate Professor in Applied Linguistics at the University of Melbourne, Australia. He was trained as a TESOL teacher and holds a PhD in Second Language Acquisition from the University of Hawai'i at Manoa. His research interests include interlanguage pragmatics, language testing, and conversation analysis.

Naoko Taguchi is an Associate Professor of Japanese and Second Language Acquisition at the Dietrich College of Modern Languages at Carnegie Mellon University. She holds a PhD from Northern Arizona University. Her primary research interests include pragmatics in Second Language Acquisition, second language education, and classroom-based research.

PRONUNCIATION **Tamara Jones** is an instructor at the English Language Center at Howard Community College in Columbia, Maryland.

INCLUSIVITY & CRITICAL THINKING **Lara Ravitch** is a senior instructor and the Intensive English Program Coordinator of the American English Institute at the University of Oregon.

ENGLISH FOR REAL VIDEOS **Pamela Vittorio** acquired a BA in English/Theater from SUNY Geneseo and is an ABD PhD in Middle Eastern Studies with an MA in Middle Eastern Literature and Languages from NYU. She also designs ESL curriculum, materials, and English language assessment tools for publishing companies and academic institutions.

MIDDLE EAST ADVISORY BOARD **Amina Saif Al Hashami**, Nizwa College of Applied Sciences, Oman; **Karen Caldwell**, Higher Colleges of Technology, Ras Al Khaimah, UAE; **Chaker Ali Mhamdi**, Buraimi University College, Oman.

LATIN AMERICA ADVISORY BOARD **Reinaldo Hernández**, Duoc, Chile; **Mauricio Miraglia**, Universidad Tecnológica de Chile INACAP, Chile; **Aideé Damián Rodríguez**, Tecnológico de Monterrey, Mexico; **Adriana Recke Duhart**, Universidad Anáhuac, Mexico; **Inés Campos**, Centro de Idiomas, Cesar Vallejo University, Peru.

SPAIN ADVISORY BOARD **Alison Alonso**, EOI Luarca, Spain; **Juan Ramón Bautista Liébana**, EOI Rivas, Spain; **Ruth Pattison**, EOI, Spain; **David Silles McLaney**, EOI Majadahonda, Spain.

We would like to acknowledge the educators from around the world who participated in the development and review of this series:

ASIA Ralph Baker, Chuo University, Japan; **Elizabeth Belcour**, Chongshin University, South Korea; **Mark Benton**, Kobe Shoin Women's University, Japan; **Jon Berry**, Kyonggi University, South Korea; **Stephen Lyall Clarke**, Vietnam-US English Training Service Centers, Vietnam; **Edo Forsythe**, Hirosaki Gakuin University, Japan; **Clifford Gibson**, Dokkyo University, Japan; **Michelle Johnson**, Nihon University, Japan; **Stephan Johnson**, Rikkyo University, Japan; **Nicholas Kemp**, Kyushu International University, Japan; **Brendyn Lane**, Core Language School, Japan; **Annaliese Mackintosh**, Kyonggi University, South Korea; **Keith Milling**, Yonsei University, Korea; **Chau Ngoc Minh Nguyen**, Vietnam - USA Society English Training Service Center, Vietnam; **Yongjun Park**, Sangi University, South Korea; **Scott Schafer**, Inha University, South Korea; **Dennis Schumacher**, Cheongju University, South Korea; **Jenay Seymour**, Hongik University, South Korea; **Joseph Staples**, Shinshu University, Japan; **Greg Stapleton**, YBM Education Inc. – Adult Academies Division, South Korea; **Le Tuam Vu**, Tan True High School, Vietnam; **Ben Underwood**, Kugenuma High School, Japan; **Quyen Vuong**, VUS English Center, Vietnam

EUROPE Marta Alonso Jerez, Mainfor Formación, Spain; **Pilar Álvarez Polvorinos**, EOI San Blas, Spain; **Peter Anderson**, Anderson House, Italy; **Ana Anglés Esquinas**, First Class Idiomes i Formació, Spain; **Keith Appleby**, CET Services, Spain; **Isabel Arranz**, CULM Universidad de Zaragoza, Spain; **Jesus Baena**, EOI Alcalá de Guadaira, Spain; **José Gabriel Barbero Férnández**, EOI de Burgos, Spain; **Carlos Bibi Fernandez**, EIO de Madrid-Ciudad Lineal, Spain; **Alex Bishop**, IH Madrid, Spain; **Nathan Leopold Blackshaw**, CCI, Italy; **Olga Bel Blesa**, EOI, Spain; **Antoinette Breutel**, Academia Language School, Switzerland; **Angel Francisco Briones Barco**, EOI Fuenlabrada, Spain; **Ida Brucciani**, Pisa University, Italy; **Julie Bystrytska**, Profi-Lingua, Poland; **Raul Cabezali**, EOI Alcala de Guadaira, Spain; **Milena Cacko-Kozera**, Profi-Lingua, Poland; **Elena Calviño**, EOI Pontevedra, Spain; **Alex Cameron**, The English House, Spain; **Rosa Cano Vallese**, EOI Prat Llobregate, Spain; **Montse Cañada**, EOI Barcelona, Spain; **Elisabetta Carraro**, WE.CO Translate, Italy; **Joaquim Andres Casamiquela**, Escola Oficial d'Idiomes – Guinardó, Spain; **Lara Ros Castillo**, Aula Campus, Spain; **Patricia Cervera Cottrell**, Centro de Idiomas White, Spain; **Sally Christopher**, Parkway S.I., Spain; **Marianne Clark**, The English Oak Tree Academy, Spain; **Helen Collins**, ELI, Spain; **María José Conde Torrado**, EOI Ferrol, Spain; **Ana Maria Costachi**, Centro de Estudios Ana Costachi S.I., Spain; **Michael Cotton**, Modern English Study Centre, Italy; **Pedro Cunado Placer**, English World, Spain; **Sarah Dague**, Universidad Carlos III, Spain; **María Pilar Delgado**, Big Ben School, Spain; **Ashley Renee Dentremont Matthäus**, Carl-Schurz Haus, Deutch-Amerikanisches-Institute Freiburg e.V., Germany; **Mary Dewhirst**, Cambridge English Systems, Spain; **Hanna Dobrzycka**, Advantage, Poland; **Laura Dolla**, E.F.E. Laura Dolla, Spain; **Paul Doncaster**, Taliesin Idiomes, Spain; **Marek Doskocz**, Lingwista Sp. z o.o., Poland; **Fiona Dunbar**, ELI Málaga, Spain; **Anna Dunin-Bzdak**, Military University of Technology, Poland; **Robin Evers**, l'Università di Modena e Reggio Emilia, Italy; **Yolanda Fernandez**, EOI, Spain; **Dolores Fernández Gavela**, EOI Gijón, Spain; **Mgr. Tomáš Fišer**, English Academy, Czech Republic; **Juan Fondón**, EOI de Langreo, Spain; **Carmen Forns**, Centro Universitario de Lenguas Modernas, Spain; **Ángela Fraga**, EOI de Ferrol, Spain; **Beatriz Freire**, Servicio de Idiomas FGULL, Spain; **Alena Fridrichova**, Palacky University in Olomouc, Faculty of Science, Department of Foreign Languages, Czech Republic; **Elena Friedrich**, Palacky University, Czech Republic; **JM Galarza**, Iruñanko Hizkuntz Eskola, Spain; **Nancie Gantenbein**, TLC-IH, Switzerland; **Gema García**, EOI, Spain; **Maria Jose Garcia Ferrer**, EOI Moratalaz, Spain; **Josefa García González**, EOI Málaga, Spain; **Maria García Hermosa**, EOI, Spain; **Jane Gelder**, The British Institute of Florence, Italy; **Aleksandra Gelner**, ELC Katowice, Bankowa 14, Poland; **Marga Gesto**, EOI Ferrol, Spain; **Juan Gil**, EOI Maria Moliner, Spain; **Eva Gil Cepero**, EOI La Laguna, Spain; **Alan Giverin**, Today School, Spain; **Tomas Gomez**, EOI Segovia, Spain; **Mónica González**, EOI Carlos V, Spain; **Elena González Diaz**, EOI, Spain; **Steve Goodman**, Language Campus, Spain; **Katy Gorman**, Study Sulmona, Italy; **Edmund Green**, The British Institute of Florence, Italy; **Elvira Guerrero**, GO! English Granada, Spain; **Lauren Hale**, The British Institute of Florence, Italy; **Maria Jose Hernandez**, EOI de Salou, Spain; **Chris Hermann**, Hermann Brown English Language Centre, Spain; **Robert Holmes**, Holmes English, Czech Republic; **José Ramón Horrillo**, EOI de Aracena, Spain; **Laura Izquierdo**, Univerisity of Zaragoza, Spain; **Marcin Jaśkiewicz**, British School Żoliborz, Poland; **Mojmír Jurák**, Albi – jazyková škola, Czech Republic; **Eva Kejdová**, BLC, Czech Republic; **Turlough Kelleher**, British Council, Callaghan School of English, Spain; **Janina Knight**, Advantage Learners, Spain; **Ewa Kowalik**, English Point Radom, Poland; **Monika Krawczuk**, Wyższa Szkoła Finansów i Zarządzania, Poland; **Milica Krisan**, Agentura Parole, Czech Republic; **Jędrzej Kucharski**, Profi-lingua, Poland; **V. Lagunilla**, EOI San Blas, Spain; **Antonio Lara Davila**, EOI La Laguna, Spain; **Ana Lecubarri**, EOI Aviles, Spain; **Lesley Lee**, Exit Language Center, Spain; **Jessica Lewis**, Lewis Academy, Spain; **Alice Llopas**, EOI Estepa, Spain; **Angela Lloyd**, SRH Hochschule Berlin, Germany; **Helena Lohrová**, University of South Bohemia, Faculty of Philosophy, Czech Republic; **Elena López Luengo**, EOI Alcalá de Henares, Spain; **Karen Lord**, Cambridge House, Spain; **Carmen Loriente Duran**, EOI Rio Vero, Spain; **Alfonso Luengo**, EOI Jesús Maestro Madrid, Spain; **Virginia Lyons**, VLEC, Spain; **Anna Łętowska-Mickiewicz**, University of Warsaw, Poland; **Ewa Malesa**, Uniwersytet SWPS, Poland; **Klara Małowiecka**, University of Warsaw, Poland; **Dott. Ssa Kim Manzi**, Università degli Studi della Tuscia – DISTU – Viterbo, Italy; **James Martin**, St. James Language Center, Spain; **Ana Martin Arista**, EOI Tarazona, Spain; **Irene Martín Gago**, NEC, Spain; **Marga Martínez**, ESIC Idiomas Valencia, Spain; **Kenny McDonnell**, McDonnell English Services S.I., Spain; **Anne Mellon**, EEOI Motilla del Palacar, Spain; **Miguel Ángel Meroño**, EOI Cartagena, Spain; **Joanna Merta**, Lingua Nova, Poland; **Victoria Mollejo**, EOI San Blas-Madrid, Spain; **Rebecca Moon**, La Janda Language Services, Spain; **Anna Morales Puigicerver**, EOI TERRASSA, Spain; **Jesús Moreno**, Centro de Lenguas Modernas, Universidad de

ix

Zaragoza, Spain; **Emilio Moreno Prieto**, EOI Albacete, Spain; **Daniel Muñoz Bravo**, Big Ben Center, Spain; **Heike Mülder**, In-House Englishtraining, Germany; **Alexandra Netea**, Albany School of English, Cordoba, Spain; **Christine M. Neubert**, Intercultural Communication, Germany; **Ignasi Nuez**, The King's Corner, Spain; **Guadalupe Núñez Barredo**, EOI de Ponferrada, Spain; **Monika Olizarowicz-Strygner**, XXII LO z OD im. Jose Marti, Poland; **A. Panter**, Oxford School of English, Italy; **Vanessa Jayne Parvin**, British School Florence, Italy; **Rachel Payne**, Academia Caledonian, Cadiz, Spain; **Olga Pelaez**, EOI Palencia, Spain; **Claudia Pellegrini**, Klubschule Migros, Switzerland; **Arantxa Pérez**, EOI Tudela, Spain; **Montse Pérez**, EOI Zamora, Spain; **Esther Pérez**, EOI Soria, Spain; **Rubén Pérez Montesinos**, EOI San Fernando de Henares, Spain; **Joss Pinches**, Servicio de Lenguas Modernas, Universidad de Huelva, Spain; **Katerina Pitrova**, FLCM TBU in Zlin, Czech Republic; **Erica Pivesso**, Komalingua, Spain; **Eva Plechackova**, Langfor CZ, Czech Republic; **Jesús Porras Santana**, JPS English School, Spain; **Adolfo Prieto**, EOI Albacete, Spain; **Sara Prieto**, Universidad Católica de Murcia, Spain; **Penelope Prodromou**, Universitá Roma Tre, Italy; **Maria Jose Pueyo**, EOI Zaragoza, Spain; **Bruce Ratcliff**, Academia Caledonian, Spain; **Jolanta Rawska**, School of English "Super Grade," Poland; **Mar Rey**, EOI Del Prat, Spain; **Silke Riegler**, HAW Landshut, Germany; **Pauline Rios**, Rivers, Spain; **Laura Rivero**, EOI La Laguna, Spain; **Carmen Rizo**, EOI Torrevieja, Spain; **Antonio F. Rocha Canizares**, EOI Talavera de la Reina, Spain; **Eva Rodellas Fontiguell**, London English School; **Sara Rojo**, EOI Elche, Spain; **Elena Romea**, UNED, Spain; **Ann Ross**, Centro Linguistico di Ateneo, Italy; **Tyler Ross**, Ingliese for you, Italy; **Susan Royo**, EOI Utebo, Spain; **Asuncion Ruiz Astruga**, EOI Maria Molinar, Spain; **Tamara Ruiz Fernandez**, English Today, Spain; **Soledat Sabate**, FIAC, Spain; **Maria Justa Saenz de Tejad**, ECI Idiomas Bailen, Spain; **Sophia Salaman**, University of Florence, Centro Linguistico de ATENEO, Italy; **Elizabeth Schiller**, Schillers Sprachstudio, Germany; **Carmen Serrano Tierz**, CULM, Spain; **Elizabeth R. Sherman**, Lexis Language Centre, Italy; **Rocio Sierra**, EOI Maspalomas, Spain; **David Silles McLaney**, EOI Majadahonda, Spain; **Alison Slade**, British School Florence, Italy; **Rachael Smith**, Accademia Britannica Toscana, Italy; **Michael Smith**, The Cultural English Centre, Spain; **Sonia Sood**, Oxford School Treviso, Italy; **Monika Stawska**, SJO Pigmalion, Poland; **Izabela Stępniewska**, ZS nr 69, Warszawa / British School Otwock, Poland; **Rocío Stevenson**, R & B Academia, Spain; **Petra Stolinova**, Magic English s.r.o., Czech Republic; **Hana Szulczewska**, UNO (Studium Języków Obcych), Poland; **Tim T.**, STP, Spain; **Vera Tauchmanova**, Univerzita Hradec Kralove, Czech Republic; **Nina Terry**, Nina School of English, Spain; **Francesca R. Thompson**, British School of East, Italy; **Pilar Tizzard**, Docklands Idiomes, Spain; **Jessica Toro**, International House Zaragoza, Spain; **Christine Tracey**, Università Roma Tre, Italy; **Loredana Trocchi**, L'Aquila, Italy; **Richard Twiggl**, International House Milan, Italy; **Natàlia Verdalet**, EOI Figueres, Spain; **Sergio Viñals**, EOI San Javier, Spain; **Edith von Sundahl-Hiller**, Supernova Idiomes, Spain; **Vanda Vyslouzilova**, Academia, Czech Republic; **Helen Waldron**, ELC, Germany; **Leslie Wallace**, Academia Language School, Switzerland; **Monika Wąsowska-Polak**, Akademia Obrony Narodowej, Poland; **Melissa Weaver**, TLC-IH, Switzerland; **Maria Watton**, Centro Lingue Estere CC, Italy; **Dr. Otto Weihs**, IMC FH Krems, Austria; **Kate Williams**, Oxford House Barcelona, Spain; **June Winterflood**, Academia Language School, Switzerland; **Ailsa Wood**, Cooperativa Babel, Italy; **Irene Zamora**, www.speakwithirene.com, Spain; **Coro Zapata**, EOIP Pamplona, Spain; **Gloria Zaragoza**, Alicante University, Spain; **Cristina Zêzere**, EOI Torrelavega, Spain

LATIN AMERICA Fernando Arcos, Santo Tomás University, Chile; **Ricardo Barreto**, Bridge School, Brazil; **Beth Bartlett**, Centro Cultural Colombo Americano, Cali, Colombia; **Julie Patricia Benito Lugo**, Universidad Central, Colombia; **Ana Luisa Bley Soriano**, Universidad UCINF, Chile; **Gabriela Brun**, I.S.F.D N 129, Argentina; **Talita Burlamaqui**, UFAM, Brazil; **Lourdes Leonides Canta Lozano**, Fac. De Ciencias Biolgicas UANL, Mexico; **Claudia Castro**, Stratford Institute – Moreno-Bs.As, Argentina; **Fabrício Cruz**, Britanic, Brazil; **Lisa Davies**, British Council, Colombia; **Adriana de Blasis**, English Studio Ciudad de Mercedes, Argentina; **Nora Abraira de Lombardo**, Cultural Inglesa de Mercedes, Argentina; **Bronwyn Donohue**, British Council, Colombia; **Andrea C. Duran**, Universidad Externado de Colombia; **Phil Elias**, British Council, Colombia; **Silvia C. Enríquez**, Escuela de Lenguas, Universidad Nacional de La Plata, Argentina; **Freddy Espinoza**, Universidad UCINF, Chile; **Maria de Lourdes Fernandes Silva**, The First Steps School, Brazil; **Doris Flores**, Santo Tomás English Program, Chile; **Hilda Flor-Páez**, Universidad Catolica Santiago de Guayaquil, Ecuador; **Lauriston Freitas**, Cooplem Idiomas, Brazil; **Alma Delia Frias Puente**, UANL, Mexico; **Sandra Gacitua Matus**, Universidad de la Frontera, Chile; **Gloria Garcia**, IPI Ushuaia-Tierra del Fuego, Argentina; **Alma Delia Garcia Ensastegui**, UAEM, Mexico; **Karina Garcia Gonzalez**, Universidad Panamericana, Mexico; **Miguel García Rojas**, UNMSM, Peru; **Macarena González Mena**, Universidad Tecnológica de Chile, Inacap, Chile; **Diana Granado**, Advanced English, Colombia; **Paul Christopher Graves**, Universidad Mayor, Chile; **Mabel Gutierrez**, British Council, Colombia; **Niamh Harnett**, Universidad Externado de Colombia, Colombia; **Elsa Hernandez**, English Time Institute, Argentina; **Reinaldo Hernández Sordo**, DUOC UC, Chile; **Eduardo Icaza**, CEN, Ecuador; **Kenel Joseph**, Haitian-American Institute, Haiti; **Joel Kellogg**, British Council, Colombia; **Sherif Ebrahim Khakil**, Universidad Autónoma Chapingo, Texcoco, Mexico; **Cynthia Marquez**, Instituto Guatemalteco Americano, Guatemala; **Aaron McCarroll**, Universidad Sergio Arboleda, Colombia; **Milagro Machado**, SISE Institute, Peru; **Marta de Faria e Cunha Monteiro**, Federal University of Amazonas – UFAM, Brazil; **Lucía Murillo Sardi**, Instituto Británico, Peru; **Ricardo A. Nausa**, Universidad de los Andes, Colombia; **Andrea Olmos Bernal**, Universidad de Guadalajara, Mexico; **M. Edu Lizzete Olvera Dominguez**, Universidad Autonoma de Baja California Sur, Mexico; **Blanca Ortecho**, Universidad Cesar Vallejo Centro de Idiomas, Peru; **Jim**

Osorio, Instituto Guatemalteco Americano, Guatemala; **Erika del Carmen Partida Velasco**, Univam, Mexico; **Mrs. Katterine Pavez**, Universidad de Atacama, Chile; **Sergio Peña**, Universidad de La Frontera, Chile; **Leonor Cristina Peñafort Camacho**, Universidad Autónoma de Occidente, Colombia; **Tom Rickman**, British Council, Colombia; **Olga Lucia Rivera**, Universidad Externado de Colombia, Colombia; **Maria-Eugenia Ruiz Brand**, DUOC UC, Chile; **Gabriela S. Eguiarte**, London School, Mexico; **Majid Safadaran**, Instituto Cultural Peruano Norteamericano, Peru; **María Ines Salinas**, UCASAL, Argentina; **Ruth Salomon-Barkmeyer**, UNILINGUAS – UNISINOS, Brazil; **Mario Castillo Sanchez Hidalgo**, Universidad Panamericana, Mexico; **Katrina J. Schmidt**, Universidad de Los Andes, Colombia; **Jacqueline Sedore**, The Language Company, Chile; **Lourdes Angelica Serrano Herrera**, Adler Schule, Mexico; **Antonio Diego Sousa de Oliveira**, Federal University of Amazonas, Brazil; **Padraig Sweeney**, Universidad Sergio Arboleda, Colombia; **Edith Urquiza Parra**, Centro Universitario México, Mexico; **Eduardo Vásquez**, Instituto Chileno Britanico de Cultura, Chile; **Patricia Villasante**, Idiomas Católica, Peru; **Malaika Wilson**, The Language Company, Chile; **Alejandra Zegpi-Pons**, Universidad Católica de Temuco, Chile; **Boris Zevallos**, Universidad Cesar Vallejo Centro de Idiomas, Peru; **Wilma Zurita Beltran**, Universidad Central del Ecuador, Ecuador

THE MIDDLE EAST Chaker Ali Mhamdi, Buraimi University College, Oman; **Salama Kamal Shohayb**, Al-Faisal International Academy, Saudi Arabia

TURKEY M. Mine Bağ, Sabanci University, School of Languages; **Suzanne Campion**, Istanbul University; **Daniel Chavez**, Istanbul University Language Center; **Asuman Cincioğlu**, Istanbul University; **Hatice Çelikkanat**, Istanbul Esenyurt University; **Güneş Yurdasiper Dal**, Maltepe University; **Angeliki Douri**, Istanbul University Language Center; **Zia Foley**, Istanbul University; **Frank Foroutan**, Istanbul University Language Center; **Nicola Frampton**, Istanbul University; **Merve Güler**, Istanbul University; **H. Ibrahim Karabulut**, Dumlupınar University; **Catherine McKimm**, Istanbul University; **Merve Oflaz**, Dogus University; **Burcu Özgül**, Istanbul University; **Yusuf Özmenekşe**, Istanbul University Language Center; **Lanlo Pinter**, Istanbul University Language Center; **Ahmet Rasim**, Amasya University; **Diana Maria Rios Hoyos**, Istanbul University Language Center; **Jose Rodrigues**, Istanbul University; **Dilek Eryılmaz Salkı**, Ozyegin University; **Merve Selcuk**, Istanbul Kemerburgaz University; **Mehdi Solhi Andarab**, Istanbul Medipol University; **Jennifer Stephens**, Istanbul University; **Özgür Şahan**, Bursa Technical University; **Fatih Yücel**, Beykent University

UNITED KINGDOM Sarah Ali, Nottingham Trent International College, Nottingham; **Rolf Donald**, Eastbourne School of English, Eastbourne, East Sussex; **Nadine Early**, ATC Language Schools, Dublin, Ireland; **Dr. Sarah Ekdawi**, Oxford School of English, Oxford; **Glynis Ferrer**, LAL Torbay, Paignton Devon; **Diarmuid Fogarty**,

INTO Manchester, Manchester; **Ryan Hannan**, Hampstead School of English, London; **Neil Harris**, ELTS, Swansea University, Swansea; **Claire Hunter**, Edinburgh School of English, Edinburgh, Scotland; **Becky Ilk**, LAL Torbay, Paignton; **Kirsty Matthews**, Ealing, Hammersmith & West London's college, London; **Amanda Mollaghan**, British Study Centres London, London; **Shila Nadar**, Twin ECL, London; **Sue Owens**, Cambridge Academy of English, Girton, Cambridge; **Caroline Preston**, International House Newcastle, Newcastle upon Tyne; **Ruby Rennie**, University of Edinburgh, Edinburgh, Scotland; **Howard Smith**, Oxford House College, London; **Yijie Wang**, The University of Edinburgh, Scotland; **Alex Warren**, Eurotraining, Bournemouth

UNITED STATES Christina H. Appel, ELS Educational Services, Manhattan, NY; **Nicole Bollhalder**, Stafford House, Chicago, IL; **Rachel Bricker**, Arizona State University, Tempe, AZ; **Kristen Brown**, Massachusetts International Academy, Marlborough, MA; **Tracey Brown**, Parkland College, Champaign, IL; **Peter Campisi**, ELS Educational Services, Manhattan, NY; **Teresa Cheung**, North Shore Community College, Lynn, MA; **Tyler Clancy**, ASC English, Boston, MA; **Rachael David**, Talk International, Miami, FL; **Danielle De Koker**, ELS Educational Services, New York, NY; **Diana Djaboury**, Mesa Community College, Mesa, AZ; **Mark Elman**, Talk International, Miami, FL; **Dan Gauran**, EC English, Boston, MA; **Kerry Gilman**, ASC English, Boston, MA; **Heidi Guenther**, ELS Educational Services, Manhattan, NY; **Emily Herrick**, University of Nebraska-Lincoln, Lincoln, NE; **Kristin Homuth**, Language Center International, Southfield, MI; **Alexander Ingle**, ALPS Language School, Seattle, WA; **Eugenio Jimenez**, Lingua Language Center at Broward College, Miami, FL; **Mahalia Joeseph**, Lingua Language Center at Broward College, Miami, FL; **Melissa Kaufman**, ELS Educational Services, Manhattan, NY; **Kristin Kradolfer Espinar**, MILA, Miami, FL; **Larissa Long**, TALK International, Fort Lauderdale, FL; **Mercedes Martinez**, Global Language Institute, Minneapolis, MN; **Ann McCrory**, San Diego Continuing Education, San Diego, CA; **Simon McDonough**, ASC English, Boston, MA; **Dr. June Ohrnberger**, Suffolk County Community College, Brentwood, NY; **Fernanda Ortiz**, Center for English as a Second Language at the University of Arizona, Tuscon, AZ; **Roberto S. Quintans**, Talk International, Miami, FL; **Terri J. Rapoport**, ELS, Princeton, NJ; **Alex Sanchez Silva**, Talk International, Miami, FL; **Cary B. Sands**, Talk International, Miami, FL; **Joseph Santaella Vidal**, EC English, Boston, MA; **Angel Serrano**, Lingua Language Center at Broward College, Miami, FL; **Timothy Alan Shaw**, New England School of English, Boston, MA; **Devinder Singh**, The University of Tulsa, Tulsa, OK; **Daniel Stein**, Lingua Language Center at Broward College, Miami, FL; **Christine R. Stesau**, Lingua Language Center at Broward College, Miami, FL; **David Stock**, ELS Educational Services, Manhattan, NY; **Joshua Stone**, Approach International Student Center, Allston, MA; **Maria-Virginia Tanash**, EC English, Boston, MA; **Noraina Vazquez Huyke**, Talk International, Miami, FL

Overview

A REAL-WORLD VIEWPOINT

Whatever your goals and aspirations, *Wide Angle* helps you use English to connect with the world around you. It empowers you to join any conversation and say the right thing at the right time, with confidence.

9 Development

Start thinking about the topic with relevant, interesting **introduction questions.**

blink

Be inspired by the **vibrant unit opener images** from Blink photography. The international, award-winning photographers bring stories from around the world to life on the page.

What kinds of development does the image show?

Is development always a good thing?

What can we do to develop our careers?

BEHIND THE PHOTO

Work with a partner. Imagine that you had the power to change the world.

1 What would you change?
2 What technology would you need?
3 How will people need to change to help you reach your goal?

REAL-WORLD GOAL

Practice a new skill every day for a week

Apply learning to your own needs with **Real-World Goals**, instantly seeing the benefit of the English you are learning.

Watch the **"Behind the Photo"** video from the photographer.

"In the distance, we also can see the windmills. They represent a modern economic alternative for many farmers who find no future in working the land. It might be sad, but they make more money selling the electricity than harvesting the crops."

Edu Bayer

Enjoy learning with the huge variety of **up-to-date, inventive and engaging audio and video.**

9.4 If You Ask Me

Understand what to say and how to say it with **English For Real**.

These lessons equip you to choose and adapt appropriate language to communicate effectively in any situation.

ENGLISH FOR REAL

1 ACTIVATE In which situation(s) do you feel most comfortable talking about your beliefs? Discuss with a partner.

- With a friend at a coffee shop
- With a colleague at work while working on a project
- With a fellow student at a library
- With a fellow passenger on the subway
- With your boss outside of work
- With your professor during his or her office hours

2 EXPAND Do you agree that everyone should eat with chopsticks all the time? How would you respond to the following people if they said this to you?

	Colleague/Classmate	Professor/Boss
1. Don't say anything	☐	☐
2. "That's the worst idea I've ever heard."	☐	☐
3. "NO!"	☐	☐
4. "I don't agree, but sure."	☐	☐
5. "Hmm…I guess."	☐	☐
6. "I'll consider trying it."	☐	☐
7. "I agree with you 100%!"	☐	☐
8. "I don't want to talk about this."	☐	☐

3 ▶ IDENTIFY Watch the video, and find out what happened.

1 What are Kevin, Phil, and Andy discussing?
2 Do they all agree? How do you know?
3 Do you think Andy changes his opinion? Why or why not?

REAL-WORLD ENGLISH Defending a belief

Whenever you propose an idea you believe in, some people may either
can defend your belief without getting caught up in criticizing naysaye

After introducing your belief, demonstrate experience that establishes y

*Eating with chopsticks for the entire month I was traveling through Japan
appreciation for taking my time while eating because I had to concentrate
things at once.*

You may need to clarify your purpose if someone disagrees with the va

A: There's nothing wrong with multitasking while eating. Not everyone ha
*B: It's not about doing as much as you can within a given timeframe. It's
time out.*

If asked, you can list more reasons for your belief.

*Well, I'm a huge believer in not overeating, and eating with chopsticks pre
if I had shoveled food in my mouth with a fork. I was forced to eat slower,
have because I felt fuller faster.*

When it appears that the conversation is ending, sometimes you can
takeaway.

A: Sounds like you're overthinking this.
B: Yeah, well using chopsticks meant a smaller pant size and a happier s

However, be sensitive about other people's beliefs. Sometimes, insisti
In such situations, it may be better to acknowledge that people's opir
convince the other person that you are right.

Well, personally, I prefer to eat with chopsticks, but I understand that othe

4 NOTICE During a conversation, if someone states a belief and you disagree with it, do you normally let it go, or do you talk about it?

5 ▶ ANALYZE Watch the video again. Write which function of defending a belief is used.

providing a takeaway	clarify your purpose
introduce your belief	demonstrate experience
list reasons for your belief	

1 I wore one from kindergarten through high school. _____

2 Choosing what to wear can be stressful and a big waste of time! _____

3 When you wear a uniform, you don't have to think about what to wear! _____

4 Fewer items of clothing means less maintenance! _____

5 I think there are more benefits to wearing uniforms than there are to being trendy. _____

6 ASSESS Do you think Phil would defend his belief to a professor the same way he did with Andy and Kevin? Why or why not?

- Your choice

8 INTEGRATE Work with a partner, and take turns defending your beliefs from Exercise 7 in an active conversation.

9 SHARE With your partner, role-play your conversation.

 **GO ONLINE**
to create your own version
of the English For Real video.

Step into the course with **English For Real videos** that mimic real-life interactions. You can record your voice and respond in real time for out-of-class practice that is relevant to your life.

109

COMPREHENSIVE SYLLABUS

Ensure progress in all skills with a pedagogically consistent and appropriately leveled syllabus.

3 Experts need to begin with a natural talent.

4 Preparation is more important than talent in developing expertise.

5 Anyone can become an expert.

3 🔊 **ASSESS** Listen to the podcast. Check your answers to Exercise 2.

LISTENING SKILL Taking notes

When you take notes from a talk, lecture, or podcast, you will not have enough time to write every word the speaker says. Use abbreviations and symbols where possible. Also focus on the main ideas and key details.

The speaker will usually indicate main ideas through repetition, restatement, and summary, and may also use certain expressions. Main ideas are supported by examples, explanations, reasons, and other details.

You hear:
True expertise depends on three things.

You write:
Expert, 3 things
1.   2.   3.

The speaker may indicate supporting details with certain signal words. Listen for these expressions to take notes on important details.

Examples: *for example, for instance, such as, like*
Reasons: *because, because of, due to, as a result, so*
Explanation: *that means, what I mean*
Listing: *first, second, third, next, finally*

VOCABULARY DEVELOPMENT
Synonyms of change

There are many synonyms for the verb *to change*. We use some in particular contexts and others with certain collocations.

Change part but not all: **modify** *behavior / rules / design,* alter *behavior,* **adjust** *accordingly,* revise *plans / writing / ideas,* amend *laws / legislation / laws*

Change gradually: continue to *evolve,* **transition** to adulthood

Change dramatically: *transform* or **revolutionize** *society,* **convert** *energy,* undergo **transformation**, surgery, or testing

Some verbs indicate the subject is undergoing change (*evolve, transition*), some indicate that the object is undergoing change (*revise, amend, modify*), and others can be used in both ways depending on the context.

💡+ Oxford 5000™

5 🔊 **BUILD** Choose the best word to complete each sentence. Then listen and check your answers.

1 Through practice, they were able to *transform / adjust* into super-memorizers.

2 You can become much better, providing you *revolutionize / adjust* your practice.

3 They had to keep *converting / modifying* their techniques.

4 Deliberate practice involves using feedback to *adjust / transition* your technique or strategy accordingly.

6 WHAT'S YOUR ANGLE? Answer the questions. Then discuss them in a group.

1 After listening to the podcast, have you modified your ideas about expertise? Why or why not?

2 What methods do coaches usually use to help people develop their skills?

3 Think about a new situation you have been in recently. How did you adapt?

GRAMMAR IN CONTEXT Passive voice

We use passive voice when we want to focus on the action rather than the performer of the action. We form the passive with the verb *be* + past participle. We can use the passive in all tenses, with modal verbs, and in the infinitive.

I can see how athletes' performances **can be evaluated**.
Of course, the paintings **have to be judged**.
But some of the participants in the study **were trained** *to remember many more numbers after hearing them only once.*
Deliberate practice involves **being coached** *and using feedback to revise your technique or strategy.*
When you **are being coached***, you* **are forced** *to look at your performance in a new way.*

See Grammar focus on page 167.

7 IDENTIFY Read the text about the development of musical ability. Choose the active or passive voice.

8 INTEGRATE Rewrite the sentences in passive voice.

1 People can develop expertise through deliberate practice.

_____ through deliberate practice.

2 Someone will give awards to the winning athletes.

_____ to the winning athletes.

3 People often acquire musical skills through early training.

_____ through early training.

4 Scientists have done research on memorization techniques.

_____ on memorization techniques.

9 🔊 **ASSESS** Listen and check your answers to Exercise 8.

10 WHAT'S YOUR ANGLE? Answer the questions. Then discuss your ideas in a group.

1 Do you think any skill can be developed into expertise? Why or why not?

2 What is something you have spent a lot of time practicing? How did you practice?

3 How would you apply the ideas in the podcast to trying to change in some other way?

▼ VOCABULARY

The 💡+ Oxford 5000™ is a word list containing the most important words to learn in English. The words are chosen based on frequency in the Oxford English Corpus and relevance to learners of English. Every word is aligned to the CEFR, guiding you on the words you should know at each level.

▼ GRAMMAR

The carefully graded grammar syllabus ensures you encounter the most relevant language at the right point in your learning.

Children and Music

The developmental psychology of music focuses on change in musical skills as children age. Change due to growth or development [1] *may distinguish / may be distinguished* from that due to training, but there is evidence that training may be more effective at particular stages or ages.

By the time children go to school they already have some experience with music. Infants [2] *expose / are exposed* to music (and music-like sounds) in the home (for example, through recordings, radio, and television), speech, and play songs and lullabies sung by adults. Adult speech and song [3] *provide / are provided* infants with pleasurable musical interaction and a possible basis for their later engagement with music.

The main method researchers use to study infants [4] *involves / is involved* observation of head turning, in which the infant [5] *shows / is shown* awareness of something new or interesting. Such studies [6] *indicate / is indicated* that infants are sensitive to many aspects of music; these results [7] *have led / have been led* some investigators to conclude that biology rather than culture-specific learning is the main factor in infant music perception.

Research beyond infancy focuses on changes in musical ability acquired through training and environment, rather than age. Within western culture, high levels of performance skill [8] *commonly attribute / are commonly attributed* to innate talents, even though there's no strong evidence of a genetic basis for musical ability. One of the best predictors of musical skill is the amount and type of instrumental practice in which a performer [9] *engages / is engaged*. Estimates of practice time and biographical accounts suggest that highly skilled performers [10] *have practiced / have been practiced* 10,000 hours by the age of 21; this highlights the role that motivation plays.

Assessment of musical ability [11] *has shown / has been shown* to be unreliable: for example, musically expert judges [12] *influence / are influenced* by such factors as gender and attractiveness. Objective measures of musical ability [13] *have attempted / have been attempted*, but the use of standardized tests to predict musical aptitude has been largely unsuccessful.

—adapted from *The Oxford Companion to Music*, by Alison Latham

Oxford Reference is a trusted source of over two million authentic academic texts.

Free access to the Oxford Reference site is included with Student Books 4, 5, and 6.

Personalize the lesson topics and see how the language can work for you with **What's Your Angle** activities.

9.2 The Powers of a Superhero

1 ACTIVATE Look at the photos. What superpowers does each character possess? Discuss in a small group.

2 WHAT'S YOUR ANGLE? Which of the powers in Exercise 1 would you most like to have and why? Discuss with a partner.

3 VOCABULARY Read the sentences. Choose the best definition for the word or phrase in bold.

1 Glasses are one way to **enhance** vision.
  a increase or further improve
  b control or restrict

2 Deliberate practice **facilitates** the development of expertise.
  a makes possible or easier
  b leads a discussion

3 The surgery will improve the heart's ability to **function**.
  a to grow or develop
  b to work in the correct way

4 **Biomedical** interventions are sometimes necessary to save a life.
  a the act of interrupting
  b action taken to improve a situation or condition

5 Completely driverless cars are **on the horizon**.
  a able to lift off the ground
  b likely to happen soon

6 The city should **devise** a better system to control traffic.
  a invent a new way of doing something
  b behave in a dishonest way

7 Firefighters need breathing **apparatus** to enter the burning building.
  a equipment needed for a task
  b the structure of an organization

8 If you are a surgeon, you have **specialized** skills.
  a developed for a particular purpose
  b different from normal

ℝ+ Oxford 5000™

4 IDENTIFY Read the article. What kind of abilities are currently being enhanced? Discuss your ideas with a partner.

5 BUILD Complete each sentence with the correct form of a word from Exercise 3.

1 With the help of biomedical _____, people can _____ beyond what is necessary to live.

2 Eating certain things can _____ someone's ability to see at night.

3 One technology _____ is a prosthetic limb that can feel.

4 Engineers work with doctors to _____ equipment that can help patients in new ways.

5 The cost of a cutting-edge _____, like the one that helps people carry heavy loads, can be high.

6 USE Answer the questions. Then discuss your ideas in a group.

1 How is human enhancement different from other medical interventions?

2 What are some ways that the medical field can help people with physical disabilities function more independently?

3 What kinds of apparatuses can help people perform their jobs more effectively?

4 Scientists are devising a variety of solutions in the area of human enhancement. How might they improve your life?

5 In what ways does technology facilitate better performance (e.g., at work, on teams)?

READING SKILL Recognizing and understanding rhetorical questions

Writers use rhetorical questions in order to make a point without the expectation of a reply. These questions often act to engage the reader's interest and to present the writer's main ideas.

Have you ever wanted the powers of a superhero? (The writer is engaging the reader's interest.)
What is human enhancement? (The answer is one of the writer's main ideas.)

You can use rhetorical questions to assert or rebut an argument, to obtain agreement, or to effect a response.

It sounds scary, doesn't it? (The writer goes on to argue against this.)
You remember the movie Iron Man, right? (The writer is obtaining agreement.)

7 ASSESS Find the rhetorical questions in the article. Why is the writer using each one? Discuss your ideas with a partner.

102

THE AGE OF
SUPERHEROES

Have you ever wanted the powers of a superhero? Most people would like to fly, wouldn't they? Or climb buildings or lift cars? Maybe to see through walls or hear in color? What used to be considered science fiction or fantasy is now within reach. The era of human enhancement is upon us.

What is human enhancement? It is generally considered to be any biomedical intervention that is used to improve someone's functioning and condition beyond what is required for health and survival. A biomedical intervention could include implanting sensors in a prosthetic limb to facilitate the sense of touch, attaching electrodes to your brain to stimulate learning, introducing beneficial bacteria into the gut, or even changing your diet to enhance night vision.

Professor Maciej Henneberg and Dr. Aurthur Saniotis, both at the University of Adelaide, maintain that human adaptation, including methods of enhancement, is an ongoing process, part of a complex system that is continuously changing. These enhancement methods themselves are complex and ever changing.

Take the topic of brain–computer interfaces. It sounds scary, doesn't it? But it may solve some difficult problems. Using such an interface, a monkey in the United States can move an object on a computer in Japan. The same kind of brain–computer connection has been used by a paralyzed woman to feed herself chocolate. The uses for this kind of technology are impressive, particularly for people with locked-in syndrome. If you have this syndrome, you are aware of everything going on around you but completely unable to move anything except your eyes. Imagine if these patients could use their brains to not only communicate with other people but to control technology that might help them be more self-sufficient.

You remember the movie *Iron Man*, right? With the scientist in a special robotic suit? Robotics are another way we can enhance human performance. Robotic exoskeletons are already helping people with paralysis. For example, a paraplegic woman walked the London Marathon in a robotic exoskeleton. However, the same kind of technology is being used in other situations. Scientists are devising equipment that would allow someone to carry 200 pounds for several hours without fatiguing. This kind of apparatus could be used by the military, construction workers, recreational climbers, or rescue personnel. A body-extender robot has also been used by rescue workers in Italy to lift walls off earthquake survivors.

Such robotics are a logical extension of the technology developed first for prosthetics. Prosthetic devices have been around for centuries. They take the place of a missing body part. The first time someone strapped on a wooden stick in place of an amputated leg, he wore a prosthetic. The field of prosthetics has come a long way since then. Take the case of Josef Metelka, an exceptional athlete with 13 legs, 12 of them specialized for specific sports such as snowboarding and biking. Each is tailored to the environment (e.g., snow) and task (e.g., twisting and landing).

What is on the horizon for these replacement body parts? It is hoped that soon they may be able to feel. A Danish man recently underwent surgery to test out a new technology. A team of robotics experts, engineers, neuroscientists, and surgeons from Italy, Switzerland, and Germany implanted electrodes into nerves in the man's upper arm. These were connected to artificial sensors in a prosthetic hand. Through electronics and software, touch and pressure feedback was delivered to the man's brain, allowing the patient to "feel"—at least, to tell the shape and stiffness of an object through touch.

How else might a person take advantage of enhancement technology? One area of research that seems to have practical application for almost anyone is *transcranial direct current stimulation* (TDCS). TDCS changes the way the neurons in our brain send signals. Electrodes are attached to the head to stimulate the brain. Almost everyone shows improvement in learning and reduction in anxiety. And if you had access to Ce6, a compound found in deep-sea fish, you could do what Gabriel Licina did—he added it to eyedrops to improve his ability to see in the dark.

We may be at the very beginning of the era of human enhancement. There's no way to predict how far we can go, is there?

103

▼ READING AND LISTENING

Explicit reading and listening skills focus on helping you access and assimilate information confidently in this age of rapid information.

Build confidence with the **activation-presentation-practice-production** method, with activities moving from controlled to less controlled, with an increasing level of challenge.

vacation are most important to you?
o you think you would get along with
r why not?

NTEXT
 in impersonal reporting

create a more impersonal or
lly in business or academic
 do this with reporting verbs such
recommend, consider, report, hope,
d.

orting verbs is:

+ infinitive/*that* clause

onials on your website, **your service**
ne of the best in this field.
esn't kill you makes you stronger,"
ut it's not what I'm looking for in a

WRITING SKILL Using formal email language

In many situations, email has taken the place of the formal business letter. Although emails can be informal when between friends and family, in formal contexts you must use formal language and conventions.

1 Begin the body of the email with a formal greeting or salutation:
  Dear Mr. / Ms. Sanders,

2 Explain your reason for writing:
  I'm writing to express my dissatisfaction with my recent Personal and Planetary Productivity Retreat.

3 Use appropriate vocabulary:
  While many aspects of the retreat were enjoyable, I don't feel it lived up to its description on your website.

4 Conclude with a closing and your name (your full name if you are strangers):
  Sincerely,   Best regards,

he rhetorical question to the idea.
anted the powers of a superhero? ___
nhancement? ___
doesn't it? ___
he movie *Iron Man*, right? ___
orizon for these replacement parts? ___
verage person take advantage of
chnology? ___

ther way we can enhance human

some difficult problems.
n enhancement is upon us.
e able to feel.
intervention that improves a person's
condition.
s, which can improve learning.

PRONUNCIATION SKILL Intonation in tag questions

There are two intonation patterns for tag questions. In tag questions that elicit agreement, the speaker is requesting confirmation from the other person. The speaker is certain, or fairly certain of the listener's agreement. In these tag questions, the intonation falls in a way that is similar to the falling intonation of statements.

It sounds scary, doesn't it?

However, in other tag questions, the speaker is unsure of the listener's response. The rising intonation pattern signals uncertainty, as in true *yes/no* questions.

Superman has X-ray vision, doesn't he?

Be careful! If the rising intonation is too extreme, it can sound like the speaker doesn't believe something or is making an accusation.

▼ WRITING

The writing syllabus focuses on the writing styles needed for today, using a **process writing approach** of **prepare-plan-draft-review-correct** to produce the best possible writing.

▼ SPEAKING

Speaking and **pronunciation skills** build the functional language you need outside of class.

A BLENDED LEARNING APPROACH

Make the most of *Wide Angle* with opportunities for relevant, personalized learning outside of class.

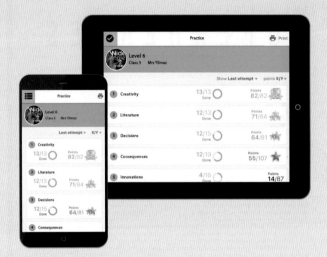

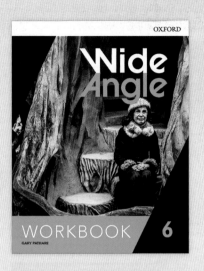

ONLINE PRACTICE

 When you see this icon in your Student Book, go online to extend your learning.

With Online Practice you can:

- Review the skills taught in every lesson and get **instant feedback**.
- Practice grammar and vocabulary through **fun games**.
- Access **all audio and video** material. Use the Access Code in the front of this Student Book to log in for the first time at wideangle.oxfordonlinepractice.com.

WORKBOOK

Your Workbook provides additional practice for every unit of the Student Book.

Each unit includes:

- An entirely new reading with skill practice linked to **Oxford Reference**.
- Support for the **Discussion Board**, helping students to master online writing.
- Listening comprehension and skill practice using the **Unit Review Podcast**.
- Real-life English practice linked to the **English For Real** videos.
- **Grammar** and **vocabulary** exercises related to the unit topic.

Use your Workbook for homework or self-study.

FOCUS ON THE TEACHER

The Teacher's Resource Center at wideangle.oxfordonlinepractice.com saves teachers time by integrating and streamlining access to the following support:

- **Teacher's Guide**, including fun **More to Say** pronunciation activities and **professional development** materials.
- **Easy-to-use** learning management system for the student Online Practice, **answer keys**, **audio**, lots of **extra activities**, **videos**, and so much more.

The **Classroom Presentation Tool** brings the Student Book to life for heads-up lessons. Class audio, video, and answer keys, as well as teaching notes, are available online or offline, and are updated across your devices.

1 Creativity

Who is more creative, a potter, an author, or a painter? Why?

How does creativity play a role in what this person is doing?

BEHIND THE PHOTO

REAL-WORLD GOAL

Go see art in a formal or informal venue

1 Answer the questions. Then share your answers with the class.

2 What is the purpose of art? See the list below, and add to it if you have other ideas. Choose three that you think are the most important. Compare your answers in a small group, giving reasons.

inspire	please	excite	impress	make you think
distract	shock	surprise	comfort	amuse

1.1 Walking on Art

1 ACTIVATE Finish these sentence starters, so they are true for you. Compare your answers with a partner.

1 I'm particularly interested in art that...
2 I don't like art that...
3 The last time I viewed some form of art was...
4 My interests in art have changed from...to...
5 My own artistic ability is...
6 If I had the chance, I would go to see or watch...

2 INTERACT Look at the 3-D sidewalk art in the photo below. Discuss the questions with a partner.

Have you ever seen artwork like this? What might some of the difficulties be in creating a piece of art of this type?

3 IDENTIFY Read the online comments posted in reaction to this 3-D sidewalk art, *The Crevasse*, created by Edgar Müller on the East Pier in Dún Laoghaire, Ireland, for the Festival of World Cultures (August 2008). Do you agree with any of the comments? Why or why not?

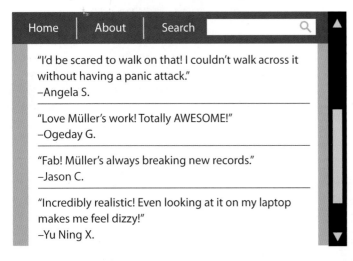

| Home | About | Search | 🔍 |

"I'd be scared to walk on that! I couldn't walk across it without having a panic attack."
–Angela S.

"Love Müller's work! Totally AWESOME!"
–Ogeday G.

"Fab! Müller's always breaking new records."
–Jason C.

"Incredibly realistic! Even looking at it on my laptop makes me feel dizzy!"
–Yu Ning X.

READING SKILL Recognizing and understanding register and style

It is important to recognize differences in style and register when reading to help understand the purpose of the text and the kind of audience it is aimed at.

For example, in informal written language, such as online comments, users' language is often closer to conversational English. Some features of informal written language are word choice (such as use of slang), missing or incomplete words (including abbreviations and contractions), incomplete sentences, a high frequency of exclamation marks and dashes, use of extreme adjectives and adverbs, and so on.

4 APPLY Find some examples of informal language in the online comments from Exercise 3.

5 IDENTIFY Read the article on the next page, taken from an art magazine. What are the "old" and "new" angles mentioned in the title?

6 INTEGRATE Read the article again and find the following information.

1 Name two historical examples of street art. *medo mmens / roman mosaics*
2 Name three difficulties that 3-D artists face while a work is in progress. *weather / surfaces / poses problems*
3 Name three other pieces that Müller has produced, besides *The Crevasse*. *lava burst / Ice age 3*
4 Name two ways in which the public interacts with two of Müller's pieces.
5 Name three groups of people who might go to the Venice street art festival.
6 Name two facts about the festival regarding its size.

Sidewalk Art: Old and New Angles

What's happening with sidewalk art?

Few art festivals allow you to participate in the process of art, but the International Chalk Festival in Venice, Florida, is different. **Enthusiasts** can actually watch the artists at work over the four-day event, which takes place every fall. This year marks the tenth anniversary, and over 1,000 street artists will apply to exhibit their work at the festival, which has the world's largest collection of 3-D pavement art in a single location.

3-D Art: Two leading lights

Art in 3-D, which is designed to be viewed from a particular angle, has been popularized in recent decades by the American artist Kurt Wenner, a regular participant at the festival and the first to establish a 3-D art festival in America.

Wenner spent years in Italy studying classical art to learn about perspective, and his **compositions** have been very influential with other artists. One of the best known of these is the German painter Edgar Müller, another **high-profile** figure in sidewalk art, who has also contributed to this festival. Müller has been creating street art since his teenage years and now concentrates purely on this art form. He paints 3-D street art on a huge scale, often with **vibrant** colors, aiming to give public areas a shockingly different appearance.

Close-up: An example of 3-D art

Artists who work in 3-D, such as Wenner and Müller, use imagination, mathematics, and skill to produce images that appear to rise and dip below ground when seen from a specific point. A particularly striking example of Müller's work, where he managed to produce a sense of genuine depth on a flat surface, is *The Crevasse*. This took five days to create, with the help of several assistants, and it covered 250 square meters.

It was a challenging piece, due to the unpredictable weather conditions and the difficulties of painting on the sidewalk and other surfaces, which can have various **textures**. Street art of this kind clearly poses problems: in the past, chalks and pastels were used as the **medium**, but now Müller and other sidewalk artists often use wall paint, which is more durable.

Müller has commented on both the negative and positive aspects of creating such vast pieces in a public space. People who go past tend to comment on the work in progress, which can be overwhelming—but also potentially informative, creatively speaking. However, it is when the work is complete that it becomes truly interactive. In the case of *The Crevasse*, passersby would play with the image and pose for photographs on the "edge," pretending to fall into the icy depths. As such, in this and other 3-D works of size, the public becomes part of the illusion itself.

His other works include the record-breaking 330-square-meter image representing the film *Ice Age 3* and an impressive image of a bright blue phoenix, where passersby would frequently "ride" on the bird's back. One of Müller's best-known works is his striking painting of a volcanic lava flow, *Lava Burst*, painted against the **backdrop** of a German street in the city of Geldern.

The history of sidewalk art

Sidewalk art has now acquired a status of its own, so images are becoming increasingly ambitious in terms of size and **scope**. However, although it has gained particular significance in recent decades, artists have actually been creating art works on the ground since the Middle Ages in Europe, such as the **sacred** works drawn by traveling artists in Italy, known as madonnari. In fact, sidewalks have been used to display works of art since Roman times, when they were often decorated with mosaics. Jumping to the twenty-first century, Wenner is known as the first American madonnaro, and Müller holds the title of maestro madonnaro, or **master** street painter.

The festival

The chalk festival in Venice attracts gifted and **prominent** artists from all over the world and allows visitors to interact with the artists and their images. Novice and student artists are also invited to sign up and draw alongside their more experienced counterparts. It seems that art is being reinvented in a fascinating way.

ℙ+ Oxford 5000™

---

7 VOCABULARY Select one of the words in italics that has a different meaning and cannot fit in the sentence.

1 His *medium* / *activity* / *material* is generally chalk, but he sometimes uses watercolors.

2 You walk over the *painting* / *image* / *imagery*, and it feels like you are falling into the depths.

3 The *works* / *compositions* / *productions* can be striking and powerful.

4 Wenner, Müller, and others, such as Julian Beever, are all *masters* / *chiefs* / *experts* in this field.

5 The street itself often forms the *backdrop* / *backing* / *background* for their work.

6 The madonnari specialized in *sacred* / *religious* / *faithful* works.

7 The colors of the pieces can be very *vibrant* / *bright* / *lively*.

8 The festivals attract sidewalk art *lovers* / *enthusiasts* / *fans* from all over the world.

9 Some of the artists are very *prominent* / *high interest* / *high profile*.

5

8 ASSESS Which of the words in Exercise 7 were new to you? Compare answers with a partner.

9 WHAT'S YOUR ANGLE? Discuss these points with a partner.

If you had the opportunity, would you go and see some of Edgar Müller's works? What would you do if you went to see either *The Crevasse* or *Lava Burst*? Does the fact that they're temporary affect you?

GRAMMAR IN CONTEXT Present tenses

There are different ways to talk about the present in English that do not simply reflect the notion of time.

Present continuous:

1 Everyone's just having fun "on the ice."
2 Images are becoming increasingly ambitious.
3 Müller's always breaking new records.

Simple present:

4 Müller and other sidewalk artists use wall paint, which is more resistant.

Simple present perfect:

5 Sidewalk art has now acquired a status of its own.

Present perfect continuous:

6 He has been creating street art since his teenage years.

See Grammar focus on page 159.

10 IDENTIFY Match the descriptions below with examples 1–6 in the Grammar box.

1 Changing situation _2_

2 Something that the speaker finds annoying, strange, or noteworthy (used with adverb *always*) _3_

3 Something that happened at an unspecified point in the past, and the result is significant _5_

4 Something that happened repeatedly in the past and is still happening now, with an emphasis on duration _6_

5 Things that generally or routinely happen; facts _4_

11 ASSESS Decide which of these are correct. How can you correct the incorrect ones?

1 The artist is working on this painting for three months, and it's still incomplete. *has been working*

2 The cousins have been creating about 300 sidewalk paintings in the last two years. *ed*

3 She's usually painting in watercolors, not oils. *s*

4 My brother can be annoying. He's always leaving his half-finished pictures around.

5 My neighbor has just painted the outside of their house.

6 The paint is drying faster in warmer weather.

7 That artist gradually becomes better known, thanks to his use of social media. *dries* *ing*

12 APPLY Read this text that describes street art. Put each verb into the correct form, using the most appropriate present verb form.

Popular interest in street art and graffiti 1 *has changed* (change) over the years. Historically, they have been either ignored or dismissed, but attitudes 2 *changing* (change). In fact, these art forms 3 *have grown* (grow) in popularity since the 1980s. This is apparent from the wide range of books and articles that 4 *are* (be) available, as well as websites, festivals, and museum and gallery exhibitions that are devoted to street art and graffiti. These days, street art is an exciting and original form of artistic production that 5 *Attracting* (attract) more and more artists.

Street art and graffiti are similar, but also interestingly different. In the case of street art, it is difficult to separate it from other forms of art in the public eye, such as public sculpture and performance. Furthermore, different people 6 *use* (use) the term *street art* in different ways, applying it to graffiti, large wall paintings or murals, public sculpture, street installation, and many other art forms.

The broadest notion of street art is just that of "art in the streets." However, according to Nicholas Alden Riggle's 2010 work, "Street Art: The Transfiguration of the Commonplace," a painting that is placed on the street 7 *does not become* (not become) street art.

Street art is art whose meaning 8 *depends* (depend) on its use of the street. This definition 9 *rules out* (rule out) the example of a painting that someone 10 *has simply placed* (simply place) in the street. It also supports the view that street art cannot be removed without threatening its meaning as street art. Its home is a public arena, and so it can be freely altered or destroyed by the public.

—adapted from *Encyclopedia of Aesthetics*, 2nd ed., edited by Michael Kelly

13 INTERACT Reread the text above. In your own words, what are the main points that the excerpt talks about? When you are ready, cover the text, and share what you understand with a partner.

14 WHAT'S YOUR ANGLE? Think of a particular work of art you admire. It could be a sculpture, a photograph, a painting, and so on, and does not need to be famous. Describe the work to a partner in as much detail as possible, explaining what impresses you about it. Consider the following.

- subject of the piece
- colors
- why you like it
- medium or materials
- size
- where you have seen it

1.2 From Subway to Superstar

1 ACTIVATE Consider what makes an artist of any kind successful. Work with a partner to decide on the top three things from this list.

luck
originality
talent
personality
looks
ambition or motivation
knowing the right people
the ability to develop a fan base
knowing how to use social media to self-publicize
an ability to respond to the times you are in
identifying a "gap in the market"

2 ▶ IDENTIFY Watch part of a college lecture about the street artist Keith Haring. Then answer the questions.

1 What kind of art was he interested in?
2 How did he begin his public work?
3 What was his goal?

3 ASSESS Read the following excerpt from the lecture. What sorts of social issues was Haring drawing attention to?

Haring started by doing chalk drawings on empty spaces on the walls of subway stations. They were simple line drawings with themes and ideas most people could understand, like birth, death, war, love.

He soon had international attention, and he used his powerful style to make strong social messages. He dealt with issues like drug abuse, and he supported charities with his work. He also got involved in group art projects, especially with children, and community art projects.

But not only did he do work for social causes, for public and community causes. He also started to create art for advertising and to take some of his images and put them on T-shirts and hats and posters, you know, things like that. Then in 1986, he opened a store, the Pop Shop, to sell these things. And this is when he really became controversial.

4 ▶ IDENTIFY Watch the final part of the talk. Find out what happened to Haring in terms of his success.

5 WHAT'S YOUR ANGLE? Do you agree or disagree with these statements? Discuss with a partner.

1 Artists who want wealth above anything else are not genuine artists.
2 Art on T-shirts is no longer art.
3 Haring was both a success and a failure.

A cellist in downtown Mexico City, Mexico

Keith Haring's mural 'Tuttomondo' in Pisa, Italy

Keith Haring shop and cafe in Pisa, Italy

7

main street

6 IDENTIFY Remind yourself of your responses to Exercise 1. Then read the following essay, which was a response by a student to the question, "Why do only a few artists achieve success in their respective fields?" Does the writer have similar ideas to yours?

While homeward bound the other day after work, in the bitter cold, I approached a crowd at the entrance to the subway. Two teenage street performers were entertaining people. Their acrobatic performance took my breath away, and my enthusiasm intensified as I watched, my eyes widening in disbelief at their skill. Despite everything, I stopped to observe for several moments. Even after I'd left, the artists' grace, strength, and perfect control stayed with me. Applause filled the air; we had all enjoyed watching.

There is clearly a huge amount of creativity out there in the form of artists, performers, designers, sculptors, or whatever, yet a mere handful are recognized. It struck me that artists of such quality might never go on to become "successful." In fact, the majority must simply stop trying. So, how exactly does one stand out from the crowd?

I believe there are several reasons some artists "make it" and others do not. To start with, they need to have talent. However, they must also have the stamina to work hard and master their skill. They need to practice regularly; many start devoting time to their skill from a very young age.

In addition, I consider the personality of the artist to be of particular significance. A successful artist is often characterized by enormous drive. Attitude-wise, they need to be willing to go on trying even when faced with difficulties and criticism. Can they accept setbacks but at the same time be ready to take risks? Many would agree that having confidence is also vital: while it is true that some successful artists lack confidence, this is not the norm.

All things considered, although some would argue that aspects of a person's personality are not directly connected to success, I would argue otherwise. Self-confidence can help to stabilize individuals, and this is essential on the difficult and rocky road to success.

Moreover, I think most artists ideally need something special about them. I would go so far as to say that originality is also key, as there are so many potential new artists in all fields. In my mind, an artist needs to find a new angle: if truth be told, there can only be a limited number of artists at one time in one area with a similar style. This is why original artists like Andy Warhol and Keith Haring became successful.

In my opinion, knowing one's audience or one's context and responding effectively are also necessary for some artists, depending on the type. For example, if you're a street performer starting out, you may benefit from engaging with your audience. Developing a fan base is essential for the success of artists such as musicians.

Finally, I realize that some might disagree, but I think that a large part of becoming successful is due to luck. Some artists have gained popularity simply because they were fortunate enough to be spotted by somebody in the business. The singer Adele is an excellent example of this: one of the songs that she had uploaded onto social media was noticed by a recording company. The rest is history.

In conclusion, it seems reasonable to assume that talent is a vital part of success, but it is far from the only thing. Being successful, whatever that means exactly, requires a combination of various ingredients, but it is heavily dependent on personality and usually helped by a large dose of luck.

7 WHAT'S YOUR ANGLE? Discuss with a partner whether you agree or disagree with the writer's points. Do you have any additional ideas about what makes a particular artist successful?

GRAMMAR IN CONTEXT
Constructions with -ing or with to infinitive

Some verbs take the to infinitive.

They need to have talent.

Some take the -ing form.

We had all enjoyed watching.

Some take either with little or no change in meaning.

Many start devoting time to their skill from a very young age.
Many start to devote time to their skill from a very young age.

However, sometimes both patterns can be used but with different meanings. Verbs like *stop, remember, forget, go on, try,* and *regret* can be followed by either *to* + infinitive or *-ing*, but these have different meanings.

I stopped to observe for several moments.
I stopped observing for several moments.

See Grammar focus on page 159.

---

8 IDENTIFY Choose the correct verb form from those given in italics. Both of the options in italics exist. Select the one where the meaning fits in the sentence.

1 The presenter went on *talking / to talk* even though no one was listening.

2 That was the last gas station before the venue. We stopped *filling up / to fill up* as we were on empty.

3 Oh, no! I forgot *bringing / to bring* my glasses. I won't be able to see the stage now!

4 I remember *going / to go* to that exhibition when we were teenagers.

5 We regret *not being able / not to be able* to renew our museum membership as there have been lots of good exhibitions on.

VOCABULARY DEVELOPMENT
Word formation: verb and adverb endings

Recognizing word endings can help you recognize word families when reading, identify word class, and understand meaning. When writing, knowledge of word formation can give your English accuracy and sophistication by increasing your vocabulary.

Some common verb suffixes include:

SUFFIX	GENERAL MEANING	EXAMPLE
-ify	cause or become	intense (adj) → intensify (v)
-en	cause a change in size, shape, etc.	wide (adj) → widen (v)
-ize	cause or change via a process	stable (adj) → stabilize (v)

Some useful adverb endings include:

SUFFIX	GENERAL MEANING	EXAMPLE
-wise	as far as X is concerned	attitude (n) → attitude-wise
	in that way	clock (n) → clockwise
-ward(s)	in the direction of	home (n) → homeward(s)
		out (adv) → outward(s)

9 BUILD Look at the words below and work with a partner to make them into verbs. Each word will take only one of these verb suffix endings: -ify, -en, -ize. You may need to change the spelling of a word when adding the suffix. Check in a dictionary.

short _shorten_   false _falsify_   –industrial   – humid _humidify_   _industrialize_
beauty _beautify_   national _nationalize_ horror _horrify_   strength _strengthen_
popular _popularize_ fat   – _fatten_ – loose _loosen_   pure _purify_
minimal _minimize_ simple _simplify_   computer _computerize_
length _lengthen_ broad   – _broaden_ tight _tighten_

10 USE Use a word with one of the suffixes from the Vocabulary Development box to make each sentence more concise.

1   My jacket was too short, so the tailor made it longer.
    My jacket was too short, so the tailor lengthened it.

2   So much of art is now done on the <u>computer</u>, and this means that new forms are constantly developing.   _computerize_

3   As far as the <u>quality</u> is concerned, the photographer's skill is excellent. _Qualitwise_ _horrify_

4   If you don't put <u>humid</u> air back into the rooms, the paintings will be destroyed.

5   The director is making the routine much <u>simpler</u> for the performers.   _Simplifying_

6   Social media has made making videos more <u>popular</u>.
    popularize

WRITING SKILL Giving your opinion

When giving an opinion in a formal piece of writing, as an essay, a writer needs to be able to select appropriate phrasing so that points are clear, balanced, and strong while also being sufficiently proper. There are several ways to give an opinion.
I think…; I consider…

You can also distance yourself from your opinion.
Many would agree that…; It would be fair to say…

You can acknowledge counterarguments or others' opinions.
I realize that some might disagree, but…; I understand why some feel…, but…

11 IDENTIFY Find at least one more example for each of these in the essay.

1   Giving your opinion
2   Distancing yourself from your opinion
3   Acknowledging others' arguments or opinions

12 PREPARE Look back at the essay to examine how the writer has organized the ideas. Answer these questions with a partner.

1   How is the opening paragraph a little unusual? Is it successful?
2   What is discussed in paragraph 2?
3   What happens in paragraphs 3 to 7? Paragraph 8?

13 WRITE Write an opinion essay (225 to 300 words). Select one of these topics.

Many people believe that talent is born, not made. Discuss.
An essential quality of art is beauty. Discuss.
When one artist or a type of art is popularized, it stops being art. Discuss.
Be sure to

■   Use an interesting opening paragraph.
■   Give your points clearly with reasons.
■   Acknowledge others' opinions.
■   Plan what will go in each paragraph, and then write the first draft.

14 IMPROVE Reflect on your first draft, and ask yourself these questions. Then check your grammar, punctuation, vocabulary, and spelling before rewriting your essay.

☐   Do I have clear paragraphs?
☐   Is there a good opening paragraph?
☐   Is my point of view clear?
☐   Have I acknowledged others' opinions?

15 WHAT'S YOUR ANGLE? Think about your personality, ambition, and talents. Could you be a successful artist? Would you like to be one? Why or why not? Share with a partner.

.3 Music and the Mind

1 ACTIVATE Look at the picture below. Then ask and answer the questions with a partner.

> **1** How important is music to you, and what kind of music do you listen to?

> **2** How often do you listen to music? Where? When? Do you go to see live music?

> **3** Have you ever played a musical instrument? Would you like to? Which one?

LISTENING SKILL Listening for the main ideas and supporting evidence

Distinguishing between the main points and the supporting evidence in formal presentations, seminars, or lectures, and so on, can assist comprehension. The main idea is usually stated clearly at the beginning of each section.

Speakers may also refer to evidence to support their ideas, either (i) referring to an example, e.g., *for instance*, or (ii) referring to data, findings, or research, e.g., *research suggests*.

MAIN POINT Musical hallucinations cannot be controlled by the conscious mind.

SUPPORTING EVIDENCE Research suggests that this kind of hallucination usually happens to older people.

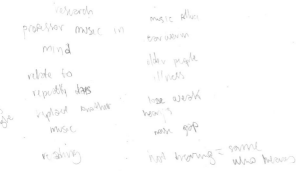

2 IDENTIFY Think about the Listening Skill. Do these phrases (A) indicate a main point or (B) start a supporting point by referring to examples or studies?

1 According to a recent study… B
2 And moving on to the next point, which is…
3 An example of this can be seen in…
4 As X states/describes/suggests…
5 Finally, I'd like to discuss X.
6 Researchers at Hamburg University showed that…

3 WHAT'S YOUR ANGLE? You are going to listen to an interview with an expert talking about music and the mind. First, discuss these questions with partner.

1 How often do you sing, hum, or whistle a song? Are you usually conscious of doing this or not? How do you react when others do this?
2 Do you often have a song replaying in your mind no matter how hard you try to stop it? (This is called an *earworm*.)
3 What kind of music or song would you most hate to have as an earworm?

4 🔊 IDENTIFY Listen to the interview podcast, and decide what the main points are. Choose the best summary.

1 A description of earworms, the causes of and cures for earworms
2 Earworms, musical hallucinations (when you imagine you hear music), an unusual case
3 How to engage your brain, how to stop musical hallucinations

5 🔊 ASSESS Listen again. Focus on the details and decide if the following statements are true (T), false (F), or if we don't know (DK).

1 To get rid of an earworm, you should do a mental task that is the right level of challenge. _T_
2 Visualization is the most popular way to get rid of an earworm. _T_ DUNNO
3 Musical hallucinations are like earworms because in both cases you believe the music to be real. _F_
4 Generally, it is older people who suffer from these hallucinations. _T_
5 Only certain types of music can be heard in a musical hallucination. _F_
6 The woman was cured of her auditory hallucinations. ___ DUNNO

The simple past is used to describe completed events, including events in sequence.

When she sang or hummed the tunes to her husband or others, they recognized them.

The past perfect describes an event that happened before the event in focus. The simple past perfect is used for completed events.

Do you think she'd just forgotten them?

In addition, the past perfect continuous focuses on duration and/or repetition.

The woman had been hearing music that sounded real.

The past continuous is used to give background information about an action in progress at the same time as the main event.

This woman…first heard the music as she was trying to fall asleep one night.

Used to and *would* are used to talk about habits or repeated actions. *Used to* can be used to talk about states, too.

She would hear one song repeatedly for three weeks.
It used to be thought that this only happened to the elderly.

See Grammar focus on page 159.

6 APPLY Complete each sentence by choosing the correct form of the verb.

1 An earworm *came / had come* into my mind last Thursday, when I *was driving / had driven* to work.

2 The scientists *would look / were looking* into an unusual case, and *had made / were making* two interesting discoveries.

3 When I was young, I *would listen / had listened* to classical music, but I prefer jazz these days.

4 I *was playing / used to play* electric guitar for several years, but after breaking my wrist, I *gave / had given* it up.

5 When I got home last night, my roommate *was practicing / had practiced* his trumpet, which meant I couldn't concentrate.

6 I *would be / used to be* upset if I couldn't master a piece of music at once, but now I just try harder.

7 VOCABULARY Look at the music-related nouns below on the right. Match each adjective with the noun it frequently precedes.

1	**folk**	a	**anthem**
2	advertising	b	tune
3	instrumental	c	song G
4	**catchy**	d	choir
5	national	e	piece
6	**school** or **male-voice**	f	jingle

Oxford 5000™

8 USE Which words are being described from Exercise 7?

1 It's a short, repeated tune that you hear on the radio or on the TV to publicize or sell something. 2-f

2 This is a song from popular and traditional culture that has a particular rhythm or style. ___

3 This describes a song or part of a song that you find yourself singing or humming a lot. ___

4 It's a group of men singing together, usually unaccompanied by musical instruments. ___

5 This describes music that has many instruments but that doesn't have a singer. ___

6 This is a song that represents your country and may be sung at formal and major sports events. ___

You can help your listeners understand you comfortably by stressing the words that carry the information and that communicate the main message. These are typically nouns, verbs (except common ones like *be* or *have*), adjectives, and adverbs. Little grammar words like articles, prepositions, and auxiliaries are generally not stressed, as they do not usually carry the main meaning.

Interestingly, the songs are often from the distant past, tunes that you used to hear a lot, like national anthems…

9 NOTICE Read the sentences below from the start of the interview. Before you listen, find the words that you think will be stressed. Then listen again and repeat the sentences.

And today, as part of our series Music and the Mind, Professor Charlotte Varga is with us from the Philadelphia Center. She's been doing research on music and the mind and has kindly agreed to talk with us. Welcome!

10 IDENTIFY Before you listen, find the stressed words in these sentences. Then listen again and repeat the sentences.

1 Now, what can you tell us about this interesting topic?

2 It can be incredibly frustrating, as the song just sticks in your mind.

3 So it's different from your earworm.

4 The songs are often from the distant past.

11 WHAT'S YOUR ANGLE? How well can you remember song lyrics? Do you sometimes try to actively learn them? If so, why? Discuss. If you can, tell a partner a few song lyrics.

When I was in Brazil I had studied in Public school. In my school they taught many subjects as science, math, history and English. I hadn't problem with history and Portuguese but math was difficult for me. Sometimes I had to take extra math classes with a tutor.

1.4 What Are You Implying?

1 ACTIVATE Imagine that someone has asked you to meet at a coffee shop because he or she needs your help with something. The person is 30 minutes late, which really annoys you. For each situation, would you say anything when the person shows up? If so, what do you say?

1 The person is a close friend.
2 The person is your boss.

2 INTERACT Compare responses with a partner. How does the relationship between you and your friend or you and your boss affect how you speak to each of them? How does the setting affect what you say?

3 ▶ IDENTIFY Watch the video and answer these questions.

1 Does Dave say anything to Max that may be interpreted as negative?
2 How does Dave non-verbally communicate a negative opinion of Max?
3 Dave talks about his art success. How does this affect the conversation?
4 How does the conversation end?

REAL-WORLD ENGLISH Picking up on implied meaning

Sometimes people avoid direct criticism of a person we are speaking to because they want to avoid overt conflict. Rather, they hint at their true meaning through a combination of intonation, sarcasm, and backhanded compliments. To avoid engaging in the same negativity, you can immediately say something that shows you understood the implied meaning but do not appreciate the person's implied insult:

A: Those glasses do a really good job of hiding the bags under your eyes.
B: I like my glasses, too. But hey, I'm a little sensitive about my wrinkles.

Another possible way to respond to such implied negative meaning is with humor:

B: Yeah, I know. That's why I chose them (and wink).

You can also neutrally communicate clear consequences if someone is speaking to you negatively:

A: Thanks for inviting me to this movie that has the worst ratings ever. What a really great way to spend my free time.
B: I invited you because I thought it would be fun. But if this is how you feel about something I invite you to do, I will just go with someone else. No big deal.

4 ▶ **ASSESS** Watch the video again and watch for the strategies described in the Real-World English box. Would any of these strategies be different in your own culture? Share with a partner.

5 **ANALYZE** Write your responses to the following sentences. What is the speaker of each sentence implying?

A: Another F on a test! Man, you are a genius!
B: I know. I tried really hard!

1 I have the top score in class, and I don't even study that hard. I guess it all comes to me naturally.

_____

2 I have *so* many friends on social media, and they always like my posts. I guess people feel that my life is really interesting.

_____

3 Can you believe that someone complimented me and then offered to buy the painting I made for class? I mean, I just slapped a few colors together without really thinking about it.

_____

4 Ugh! I was trying to be nice by offering my colleague a ride home. While we were driving, he spilled his coffee on the seat. I mean, who drinks coffee in a Lamborghini?

_____

5 Whenever I am out in public, a lot of people mistake me for that famous author. I guess I have one of those famous-looking faces!

_____

6 **NOTICE** Read the sentences in Exercise 5 out loud twice with different types of intonation. Does the meaning of each sentence change depending on the intonation?

7 **EXPAND** Work with a partner. Compare your responses. Did you choose to let the person know that you want them to stop? Did you communicate clear consequences? Did you use humor? Or did you choose another strategy? Take turns saying the sentences and your responses.

8 **BUILD** Your responses to someone's implied meaning might change depending on your relationship to the person. What you would say in the following situations? Share your responses with a partner.

1 You show a photo of you and your sibling(s) as children. Someone says: *Wow, I guess you went through an awkward stage as a kid.* Write how you would respond to this person if you are:
Not close to this person

_____

Very close to this person

_____

2 You haven't had time to reciprocate treating someone to lunch. Before your lunch break, this person starts a conversation with you and then looks at their watch and says, *Geez I'm so hungry, and I didn't pack a lunch today.* Write how you would respond to this person if you are:
Not close to this person

_____

Very close to this person

_____

9 **INTERACT** Look at the situation below and work with a partner to prepare a conversation. Keep the dialogue going for one minute, and end your conversation naturally.

You bump into a colleague you have been trying to avoid because a few months ago you promised to attend a three-hour after-work function that you consider extremely boring. You've also used the excuse of a packed schedule to get out of attending the boring event, but she or he just overheard you say to another co-worker that your schedule is wide open this week. Your colleague approaches you and says: *That thing is tomorrow after work. I'm so shy at those events, and it would make me feel better if someone came with me.*

10 **SHARE** Role-play your conversation for the class.

GO ONLINE
to create your own version
of the English For Real video.

13

1.5 Artistic Struggle

1 ACTIVATE Look at the names of these famous creative people. Can you say what they are famous for?

1 Richard Branson
2 Frank Gehry
3 J.K.Rowling
4 Walt Disney
5 Michelangelo
6 Coco Chanel
7 Ang Lee
8 Frida Kahlo

2 INTEGRATE All the creative people in Exercise 1 overcame different problems in their lives. Work with a partner to match the person to the problem.

a Learned how to sew in an orphanage ___
b Had serious problems forming relationships ___
c Initially rejected by publishers ___
d School principal thought they would end up a millionaire or a criminal ___
e Fired for lacking imagination ___
f Made money selling cardboard furniture ___
g Experienced injuries from a bus accident ___
h Unemployed for many years after moving to the United States ___

3 WHAT'S YOUR ANGLE? Tell your partner who you would most like to meet of all the creative people who came up in today's lesson. Why? Think of at least two questions you would ask them.

> ### SPEAKING Giving a presentation: Signposting, generalizing, and clarifying points
>
> To make a presentation clear, speakers use clear language to **signpost** or guide listeners, so they can follow the main points.
>
> *Now I'm going to discuss…, Moving on…*
>
> Speakers often **generalize**. As a listener, listen for clues.
>
> *Generally speaking…*
>
> Recognizing language for generalizing can help listeners pick out the main message. Speakers sometimes use this kind of language before moving to more specific language.
>
> *(general) My favorite kind of art is sculpture, due to its simplicity.* → *(specific) In fact, there is one piece that…*
>
> Speakers often **clarify** points they make, perhaps because it is complicated or because their listeners appear confused.
>
> *By that, I mean…*

4 PREPARE Match the first phrases from each stage of the presentation with the appropriate stage. The key signposting words are italicized to help you.

Stages of the presentation

1 Introduction ___
2 Background details ___
3 New life in the U.S. ___
4 From acting to directing ___
5 Finding work ___
6 Describing Lee's work ___
7 Why the speaker likes him ___
8 Summary ___
9 Closing the talk ___

First phrases from each stage

a Instead, *moving on, I'll talk briefly about* the nature of his art. How would I describe his films?
b *I hope you've enjoyed* my presentation…
c *Anyway*, during this period, Ang Lee realized that although he had a talent for acting, his English was not good enough to let him pursue this career.
d *Today, I'd like to talk to you about* one of my favorite film artists.
e *Following on from that, I'll just give you* a little background information…
f *And for my next point*, I'll explain precisely why I personally am such a big fan.
g *So* Lee began focusing on directing and screenwriting…
h *In conclusion*, I would like to explain that I find Lee admirable not only because of his gift…
i *And that brings me to my next point*: where his real story started.

5 ◀ APPLY Listen to the presentation and make notes about each part, using the signposting phrases italicized in Exercise 4 to help you identify the different stages.

6 IDENTIFY Look at the phrases below. Decide which ones are used to generalize (Z) and which to clarify (Y).

By and large… ___		In other words… ___	
As a rule… ___		What I'm trying to say is… ___	
In general… ___		By that I mean… ___	
What I mean is… ___		On the whole… ___	
…tend to… ___		Is this what is needed? ___	

7 SHARE Prepare to give a three-minute presentation about a creative person of your choice.

8 IMPROVE Watch your classmates' presentations, and write three things you like about them and three areas for improvement.

Now go to page 147 for the Unit 1 Review.

2 Literature

▼ What do you think the climber is reading?

▼ What are the benefits of reading fiction?

▼ Do you prefer to read on screen or on paper?

BEHIND THE PHOTO

Work in a small group. Find out the following, and be prepared to report back to the rest of the class.

1   Who reads the most per month on average? This could be fiction or nonfiction but should not be related to work or school.
2   When does this person prefer to read?
3   Where does this person prefer to read?

REAL-WORLD GOAL

Read a fiction or nonfiction book in English

2.1 Literature that Lasts

1 **ACTIVATE** What kind of books do you most enjoy? Choose your favorite(s), and discuss why in small groups.

classic	historical novels	comedies
poetry	popular fiction	science fiction
fantasy	detective stories	thrillers
comics	horror	(auto)biographies
short stories	nonfiction	other

2 **IDENTIFY** Read the blurb from the back cover of a novel. What kind of book is it? Which of the covers above does it go with?

INTRODUCTORY PASSAGE

On the Polar ice-cap, 640 kilometres north of the Arctic Circle, the deadly, icy winds can freeze a man to death in minutes. But the survivors of the crashed airliner are lucky—they are rescued by three scientists from a nearby weather station.

But why did the airliner crash in the first place? Who smashed the radio to pieces? And why does the dead pilot have a bullet hole in his back? The rescue quickly turns into a nightmare: a race through the endless Arctic night, a race against time, cold, hunger—and a killer with a gun.

READING SKILL Appreciating literature

Appreciating literature can help you comprehend an author's writing on different levels, leading to a deeper understanding. It can also be very informative about history, human behavior, culture, society, and so on. Many say that a deeper understanding of literature helps you in life. A good way to understand more deeply is to ask yourself questions as you read:

Why is this scene important? What does it tell us about the main character(s)?

What elements of interest are there? (history, humor, emotions, facts, attitudes, the plot, and so on)

In what way is the author's description effective or not? Consider word choice, such as adjectives, adverbs, and verbs, and how the writer creates tension and interest through his or her language, and so on.

3 **IDENTIFY** You are going to read an extract from a novel called *Night Without End* by Alistair MacLean. Read and put the events in order according to the extract.

1 They left the cabin.
2 They found warm clothes and equipment and prepared the dogs.
3 They ran through the snow to find the plane and survivors.
4 One of the scientists heard the engines of a plane.
5 They were trying to get warm in the cabin as they settled for the night.
6 They tied the metal thread from the 'homing spool' to fixed objects, to hold on to and avoid getting lost.
7 They heard the plane descend and crash.

Chapter I
Monday Midnight

It was Jackstraw who heard the sound first.

"Aeroplane," he announced.

"Aeroplane?" I asked disbelievingly.

"Come and listen."

That was the last thing I felt like doing. I had been lying in my sleeping bag for fifteen minutes and had only just succeeded in creating a little warmth inside it. My feet, which had been completely frozen, were beginning to come to life again and the idea of getting out into the sub-zero temperatures of our cabin filled me with horror.

"Can you still hear the plane?" I asked.

"Yes. It's getting louder and closer all the time." I lay there wondering what kind of plane it could possibly be.

"Dr. Mason!" His voice was urgent now. "I think the plane's in trouble! It's coming lower and closer. It's a big plane—I can hear several engines."

We lost no time getting out of the cabin. We gasped in pain as the bitter cold entered our lungs. The wind was even stronger than I had expected. Its sound, like that of a human being crying out in pain, was louder than usual, but above that sound, we could now hear the roar of the plane's engines.

And then we saw it. It was less than two kilometers away. I only saw it for five seconds, but what I saw filled me with amazement. It was not the small type of plane I was expecting. It was a huge passenger airliner.

The plane had turned a full circle and was now slowing down. It seemed to be flying at a dangerously slow speed. Then I saw its landing lights come on.

"He's going to land!" I shouted to Jackstraw. "He's looking for a place to land. Get the dogs. Tie them to the sledge. Hurry!"

"Get all the warm clothes you can find, Joss," I shouted. "And bring sleeping bags, blankets—whatever you can think of. Don't forget the fire-fighting equipment—and…don't forget the homing spool. We'll never find our way back to the cabin without that."

4 APPLY Do you think MacLean's description is successful? Consider the questions in the Reading Skill box.

5 WHAT'S YOUR ANGLE? Is this your kind of novel? Are you interested in reading more? Why or why not?

VOCABULARY DEVELOPMENT Similes

Similes are used by writers to make vivid and powerful comparisons. Similes generally use *like* or *as* to signal a comparison:

The plane came into sight, passing within two hundred meters of us like a huge, horrible bird.

The wind was even stronger than I had expected. Its sound, like that of a human being crying out in pain, was louder than usual…

Look back at the text, if necessary, and decide whether these similes are successful.

Jackstraw was busy tying the dogs to the sledge. I hurried over to the snow-tractor and with great difficulty removed the frozen searchlight that we would no doubt be needing. Then we heard the roar of the plane's engines again. The plane came into sight, passing within two hundred metres of us like a huge, horrible bird.

Our progress was slow and painful as we moved along, fighting the bitter, icy wind. We were following the line of the radio antenna that was supported at intervals by pairs of poles, four metres high. Suddenly the roar of the engines became deafeningly louder. Throwing myself to the ground, I saw the plane fly directly over us. Then the engine stopped and I heard a hissing sound, followed by another loud sound as the earth all around us shook, and then finally the sound of metal being torn apart. Then there was silence.

We set off immediately, making sure that we tied the end of the line from the spool to one of the antenna poles. Our lives now depended on that homing spool. Without it, we would never find our way back to the antenna and then the cabin. It was our only guide in the darkness and the blinding wind, over iron-hard snow, where there were never any footprints to help us find our way.

We were running now. And as I ran, desperate thoughts flooded my mind. Were the passengers trapped inside the plane or had they been thrown out onto the ice-cap? If so, they would freeze to death within five minutes. How were we going to get them back to the cabin? And how were we going to feed them all if we got them back safely?

6 BUILD There are many commonly used similes in English. Match the adjectives to the nouns they appear with in a common simile.

1	blind	→	a	button
2	cute	6	b	peacock
3	dry	9	c	ox
4	dull	4	d	dishwater
5	good	11	e	bird
6	proud	3	f	bone
7	sure	5	g	gold
8	stubborn	10	h	snow
9	strong	1	i	bat
10	white	7	j	death
11	free	8	k	mule

stubborn as a mule

dull = boring, annoyed

7 USE Finish each sentence, using one of the above similes.

1 "Are your hands warm?" "No, they're _as cold as ice!_ "

2 "Did you enjoy the novel?" "Not really! It went on and on about nothing. I found it _dull as dishwater_."

3 "Can you see this? The print's too small for me." "Me too. I'm _blind as bat_."

4 "I've given up my job and I feel so good! No more early starts and no stress. I'm _free like bird_."

5 "My grandmother's not going to change her mind." "No. She's _stubborn like mole_."

6 "Your dad lifted up the car single-handed." "I know. He's _strong like ox_."

7 "Was my little brother any trouble?" "Oh, not at all. He was _good as gold_."

Review

'S YOUR ANGLE? Think about similes in your ~~language~~guage. Do you use the same ones? Discuss.

9 SHARE In small groups, see who can make up the best similes for the following adjectives. When you have finished, decide which group's ideas are the best.

fast	black	tiny
hot	dangerous	lazy

GRAMMAR IN CONTEXT Narrative tenses

The past simple is generally used to talk about the main event or a sequence of actions or events.

Throwing myself to the ground, I saw the plane fly directly over us. Then the engine stopped and I heard a hissing sound…

The past continuous is used for background descriptions or actions that are in progress at the time of the main event(s).

We were following the line of the radio antenna that was supported at intervals by pairs of poles, four metres high. Suddenly the roar of the engines became deafeningly louder.

The past perfect is used when you want to make it clear that actions or events took place at an earlier time in the story. This might be because the actions are not in chronological order.

The wind was even stronger than I had expected.

The past perfect continuous is used to talk about ongoing activities leading up to a past event in order to give background information to the event.

"Come and listen."
That was the last thing I felt like doing. I had been lying in my sleeping bag for fifteen minutes and had only just succeeded in creating a little warmth inside it.

The future in the past is used to talk about past events that were in the future at the time of the narrative.

How were we going to get them back to the cabin?

See Grammar focus on page 160.

10 IDENTIFY Look at the sentences in the Grammar box. Translate them into your first language. Tell a partner how the languages compare. Are the forms similar or different? How are the different meanings conveyed? Can you find other examples in the text of each form?

11 APPLY Look at this summary of the novel. Put the verbs in brackets into appropriate narrative forms.

Fortunately, Mason and Jackstraw tracked down the plane in the storm and found most of the passengers on board alive. Two, including the pilot, ¹ _____ (be shot), and one was seriously injured. The scientists ² _____ (took) the survivors back to their cabin where the three men ³ _____ (live and work) for the last few weeks.

They quickly realized that there ⁴ _____ (not be) enough food for all of them to survive more than a few days. They decided they ⁵ _____ (need) to go for supplies, several hundred miles away, the next day. However, within the first few moments of being there, one of the passengers "accidentally" ⁶ _____ (break) their station radio, which was their only means of communication. That night, the injured crew member was murdered.

The scientists had an old snow-tractor and a dog sledge, but one of the passengers was elderly, and they soon discovered that another ⁷ _____ (suffer) from diabetes and needed urgent treatment. It was also evident that two of their passengers were murderers: at first, the scientists ⁸ _____ (assume) that the stewardess was guilty, but as they ⁹ _____ (travel) over the ice, their main suspects ¹⁰ _____ (kept) changing.

The scientists learned that the plane ¹¹ _____ (carry) a top-secret piece of government military equipment. Clearly, someone on the plane ¹² _____ (intend) to steal this since the plane had been hundreds of miles off course. The story ends with a frightening race across the ice and a fight between good and evil.

12 WHAT'S YOUR ANGLE? Think of a novel or story often studied in your first language that you feel positively about. Think about this book for two minutes, and prepare to tell a partner about it. Consider the author, the plot, the main characters, and the style of writing.

13 INTERACT Work with a partner and look at the following opening lines. What kind of novel could each set of lines be from? Explain.

1 Slowly, soundlessly, the snow started to fall. The flakes were thick and heavy. At the end of the drive was a tall, dark house, black as night against the white snow.

2 Maria was carefully picking out the best plums from the market stall, picking each item up and examining it closely. After about 15 minutes, she noticed the stall-holder staring at her and dropped the fruit she was holding in embarrassment.

3 There it was, number 13. The small, gold plaque read "Simpkins—Private Detective." The man knocked nervously, then waited.

4 He lay on the bed for an instant before he was overwhelmed with the strong smell of burning plastic. The room was melting.

14 WRITE Choose one of the opening lines above. Continue the story for at least 175 words. Try to include different narrative tenses and at least one simile.

2.2 Reading Graphs

1 ACTIVATE What's your preference? Compare your answers in a small group, including at least one reason for each of your answers.

- Fiction or nonfiction?
- Audio, eBook, or print book?
- Long or short?
- Modern or old?

2 INTERACT Look at the graphs about reading for two minutes. Then tell a partner what you understand about them. Start your statements with phrases like *This graph shows…* and *According to this graph…*

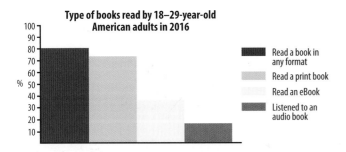

Type of books read by 18–29-year-old American adults in 2016

- Read a book in any format
- Read a print book
- Read an eBook
- Listened to an audio book

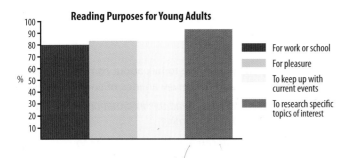

Reading Purposes for Young Adults

- For work or school
- For pleasure
- To keep up with current events
- To research specific topics of interest

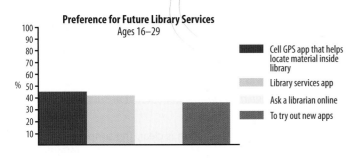

Preference for Future Library Services Ages 16–29

- Cell GPS app that helps locate material inside library
- Library services app
- Ask a librarian online
- To try out new apps

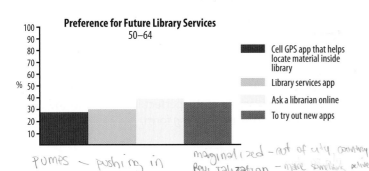

Preference for Future Library Services 50–64

- Cell GPS app that helps locate material inside library
- Library services app
- Ask a librarian online
- To try out new apps

3 IDENTIFY Read the report, and see how it compares with your own ideas in Exercise 2. Fill in the gaps with the correct phrase from below, using the information shown in the graphs.

a little under a third	approximately nine out of ten
about twice	slightly more than this
just over a third	just over a quarter
more or less	around 80%
four fifths	

This report focuses on relevant information from two recent surveys that were carried out by the Pew Research Center. The surveys were compiled in 2013 and 2016, and are available online. This report has been put together with the goal of informing funding allocation to the college library for the next three academic years.

The overall survey included data about different age groups and genders. The first graph here shows the preferred format of books for 18- to 29-year-olds. The second graph indicates the purpose of reading for the same age group. The third graph shows what future library services younger users would ideally like to be available.

With regard to book format, the first graph shows that, overall, [1] _____ of people aged 18 to 29 read a book over the 12-month period and that around 72 percent of these read a print book. Interestingly, this figure was greater than for an older age group, the 30- to 50-year-olds, where two thirds had read a print book. This suggests that paper books are still the first choice for many. However, although only 28 percent of people in total read an eBook, [2] _____ of young adults did. Audio books were also slightly more popular among young adults than the average, which was 14 percent. It appears that [3] _____ as many 18- to 29-year-olds read an eBook than listen to audio books.

The second graph indicates that the main reason for reading was to research topics of interest. [4] _____ young adults do this. This was more than any other age group in the survey. [5] _____ of young adults read for work or school, and [6] _____ percent of readers read for pleasure or for news. This suggests that the college library could usefully include a wider coverage of materials in terms of topics beyond course-related fields.

The third graph is of particular relevance to us since it describes what people want for future library services. Younger adults showed a clear preference for apps (a GPS app to use around the library) when compared to older adults. Forty-five percent of 16- to 29-year-olds said they would like a GPS library app, compared with [7] _____ of 50–64-year-olds. Similarly, whereas 42 percent stated a preference for the library services app, 8 _____ of the older age group thought the same. Reactions to having an online research service ("Ask a librarian online") were 9 _____ similar for both age groups, at 37 percent and 39 percent, respectively.

Having read these surveys, I recommend the following:

- We conduct our own survey(s) to find out the same information as the graphs described but for our own students.
- We research potential apps for our own school library service.
- We include in our survey additional questions of relevance, e.g., how our students currently use the library, how often, areas for improvement, etc.

I would be happy to be responsible for organizing this in conjunction with Marcos Ferreira, the new head librarian.

From	Harry Wheeler
Date	January 24
RE	Library Report

4 WHAT'S YOUR ANGLE? In a recent survey on reading habits in England, 1,500 adults from a range of social backgrounds and age groups were interviewed. They were asked: How much do you enjoy reading books?

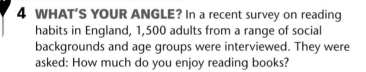
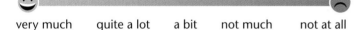

very much   quite a lot   a bit   not much   not at all

What do you think the answers were for 1,500 people? Your teacher will tell you the results.

WRITING SKILL Using vague language

When describing numbers and statistics, words or phrases such as *roughly* or *around* can be useful to give approximations, as in *around 10 percent* (see Exercise 3). This makes the data easier for a reader to interpret.

Sometimes the writer may intentionally use vague language to help make or support their specific point since phrasing can be influential. For example, 70 percent equals almost three quarters. In another situation, the writer might prefer to make the amount sound less, and therefore say "just over two-thirds."

5 APPLY Look at the graphs again carefully, and comment on any details that were not mentioned in the report such as purpose for reading and interest in future library services. Tell a partner four to six sentences. Try to include vague language.

6 ASSESS Read the college president's reply. Find out if she was pleased with the report and what the next steps are for (a) herself and (b) Harry Wheeler, the report writer.

Dear Harry,

Thanks very much for your report, which was both informative and interesting. I apologize again for having requested it at such short notice and really appreciate your hard work since I know this is a busy period for you. It was very helpful to have read this information before my preliminary meeting with the board this morning.

Having reflected on it, I'd now like to take you up on your generous offer to help with a dedicated survey for our own students. Like you, I believe it is logical and necessary at this point. As you know, we need to have decided on funding by the end of next month, so the sooner you can complete this, the better. Not having met Mr. Ferreira yet, I will arrange a meeting with him in the next couple of days and use the opportunity to inform him of this forthcoming questionnaire.

Many thanks again for your help on this.

Regards,
Eloise

GRAMMAR IN CONTEXT
Perfect infinitives and perfect -ing forms

The infinitive is used after some verbs, adjectives, and nouns.

I need to leave.

We use the perfect infinitive to talk about something that happened earlier and to convey an idea of completion.

It was very helpful to have read this information before my preliminary meeting this morning

The perfect infinitive can also be used to refer to something that will be completed at a future point.

I hope to have read it by this Friday.

We use the -ing form after some verbs (or verbs + prepositions) and in clauses of time, reason, and result. We also use the perfect -ing form to highlight that something was done or completed in the past.

I apologize again for having requested it at such short notice.

When the time of the action is clear, the simple infinitive or -ing form can be used instead of the perfect infinitive or perfect -ing form.

It was very helpful to read it.
I apologize again for requesting it at such short notice.

See Grammar focus on page 160.

7 IDENTIFY Read the email again. Find the single additional example of the perfect infinitive and the two examples of the perfect -ing form.

8 APPLY Rewrite each sentence, starting with the words given. Use a perfect infinitive or perfect *-ing* form.

1 I'm sorry I spent your book voucher!
She apologized _for having spent the book voucher_.

2 OK, I left your novel on the bus. I feel really bad!
He admitted _____.

3 Meeting that author this morning was very useful.
It was _____.

4 I felt telling her all the details about the forthcoming book wasn't actually necessary.
There was no need _____.

5 I should finish writing my new novel by the end of the week, if all goes to plan.
I hope _____.

6 It's OK, but let this be the last time you borrow my books without asking!
She was forgiven _____.

9 INTEGRATE Match clauses to make complete sentences. For each sentence, use one clause from A and one from B.

A

1 Having lost my coursework, ___

2 Having written the first chapter of my novel, ___

3 Having been told that Shakespeare was the greatest writer, ___

4 Having recognized the importance of reading to young children, ___

5 Not having brought my charger with me, ___

6 Not having remembered to buy a book at the airport, ___

B

a I began reading his works with great enthusiasm.

b I was unable to finish my book on my device.

c I wasn't awarded a certificate.

d I regularly read to my own when I became a parent.

e I just watched three films on the long-haul flight.

f I decided to rest for a little while before restarting.

10 EXPAND Work with a partner. Cover section B from Exercise 9. Together finish each sentence in A in a different and more imaginative way.

11 PREPARE Work with a partner and together discuss what the chart shows, noting anything of interest.

Types of Readers

Qualifications and Salary	Read a book in any format	Read a print book	Read an eBook	Listened to an audio book
Less than high school	45	38	11	12
High school grad	62	55	19	9
Some college	81	74	32	14
College +	86	79	41	20
Below $30,000	65	59	19	9
$30,000–$49,999	74	68	26	16
$50,000–74,999	75	69	33	19
$75,000+	81	73	40	16

12 WRITE Write a one- or two-paragraph description of the chart. Include at least three examples of vague language, but include two or three details that are incorrect. Start with an introductory sentence such as *This graph shows*….

13 SHARE Read a partner's description and identify any details that are incorrect.

14 WHAT'S YOUR ANGLE? Work in a group. Create a survey to find out details of the class's reading habits. Each group should choose one or two different aspects relating to reading or library use and devise four to six relevant questions to ask each student. Use or adapt ideas from the graphs, charts, and activities in this lesson, if you like.

A reading room at a gallery in Milan, Italy

2.3 Needing Reading

1 ACTIVATE Read these quotations from famous people about literature. Which ones do you agree with? Discuss.

"A good book is an event in my life." –Stendhal

"The person who deserves most pity is a lonesome one on a rainy day who doesn't know how to read." –Benjamin Franklin

"To acquire a habit of reading is to construct for yourself a refuge from almost all the miseries of life." –W. Somerset Maugham

2 WHAT'S YOUR ANGLE? Why do you read? Choose the most relevant reason(s) for you from the list.

to relax or de-stress   to escape   to learn   other reasons

> ## LISTENING SKILL Listening for detail
>
> Listening for detail can be challenging in a second language, especially when there is only one opportunity to listen. These three strategies may help.
>
> Anticipate: Ask yourself some questions in advance about what you are going to hear. This prediction activity, whether at a general or more intensive level, is both natural and useful.
>
> Accept: You are unlikely to understand or hear every single word and phrase; this may partly be due to cultural references, pronunciation, speed, and so on. Accept this in advance, to lower anxiety.
>
> Acknowledge: Listening is tiring, so with longer listenings, decide in advance which parts or for how long you will concentrate on.

3 IDENTIFY Read the description of an online radio talk show that you are going to listen to. What is it about?

EVENING

7:10 BOOK CLUB with Alex Heron

In this, the last program of the series, Alex talks to his guests about the importance of literature in our lives. Guests include children's author Joanne Lively, poet Suzanne Stein, and TV personality and quiz show host Zoltan Nemeth.

Charles Dickens
Great Expectations
OXFORD WORLD'S CLASSICS

One thousand and one
Arabian Nights
Geraldine McCaughrean

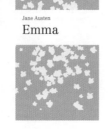
Jane Austen
Emma

4 APPLY Work in a small group. Anticipate what each guest speaker might say in response to these questions.

■ How important is literature to this person?

■ Why is or has it been so important?

■ Can you think of one or two more questions that you would be curious to have answered?

5 ◆ INTEGRATE Listen to the talk show and answer the questions from Exercise 4. Add any extra details you can to support your points.

6 INTERACT Tell your group what you heard the speakers say. Did any of the listening strategies help? Why or why not?

7 WHAT'S YOUR ANGLE? Which speaker did you agree most with? Why? Discuss with a partner.

8 VOCABULARY Match the positive adjectives for discussing literature with their closest synonyms in this context.

A
1 well-researched
2 detailed
3 realistic
4 likeable
5 exciting
6 fascinating
7 imaginative
8 understandable
9 moving
10 fast-moving

B   *touching, saddening*
a **poignant**
b intriguing
c original
d thorough
e **action-packed**
f appealing
g credible
h accessible
i compelling
j elaborate

&+ Oxford 5000™

9 INTEGRATE Insert an adjective from column B in Exercise 8 into each sentence below.

1 The novel must have taken such a long time to create because the historical elements were so accurate and _____.

2 The description of the crime and the lead-up to it are so _____ that I simply couldn't put the book down!

3 What I like about his characters is the fact that they are _____. One of them reminded me so much of an old school friend.

4 I find some of the speeches in Shakespeare's tragedies to be very _____. When I watch *Othello*, I always cry.

5 That writer looks at things in a very different way, and it's so _____. You never quite know what to expect.

6 The plots are always extremely _____, so often the books are long! But as a result, readers find them easy to picture and hard to forget.

PRONUNCIATION SKILL Word stress in adjectives

There are some general word-stress rules about adjectives that can help you in listening and speaking.

For a two-syllable adjective, the stress is much more likely to be on the first syllable (e.g., *simple*). Prefixes and suffixes are rarely stressed (e.g., in*cred*ible, *beautiful*). There are some exceptions, such as the nationality suffix *-ese*, as in *Japanese*.

For adjectives ending with *-ic*, *-ical*, *-ious*, and *-ian*, and also for most two or three syllable adjectives ending in *-ing*, the stress comes before this ending (e.g., sym*pathetic*, his*torical*, hi*larious*, Ma*laysian*, and in*triguing*).

With two-word compound adjectives, both parts are stressed, but the main stress generally falls on the second component: well-*known*, fast-*moving*, old-*fashioned*.

Note that if these compound adjectives are followed by a word where the first syllable is stressed, then the stress on the compound often changes, moving to the first syllable in the compound: an *old*-fashioned story, a *well*-known writer. This is the same with simple adjectives ending in *-ese*, so a *Japanese* novel but a novel that is Japa*nese*.

10 NOTICE Work with a partner. Categorize all the adjectives from Exercise 8 according to their word stress, noting both stresses in the compound words.

Oo	Ooo	oOo	Oooo	oOoo
moving	loveable			

ooOo	ooOoo	Ooo	oOooo	OOo

11 🔊 ASSESS Listen to the recording, and check your answers to Exercise 10. Then listen again and repeat the words.

12 INTERACT Work with a partner. Look at the two lists in Exercise 8 again. Use the adjectives to create dialogs about some of following or use your own ideas:

- plot
- main characters
- beginning/ending
- storyline
- emotions
- details

A: I thought the background details were really well researched.
B: Yes, it was really thorough!

GRAMMAR IN CONTEXT
Verb patterns after verbs of the senses

We use verbs of senses (such as *feel, see, hear, watch*) + object + infinitive (without *to*) to talk about a whole or completed action.
My mother said she watched my language grow at the same rate as my feet.

We use verb + object + *-ing* form to show a snapshot of something we saw or heard or to describe an activity as either repeated, ongoing, or incomplete.
She saw me looking at her bookshelves with curiosity on a few occasions.

See Grammar focus on page 160.

13 EXPAND Unscramble the sentences, so they are worded correctly.

1 why / intriguing / tell us / think / is / fiction / so / you

_____

2 literature / a similar / do you / about / feeling / have / ?

_____

3 writer's / process / I would like / elaborate / to see / the

_____

4 hear / sometimes / I / voices / the characters' / reading / I'm / when

_____

14 WHAT'S YOUR ANGLE? Consider a novel or author you particularly like. Do you like the novel or author because of the originality of ideas, the plot, the characters, the style of writing, or something else? Share with a partner, using some of the adjectives from Exercise 8.

2.4 I Take It Back

1 **ACTIVATE** Have you ever said something really negative about someone in the heat of the moment only to regret it later? How did other people react in that situation?

2 ▶ **IDENTIFY** Watch the video, and respond to these questions.

1 How does Andy talk about Dave?
2 How does Max talk about Dave?
3 What will Max do the next time Dave puts him down?

REAL-WORLD ENGLISH Defending someone

If someone is the topic of criticism, we can defend them and soften the criticizer's stated negative assessment. We may do this by first listening to the criticizer's comments and responding with something positive as a counterargument to each point of unpleasantness.

Bob: I don't understand why Sergio won first prize in the baking contest. He thinks his recipes are SO original when really <u>they aren't that great</u>.

Paul: Sure, but his pies always have <u>an interesting twist to them</u>.

Bob: Yeah, but he has <u>an overinflated ego</u> because of how he designs his cakes. Just because he has a background in <u>graphic design, doesn't mean his cakes are the best</u>.

Paul: I would be proud of my cakes <u>if they looked as beautiful</u> as his. And he really puts <u>a lot of thought into the appearance</u> of his creations.

When defending someone, you can soften a critique at any time, but be sure to respond only to the criticism about the subject of conversation and not criticize the person speaking.

3 ▶ **ANALYZE** Watch the video again. What does Max say to Andy in order to defend Dave?

4 **ASSESS** What does Andy say about Dave to Max? What could be a possible consequence if Dave found out that Andy said this?

ENGLISH FOR REAL

5 NOTICE How much would you defend the people in the following situations? Why do you think so?

Very little				A great deal
1	2	3	4	5

1 You and your best friend are in a smelly taxi during rush hour. Your friend has a headache, and the taxi driver is constantly honking and abruptly pressing on the brakes. While getting out of a cab at your destination, your best friend is in a bad mood and says to you in a very loud voice, "Someone needs to go back to driving school and buy some air freshener."

2 During a meeting, all of your colleagues update the boss on what you're all working on. It's clear that your co-worker, Yuri, is already extremely busy with a multitude of time-sensitive tasks, but your boss assigns more work to him. Yuri is visibly stressed during the meeting, and afterwards, when you ask him about it, he says to you, "It's pretty clear that the boss is out of touch with the type of work I do. I'm already so overloaded and I don't think he understands how busy I am. I wish he would stop treating me like his personal secretary."

3 You and your two best friends, Miryam and Prudence, choose a restaurant based on Prudence's extremely picky eating habits. Before ordering, Miryam announces that the meal is on her. Prudence orders herself a large cheese pizza and a large pasta with plain tomato sauce. Once the meal is served, Prudence asks for an extra plate on which she puts the cheese she scrapes off the pizza. She eats all of the crust, sauce, and a small amount of cheese. Then she takes one bite of the pasta and declares she is full before you and Miryam are finished eating. At the end of the meal, Prudence declines taking anything home even though most of her meal is untouched. The check comes at the same time Prudence excuses herself from the table. Miryam says to you, "I think it's really rude when she wastes so much food, especially when someone is offering to foot the bill. Plus we're always bending over backwards to make sure she approves of the menu first."

foot the bill → Take over the bill

Bending over backwards → make sure the person is being pleasent

4 You and six of your friends who you haven't seen in a while are on vacation together. It's the afternoon, and your friend Frederich really wants to go hiking, but the others don't. When asked what everyone wants to do instead, no one offers any suggestions. Your group ends up sitting in the hotel room catching up until it's time for dinner. Frederich is perturbed. On your way to the restaurant, Frederich says to you, "It's annoying when people can't decide on what they want to do and waste a bunch of time."

6 DEVELOP Write an effective softener to defend each of the people in situations in Exercise 5.

7 EXPAND Choose two situations from Exercise 5 and review the softeners you came up with in Exercise 6. Develop the interaction further. What counter-criticism could you expect to your softener? And how could you respond to further criticism? Provide a critique for each situation, and soften it. Create at least two turns of conversation.

Situation 1
Positive (your original softener): _____
Further critique: _____
Positive: _____

Situation 2
Positive (your original softener): _____
Further critique: _____
Positive: _____

8 INTERACT Compare your softened critiques to a partner's. Is there a difference in the degree of softening?

9 BUILD With a partner, prepare a one-minute role play of one of your chosen situations.

10 SHARE Role-play your conversation for the class.

11 IMPROVE Watch your classmates' role plays. Do they use an appropriate degree of softening?

GO ONLINE
to create your own version
of the English For Real video.

25

2.5 Unusual Developments

1 ACTIVATE In small groups, (a) brainstorm as many fairy tales as you can think of, using the English titles if possible, and (b) think of at least four typical "ingredients" of a typical fairy tale, such as "a happy ending."

2 **IDENTIFY** Read the following extract about Franz Kafka. Complete each sentence using a word in the box.

protagonist	theme	works	twist	classical
creature	human	society	fiction	characters

Kafka, Franz (1883–1924)

Franz Kafka was an influential 20th-century writer from Prague. His life and works focus on the alienated individual in the modern world. In his ¹ _fiction_, Kafka adapted the dreamlike conditions of the fairy tale with an ironic ² _twist_. Kafka's mix of the fantastical and the realistic confuses his ³ _characters_ and alienates them from the ⁴ _society_ they are trying to join. By turning upside down the ⁵ _classical_ fairy tale and playing with its themes and motifs, Kafka created what has been called the *anti-fairy tale*, which questions the certainties and optimism of the original form.

For example, the ⁶ _protagonist_ of his novel *The Castle* (1926) does not progress like the fairy-tale hero from the peasant village to the castle but remains stuck between the two. In *The Metamorphosis* (1915), Kafka adapted the fairy tale ⁷ _theme_ of transformation by describing a traveling salesman who has been transformed into a giant insect-like ⁸ _creature_. His one-way transformation from ⁹ _human_ to monster strangely frees him from life in modern society and liberates his family. In many of his ¹⁰ _works_, Kafka explores the difficulties of life in the early 20th century.

—adapted from *The Oxford Companion to Fairy Tales*, 2nd ed., by Jack Zipes

3 ◀) **IDENTIFY** Listen to an extract from the first page of *Metamorphosis*. What does Gregor Samsa discover when he wakes up one morning?

SPEAKING
Critiquing and reviewing constructively

Being able to criticize constructively is an important skill in many different fields. You can aim to be balanced and informed by considering several different aspects, both positive and negative. Looking at the bigger picture may be helpful, too, instead of focusing just on smaller elements.

When considering a novel, for example, different topic areas can help you to give a balanced picture overall. Even if some elements are weak, it is likely that other elements are stronger.

Common elements of a novel:

Overall impression	Plot or story line
Dialogue between characters	Language used
Authenticity of setting	Author's purpose
Characterization (how characters are drawn)	

4 ◀) **IDENTIFY** Listen to two book enthusiasts discussing Kafka's story. What are their opinions about the elements of a novel listed in the Speaking box? Complete the table. One aspect is not discussed.

	George	Marilyn
Overall impression		
Plot/storyline		
Characterization		
Dialogue		
Language used		
Setting: authentic or not		
Author's purpose		

5 INTEGRATE Compare your notes with a partner. Decide (a) if you need to listen again and (b) if the two speakers' views were balanced overall.

6 PREPARE Prepare to critique a book, story, or play that you have read or watched lately.

- Make brief notes on relevant different categories from the Speaking box, including strengths as well as weaknesses where appropriate.
- Reflect on what you will say.

7 SHARE Work in a small group. Tell each other about the piece of literature. At the end, listeners should decide if they would like to read or see it, giving reasons.

Now go to page 148 for the Unit 2 Review.

3 Decisions

Where is the woman going?

How do people make decisions?

What's the best decision
you ever made?

BEHIND THE PHOTO

1 Imagine being the leader of your community or country. What changes
would you like to make in some of the following areas?

health	security	education	employment
taxes	crime and justice	the environment	the law

2 Share your ideas in a small group.

REAL-
WORLD
GOAL

Find out about the
experience of someone

3.1 Rational Human Beings

1 ACTIVATE Complete the questionnaire.

1 If you throw a coin and it lands heads five times, what do you think the next throw will be?

   a Heads

   b Tails

   c Either

2 You are told that you can save money on your bills by changing suppliers. What do you do?

   a Change to the new provider

   b Stick with the original

   c Neither

3 Do you think the amount of violence has increased or decreased in your community in the last 50 years?

   a Stayed the same

   b Decreased

   c Increased

4 You realize you have a 1.5-inch tear in the back of your shirt at work. What do you assume?

   a Nearly everyone notices

   b A few people notice

   c No one notices

5 Which would you do if you wanted to lose weight?

   a Choose a diet program that has immediate results but is less likely to work in the long term

   b Choose a diet program that is three times the length but is likely to have lasting results

   c Neither of the above

6 Even if they are still too expensive, do you buy items in stores that are reduced or on sale when you are told the original retail price?

   a Often

   b Rarely

   c Never

7 In which of these situations do you think you would feel happier?

   a To find $20 on the street

   b To find $20 outside your house that you had lost the previous day

   c I would feel just as pleased in each case

2 INTERACT Reflect on your choices in Exercise 1 and why you made them. Then work with a partner to see if you made the same choices and for the same reasons.

3 🔊 Listen to the explanations of the biases shown in the questionnaire. Listen again to understand the explanations given if necessary. What does the word *bias* mean? Use a dictionary if needed.

4 INTEGRATE Work with a partner, and match each of the questions (1–7) from the questionnaire to the relevant bias listed below. The first one has been done for you.

   a loss aversion   7

   b the fallacy of the maturity of chances   1

   c spotlight effect   4

   d status quo bias   2

   e negativity bias   3

   f anchoring effect   6

   g present bias   5

5 WHAT'S YOUR ANGLE? Discuss what you heard in a small group. From your answers to Exercise 1, did you behave in a typical human way? Is this a good or a bad thing? Can you think of other examples of your own behavior that reflect these biases?

6 EXPAND Read the text about behavioral economics. Complete each sentence using a phrase from the box below.

surveys	psychology and sociology
crises and crashes	ways of working
the weaknesses	important decisions

Studies in behavioral economics question the beliefs we have in relation to human decision-making. Behavioral economists use findings from fields such as [1] psychology and socio__ to show how economic and financial "experts" use intuition rather than more scientific methods to make [2] important decisions__. Using laboratory experiments and [3] surveys__, they have shown the behavioral importance of concepts such as loss aversion as well as present and future bias.

Behavioral economics rose as a response to the limitations of the standard psychological models in explaining important phenomena and problems such as strikes in labor markets, [4] crises in crashes__ in financial markets, and issues such as unemployment in macroeconomics.

Behavioral economics has been controversial within economics because of its challenge to the dominant model. The field has been attacked because of its suggestion that reliable and stable outcomes cannot actually be predicted.

Behavioral economics has been impressively successful in demonstrating [5] the weaknesses__ in the dominant theory. Its future significance depends on whether it can be used effectively to give alternative [6] ways to working na__, offer explanations, provide accurate predictions, and guide research and policy.

—adapted from *The Oxford Encyclopedia of American Business, Labor, and Economic History*, by Melvin Dubofsky

7 🔊 **INTEGRATE** Listen to the first part of a lecture on decision-making and biases. The speaker talks about "System 1" and "System 2" in the brain. What are these? Which system do we use much more often?

8 🔊 **IDENTIFY** Listen to the second part of the lecture and answer the questions.

1 Which three biases from Exercise 4 are mentioned? Give details.

2 What did the monkeys do in the experiment?

> **LISTENING SKILL Distinguishing between fact-based opinion and speculation**
>
> When listening to a fact-based genre such as a lecture, speakers often use a mixture of fact-based opinion and speculation, so it may be necessary to think about the difference between the two.
>
> Fact-based opinion is based on reflection, research, and supported by evidence. This is different from speculation, which is not always based on evidence and is hypothetical. Speculation is often indicated by:
>
> - modals, e.g., *might, may, could*
> - adjective or adverbial phrases, e.g., *It's possible that…, Perhaps…, Possibly…*
> - Certain verbs, e.g., *I imagine, I guess, I presume*

9 **APPLY** Read the following paragraph from the lecture. For each statement, decide whether the speaker is giving a fact-based opinion (O) or is speculating (S).

Why do we rely so much on system one? Well, it is thought that evolution may provide a reason, particularly because of the findings with monkeys. ¹___ It could be that in evolutionary terms, you would have been more worried about losing one day's food than gaining several for the future. ²___ I wonder if it may also be because of our current pace of life: we simply don't have time to think things through. ³___

10 🔊 **IDENTIFY** Listen to the third part of the lecture and answer the questions.

1 Why do we tend to rely on System 1 if it is not logical or rational?

2 Which professionals are affected by our overreliance on System 1?

3 Who is Daniel Kahneman, and how was his work recognized?

4 What can we learn from these psychological insights?

11 **WHAT'S YOUR ANGLE?** What were the most interesting elements of the lecture? Did you learn anything new? Can you think of any ways that the findings from behavioral economics might be useful?

12 **VOCABULARY** Choose the words in italics collocate with the noun *decision*.

1 I think the government may regret this *va expensive* decision.

2 We *came to / made / placed* the decision to move abroad.

3 It was a very *simple / straightforward / basic* decision.

4 We finally reached a decision *on / about / around* the finances.

5 The decision to leave the area was *disastrous / fatal / deathly*.

6 We haven't yet *come to / reached / gone to* a decision, but we are still considering.

7 The two managers made a *joint / mutual / double* decision after two weeks.

8 They *reversed / turned over / overturned* the decision in the end.

9 It's difficult to make a *conscious / mental / rational* decision if you are under pressure.

🔲+ Oxford 5000™

> **GRAMMAR IN CONTEXT Quantifiers**
>
> Quantifiers are used before a noun and indicate amount or number.
>
> We use *either / neither* + singular noun + singular verb
> *It's possible that neither the subway nor the bus was working, so you had to find an alternative route either by taxi or on foot.*
>
> We use (*n*)*either of* + object pronoun
> *I don't know if you came to either of the presentations.*
>
> We use *every* and *each* + singular noun + singular verb
> *It seems that each person is programmed to find losing money much more powerful than gaining money.*
>
> We can say *each / every one of* and *each of*, but not *every of*.
> *Each one of our simple decisions is made by our quick-thinking system.* ~~Every of our decisions is made by our quick-thinking system.~~

See Grammar focus on page 161.

13 **INTEGRATE** Choose the correct quantifier.

1 Unfortunately, we have *neither / either / every* awareness nor the ability to stop these tendencies.

2 I would feel happy *all of / either / neither* finding $20 on the street or finding $20 inside my house.

3 I can save money on my bills by *every / all the / either* swapping to a new provider or sticking with the original.

4 *Neither of / Each one / Either* I buy things on sale or at full price.

Independent Thinking

1 ACTIVATE Discuss these questions. If you don't know an answer, make a logical guess.

1 Approximately what percentage of start-up businesses fail within five years?
- a 10%
- c 50% ⓒ
- b 25%
- d 75%

2 Which business area is most likely to succeed as a start-up?
- a construction
- c information
- b retail
- d finance, insurance, and real estate ⓓ

3 Why do most new businesses fail?
- a insufficient knowledge of the market ⓐ
- c lack of experience of owner
- b incompetence
- d poor products

4 All but one of the following types of businesses have very poor success rates after five years. Which is the successful one?
- a eating places ⓐ
- c plumbing and heating
- b child day-care services
- d grocery stores

2 SHARE To set up your own business, which of the following are essential? Choose the three most important things, and then share ideas in a small group.

- plenty of cash to start the company
- 100 percent knowledge of your product
- a ready-made selection of clients
- support from family and friends
- excellent understanding of the market
- additional money for later expansion and as a "security blanket"
- a willingness to take risks
- multiple skills, e.g., financial, management, legal, marketing, etc.

A barber at work in New York City, U.S.A.

3 WHAT'S YOUR ANGLE? Imagine you have enough money to set up your own company. What kind of company would you like to start? Do you know anyone who has done this? What happened?

4 INTERACT You are going to read about franchises. First, discuss these questions with a partner.

1 What do you already know about franchises and how they operate?
2 Can you think of any well-known national or international franchises?
3 Name one advantage and one disadvantage of becoming a franchisee rather than setting up alone.

5 IDENTIFY Read the advice column of a business magazine. Spend two minutes only. What is the problem? How does the expert help?

READING SKILL
Locating advantages and disadvantages

Knowing how to find and identify advantages and disadvantages is a useful strategy when reading some texts.

The writer may list all the advantages and all the disadvantages together but not necessarily. Look at the topic sentences in each paragraph, which is nearly always the first one. This sentence gives an overview of the paragraph.

With a franchise, you don't take nearly as many risks as being independent.

From this topic sentence, you can infer that the paragraph is likely to give the reasons that risks are lower and is, therefore, about advantages of a franchise.

Look for key words such as *advantage*, *benefit*, and *positive*, as well as *disadvantages*. Notice additive words like *also*, *in addition*, *what's more*, and *too*, indicating additional arguments on the same side. Contrasting words, showing the opposite argument, include *while*, *however*, *on the other hand*, *but*, *yet*, and so on.

6 INTEGRATE Reread the expert's response on the next page, and see if you can find two advantages and two disadvantages. Identify the topic sentences and/or key words that helped you.

7 WHAT'S YOUR ANGLE? Discuss these questions with a partner or in a small group.

1 What do you think of the expert's advice?
2 What do you think the expert's preference is?
3 What would you do if you were in this young business person's shoes?

Ask the expert!

I'm 22, just out of college, and eager to start earning money and paying off my debts! I also have a passion: hair. I have always wanted to start my own hairdressing business. I've been cutting and styling my relatives' and friends' hair as long as I can remember and am now qualified.

My question is, do you think I should set up on my own or go into a franchise? I'm being very indecisive. I have some capital since I have recently inherited some money. There are a couple of good hairdressing franchises in the area. My online research has left me frustrated. I am impatient to start, but much of the information seems irrelevant to me.

That's an interesting question and, unfortunately, the answer is nowhere near as simple as you might hope. There are pros and cons to each option.

The most obvious disadvantage to a franchise is the amount of capital you'll need. You can set up your own company as small as you like, so it could even cost just a few thousand dollars, but with a franchise—particularly with a large brand name—it could cost ten times the amount. In addition, as well as the initial cost to join, there are also the regular royalty payments, which are often paid per month (usually a percentage of your gross revenue). You're certainly likely to spend far more on a franchise. However, in the long term you may feel it is worth it.

With a franchise, you don't take nearly as many risks as being independent. You are not going into unknown territory. You are part of a known, respected brand. The product is ready-made, as are the marketing, the outfitting, the uniforms, customer service policies, and so on. Consider the time and stress that this saves! Without a doubt, being a franchisee is considerably more secure.

What's more, the franchise can save you much more money in the long term, not just for the above reasons, but because you can avoid problems by getting regular advice from your franchisor and fellow franchisees, which is vital at the start-up stage. For example, imagine the costs if you accidentally did something illegal! Franchisors can even advise you on issues such as where to locate your business.

When purchasing items, you can receive discounts, since the franchisor can bulk buy and pass on savings to you. In addition, banks are often more willing to lend to franchisees.

The first couple of years can be extremely challenging for an *inexperienced* entrepreneur, but your franchisor is an expert, with intimate knowledge of the business. In addition, as a franchise, the cash flow starts more rapidly since you already have a client base familiar with your product.

However, there are some drawbacks. The largest one, aside from cost, is the restrictions. This is where your own personality is significant. Would you object to having to closely follow a franchise operations manual? Being in a franchise doesn't allow you as much creativity as being independent. On your own, your business can become what you want it to become, and you have a great deal more flexibility. The more flexibility you have, the easier it is to adapt to customer demand, which might mean a potentially greater turnover.

While the majority of start-ups take several years to begin making a profit, you may find that your company actually succeeds earlier. In this case, would you feel frustrated or discouraged having to give a percentage of your hard-earned profits away to your franchisor?

Finally, one could simply take a very pragmatic approach. A compromise might be to learn from a franchise for a few years and then to branch out on your own later.

Ultimately, the choice is yours, but it's often impossible and perhaps irresponsible to try and make this decision hastily. Don't be dissatisfied with your decision-making skills. This period of information gathering is key. Discuss the issue with a range of individuals, particularly those in similar businesses. Consider it from as many angles as possible: your capital, your business model, your hopes, your personality, and your own philosophy. The more knowledge you gain at this stage, the more reliable your final decision will be.

GRAMMAR IN CONTEXT Comparative sayings

There are many different ways to modify your comparisons to show the degree of difference.

1 Modifier of degree
(*nowhere / every bit / nearly / almost / twice*) *as* + adjective or adverb + *as*

The answer is nowhere near as simple as you might hope.

2 Modifier of degree
(*far / a great deal / considerably / slightly / a bit / no*) + comparative adjective or comparative adverb

Without a doubt, being a franchisee is considerably more secure.

3 Modifier of degree
(*much / many / far / a great deal / a lot / a little / a bit*) + *more / fewer / less* + noun

So it gives you a great deal more flexibility.

4 as *much / many* + nouns + *as*

Being in a franchise doesn't allow you as much creativity as being independent.

5 *the more…, the more…*

The more knowledge you gain at this stage, the more reliable your final decision will be.

See Grammar focus on page 161.

8 APPLY Compare students in the class, considering the areas listed below. Work with a partner to write at least five sentences using some of the modifiers of degree from the Grammar box.

Saima's house is nowhere near as close to the college as Fatima's.

- proximity of home to class
- journey to school
- height
- neatness of handwriting
- pronunciation in English
- punctuality
- size of bag
- general attitude/organization
- English skills
- your own ideas

9 EXPAND Which is better? Consider two of the following for two minutes on your own, using modifiers of degree. Then share with a partner.

1 Learning in a class versus learning on your own
2 Using a tablet versus using a PC
3 Living at home as a student versus living away

VOCABULARY DEVELOPMENT Prefixes

There are many prefixes added to adjectives or adverbs that indicate opposite, negative, or "not" meaning:

dis- in- un- im- il- ir-

I am impatient to start, but much of the information seems irrelevant to me.
For example, imagine the costs if you accidentally did something illegal.
Don't be dissatisfied with your decision-making skills.
The first couple of years can be extremely challenging for an inexperienced entrepreneur.
You are not going into unknown territory.

10 IDENTIFY Look at the examples in the Vocabulary Development box, and use some of these to make the rules about prefix use.

Adjectives starting with *r* often take the prefixes [1] __IR__ or __DIS__.

Adjectives beginning with *p* or *m* often take the prefix [2] __IM__.

Adjectives beginning with *l* often take the prefix [3] __IL__.

Adjectives beginning with vowels or consonants can take the prefix [4] __UN__, __IN__, or __DIS__. These are the most common prefixes.

11 USE Fill in the gaps with an appropriate prefix.

1 I was very __UN/DIS__ satisfied with my meal. It was awful.
2 He can't read or write because of the problems he had in his childhood, so he is __IL__ literate.
3 She seems much younger than her age because she behaves very __IM__ maturely.
4 The people at the party were really __UN__ sociable, so after about an hour standing on my own, I left.
5 Our profit for this year really isn't worth discussing because the figures are so __IN__ significant.
6 The doctor said my heart was beating very __IR__ regularly, so I had to go for some tests at the hospital.

12 SHARE Work with a partner. Choose one of the topics below to talk about. Use some adjectives with prefixes and, if possible, modifiers to describe yourself. Think for one minute, then talk for at least 1.5 minutes each. Your partner should listen but can interrupt occasionally to ask you questions.

- Tell your partner why you think you would be good or not so good at starting up your own business.
- Compare yourself with a sibling, parent, or very close friend. Think about appearance, personality, and behavior.

3.3 Big Steps

1 ACTIVATE Work with a partner. Think about the different stages in a person's life, such as teenage years, middle age, and so on.

At what age do you typically have to make big decisions about the following?

relationships	studies	leaving home	job
buying a home	health	a career	

2 WHAT'S YOUR ANGLE? Work in a small group. Discuss any big decisions you have had to make in your life. What happened? What were the options? How did you decide?

3 IDENTIFY Read the blog post, written by a farmer in Scotland. What decision did she make, and why was it so difficult?

Home | About   Search 🔍 ▲

The week has been exhausting. It's the height of the calving season, so we woke up at 4:30 a.m. to go in search of new calves. We check three times a day because of the low temperatures, even though the Highland cow is one of the hardiest breeds.

This morning, there was a crisp frost on the ground, and we walked down the hilly, hardened tracks, breathing puffs of "smoke" into the freezing air. Luckily, the pregnant cows are brought much closer to the farm when they are about to give birth.

This routine has been part of my life on the farm for as long as I can remember. When I was four, I remember feeding a tiny newborn calf by hand in the farmhouse. For three days, I fed it, while the snow reached the height of the roof and I couldn't get to school.

Frankly, despite the hardships, I love the predictability of this way of life. There is always a sense of hyperactivity and excitement at this time of year. And, very often, I can't help reflecting on how my life might have been so different.

Twenty years ago, I made the huge decision to leave this place where my family has lived for over two centuries. Astonishingly, I was the first person in our family to get a degree, and there was always the silent assumption that I would break tradition and move away. My parents and grandparents were unbelievably proud of me—I earned a degree in Agriculture, and after doing a master's degree in Food Security, I was presented with a wonderful opportunity to work for a well-respected company in Sydney, Australia, for two years. To be honest, we all silently viewed it as an opportunity to "escape" from the demanding life on a Scottish hill farm.

Not surprisingly, everything was very different in Sydney. The job was good, my colleagues friendly, and I felt positive, initially. Then—funnily enough, as spring drew near—I started to get homesick. People around me were unaware because I worked hard and my contributions were valued. Life was comfortable, but actually, I often felt miserable inside.

Naturally, I kept thinking that these feelings would pass. The Scottish don't like to admit defeat! I mentioned my concerns to my family and friends when we spoke on Skype, but I wasn't 100 percent honest, unfortunately. They assured me it was natural and that I simply needed more time. So I waited. I have to admit, the work continued to be interesting, and I was gaining a number of skills—I can't in all honesty say I felt unhappy all of the time; it was more an absence of genuine happiness.

At the end of my first year, I was offered a promotion, a healthy pay increase, and a permanent contract. Of course, I was flattered, but I felt torn in two directions: my heart wanted to leave, but my head told me to stay. After all, life as a hill farmer didn't seem a realistic option, and jobs in my field in Scotland are scarce. My family understandably advised me to accept.

Eighteen months after I'd left, I took a month's vacation for my first trip home. As soon as we landed in Edinburgh, all tension left me, and I started to sob uncontrollably. I was home, I was staying, and I never went back. It was the best decision of my life.

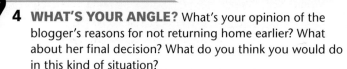

4 WHAT'S YOUR ANGLE? What's your opinion of the blogger's reasons for not returning home earlier? What about her final decision? What do you think you would do in this kind of situation?

WRITING SKILL Using attitude adverbs

When writing, you can help your reader to understand your attitude by using certain adverbs. These give the writer's viewpoint and modify a whole clause, not just a verb.

Naturally, I kept thinking that these feelings would pass.

Adverbial phrases can be used too, such as:

of course, funnily enough

Usually, attitude adverbs are placed at the start of the clause or sentence, followed by a comma. However, they may also occur before the main verb, or even at the end of a clause, especially if the writing is informal and closer to informal spoken English.

I wasn't 100 percent honest, unfortunately.
I can't in all honesty say I felt unhappy all of the time.

5 IDENTIFY Find at least five more adverbs or phrases in the blog entry. Put these and the adverbs in the Writing Skill box into categories.

Adverbs I know and use	Adverbs I have heard or read but haven't used	Adverbs I'm completely unfamiliar with
usually		
Always	frequently	scarcely
sometimes	towards	virtually
Already	backwards	fairly
later		presumably

6 PREPARE Match the attitude adverbs that have a very similar meaning.

A
c 1 frankly
d 2 from my own perspective
h 3 unfortunately
b 4 clearly
e 5 surprisingly
a 6 bizarrely
f 7 naturally
g 8 fortunately

B
a strangely
b evidently
c to be honest
d personally
e astonishingly
f of course
g luckily
h sadly

7 APPLY Choose an appropriate adverb from column A in Exercise 6 to complete each sentence. Try to use a different one each time.

1 When I got my first job I was nervous, but ___fortunately___ I felt instantly "at home."

2 ___Frankly___, I'm not surprised that they found life in the countryside can be challenging.

3 ___Surprisingly___, I find that living abroad gets easier and easier to cope with the longer you are away.

4 Most people feel some sort of sadness, but ___clearly___ some people simply feel relief to get away!

5 ___Naturally___, it's easier for some people to get over the sense of homesickness than others.

6 It seems, perhaps ___bizarrely___, that some individuals get more homesick with time, not less.

PRONUNCIATION SKILL Dropped syllables

Often speakers don't pronounce every vowel sound in a word clearly, unless they are doing so for emphasis. We reduce many unstressed syllables to /ə/ (schwa).

In some words, the reduced syllable may even totally disappear. This may make the word harder to understand when listening. For example, *business* is pronounced as only two syllables. In the word *basically*, the second *a* is dropped when saying it, leaving only three syllables.

8 ◄ NOTICE Look at these phrases from the blog entry. Focus on the words in italics. With a partner, see if you can predict how the word will be pronounced and which syllable might be omitted. Then listen and repeat.

1 My life might have been so *different*.
2 I felt *reasonably* positive at first.
3 Life was *comfortable*, but *actually*, I often felt *miserable* inside.
4 *Naturally*, I kept thinking that these feelings would pass.
5 I mentioned my concerns to my *family*.

9 EXPAND Choose any three of the questions below. Each one includes a word with a dropped syllable. Identify the word, then practice saying it in your head. Then work in a small group to ask and answer the questions.

What is the most interesting show on TV these days?

What kind of chocolate do you like best?

What is the most extraordinary vacation you have ever been on?

What is your ideal restaurant?

What vegetable do you eat most frequently?

Who's your favorite relative, outside your immediate family?

Astonishing = sorpreendente

a/an The **indefinite article** is used when we don't specify the exact thing (it is one example of a class), when it is mentioned for the first time, or when we mean one.

I remember feeding a tiny newborn calf.

the The **definite article** is used when the thing is specific and/or known, or it is unique.

the farm, the first person, the (Sydney) Opera House

Since there can be only one, superlatives take *the* with a singular countable noun to talk generally about a group…

the Highland cow

…and also with adjectives used as nouns to talk about groups.

the Scottish, the young

It's also used with the physical environment…

the snow, the ground

…and in prepositional phrases with an uncountable or plural noun + *of*.

the predictability of this way of life

zero The **zero article** is used with uncountable or plural nouns to talk generally…

people around me were unaware

…with abstract nouns…

happiness

…and with most proper nouns, including languages and nationalities.

Skype, Sydney

Most country names are used with no article unless they are plural.

Scotland, but *the United States*

In addition, there are many fixed phrases that take *a*…

four times a day

…or zero article.

I went to Ø college immediately after high school.

See Grammar focus on page 161.

10 **APPLY** Read this comment, written in response to the blog that you read in Exercise 3. Decide which article you need to add in each case: *a, the,* or Ø (none).

I enjoyed reading your frank account. I think ¹ __the__ homesickness is not discussed enough, and I know that a great number of ² __Ø__ people often feel this.

In my own case, moving to ³ __Ø__ Egypt was ⁴ __a__ big step, but luckily, it turned out well. After six months, I had made ⁵ __Ø__ friends and was able to speak ⁶ __Ø__ Arabic, though with a very poor accent! I was fortunate enough to live in ⁷ __the__ beautiful apartment owned by ⁸ __the__ company I worked for. It was bright and airy, shaded from ⁹ __a__ sun by ¹⁰ _____ large trees just outside ¹¹ _____ balcony.

Personally, I found ¹² _____ best thing about living abroad was ¹³ _____ excitement of being in ¹⁴ _____ totally different culture with wonderful food.

11 **APPLY** Read these sentences and find any problems with article use. There may be more than one problem in each sentence. Then discuss with a partner, giving reasons.

1 I think the happiness is most important thing in life.
2 Most of people I know have lived away from the home and survived!
3 I wouldn't like to live permanently in the faraway place.
4 I was happy living in the Indonesia, and when I moved to the Philippines, a difference was huge.
5 A truth is that beauty of a place is often connected with people there.
6 My sister would like to work for FBI or CIA to protect American people and the president.
7 While in the Britain last year, we saw queen and we had the tea at the Ritz, one of nicest hotels in London.

12 **EXPAND** Consider the following topics. Write at least two sentences about each one. Think about your use of articles.

- Your thoughts on whether homesickness is a harmless "illness"
- Advice for young people who are about to leave home
- Recommendations for someone about to move abroad

13 **PREPARE** In a small group, discuss your answers and prepare to give feedback to the class on one of the topics.

14 **CREATE** Write a reply of 140–200 words to the blogger presented as a comment. Use the examples from Exercises 7 and 10 to help you. Try to use at least three attitude adverbs. Include the following:

☐ Your own reaction to her personal blog
☐ Your personal experience of moving away or making a big change in your life
☐ Your own feelings about homesickness.

15 **IMPROVE** Trade comment drafts with a partner and check each other's work for accuracy, including attitude adverbs and article use. When ready, rewrite your comment using your partner's feedback.

3.4 Hey, Are You Busy?

1 ACTIVATE When is it OK to interrupt a conversation? Decide if each situation is OK (O) or not OK (N).

1 In an emergency ___
2 During a presentation ___
3 While dining with family ___
4 When someone is in an argument ___
5 When someone is on the phone ___

2 ASSESS Have you ever had something to share in a conversation but weren't sure how to jump in with your thoughts? Have you ever had a hard time expressing your thoughts and needed someone to help you?

3 ▶ IDENTIFY Watch the video to find out what happened among Kevin, Andy, and Emma. Respond to the following questions.

1 What does Kevin need help with?
2 How would you describe Kevin's mood?
3 Is Andy helpful to Kevin?
4 Is Kevin satisfied with Emma's response?

4 ASSESS Why do you think Andy doesn't let Kevin finish his own sentences?

REAL-WORLD ENGLISH Interrupting versus Interjection

When we interrupt, we are disturbing or stopping an ongoing conversation.

A: *The point of this meeting is so that we can go over...*
B: *Uh, **sorry**, but before we get into that, can we talk about when everyone is taking their vacations?*
C: *Uh, sure, I've requested June 10 to June 25.*
A: ***Wait!** Let's go over our vacation shcedule later. What we need to talk about in this meeting is...*
C: ***I have a question**. Some of us are taking longer vacations than others, so should we cancel all meetings until we can all attend?*
A: *Yes, that's a good point. I think we should decide that...*
B: ***Can I say something**. I think we should have these meetings in the afternoons from now on.*

Interjecting, on the other hand, can help move the conversation along by completing someone's utterance. We can interject with words.

A: *I went kayaking last summer and it was so fun that...*
B: *That you're going again!*

We can also interject with actions.

A: *I just started using this new app that helps me practice English and...*
B: *[shows cell phone screen to Speaker A displaying app]*
A: *How do you like it? It has really helped me remember what I've learned in class.*

5 ▶ **NOTICE** Watch the video again and pay attention to the interjections.

6 **ANALYZE** What is the difference between Kevin's interjections with Andy versus his interjections with Emma?

7 **APPLY** Write down how you would interrupt the people in the following situations

1 During lunch, people start talking about the latest episode of your favorite TV show, and you haven't had a chance to watch it yet. You are really looking forward to the episode, and you don't want it to be ruined for you.

2 At the start of class, your teacher begins by lecturing on a topic that is built upon information from a class you missed. You are completely lost, and you don't want to be in a 90-minute class without knowing what's going on.

3 You are on the phone with someone who is crying and telling you about a horrible experience they just had. While they are speaking, you get another phone call that you need to take, but you don't want your friend to think that you are not willing to comfort them.

4 At a party, one of your friends is enthusiastically telling a story to a group of people about an event at which someone embarrassed themselves. You know his depiction is inaccurate because you were at the event he is talking about, and you don't want the group of listeners to get the wrong idea.

5 A doctor is very quickly explaining to you your test results and your course of treatment. She is using a lot of medical jargon you aren't familiar with while also intermittently speaking to a nurse about another patient. You want to make sure you are completely clear on your understanding of what the doctor is telling you.

8 **EXPAND** Read the conversations and label whether there is an example of Interruption (R) or Interjection (I).

Conversation 1

A: Hmm, this sauce tastes amazing. What's your secret?
B: Well, I don't use a lot of salt and…
A: I try to stay away from salt. [1] ___
B: And I mix all the ingredients together the night before, so I…

A: That reminds me, did you watch that show last night? [2]___
B: No, which show are you talking about?
A: The one with the dragons and all the different people, and…
B: Oh, yeah. I know what you're talking about. [3] ___

Conversation 2

A: I had so much fun on my vacation.
B: Oh yeah? What did you do?
A: Well, I went zip lining and…
B: Oh wow! I've wanted to do that for so long! [1]___
A: Yeah, I'd highly recommend it to anyone. But there was this person next to me who was afraid of heights and…
B: What? What was this person doing if they were scared? [2]___
A: She said she was trying to conquer one of her fears…
B: That's pretty brave. I'm not sure I could do that if I were…[3]___
C: Hey guys! I just saw that famous guy walking down the street. [4] ___
B: Really? Who did…
A: I saw a famous person once at the mall. [5]___
C: Who?
A: The one who's on TV all the time.

9 **NOTICE** In your own culture, is interrupting or interjecting socially acceptable?

10 **INTERACT** Work with a partner. Imagine that you both have exciting news you want to share. Create a conversation in which you each interject three times.

11 **DEVELOP** Prepare a role play of your exciting conversation.

12 **SHARE** Role-play your conversation for the class.

GO ONLINE
to create your own version
of the English For Real video.

3.5 Examining Pros and Cons

1 ACTIVATE Which of these things are most important to you in a job? Choose three. Then compare your choices in a small group, giving reasons.

pay	career advancement
colleagues	status/power
bonuses/perks	enjoyable/stimulating work
environment	an easy commute
opportunities to travel	opportunities to gain new skills
flexible hours	a reasonable workload

2 ◄)) IDENTIFY Listen to the conversation between two friends, Freya and Dan. Then discuss with a partner whether the following statements are true or false.

1 Freya wants to leave her current job because the pay is bad.

2 Both Freya and Dan agree that the cost of studying is very high.

3 The first expert Freya mentions believes having a master's improves job prospects greatly.

4 Some universities advertise very positive outcomes in terms of jobs, for people who have a master's.

5 The second expert, Freya's college lecturer, believes it is worth getting a master's.

3 ◄)) ASSESS In the end, how does Freya feel about her options? Do you think she will do a master's degree? Listen again, if necessary.

SPEAKING Paraphrasing

Paraphrasing is when you repeat an idea that your source or someone else (or yourself) has said, but using your own words to make it easier to understand, or for emphasis. It may involve one or more of the following.

Synonyms

*It's not the increased knowledge you **gain** (original) → It's not the increased knowledge you **get** (paraphrase)*

Word class changes

*It's not that employers might see a master's as evidence of your **high motivation** → It's not the fact that employers might see a master's as evidence that you're **very motivated***

Shifting the focus

A bachelor's degree is only the starting point since the market is now flooded. (consequence → cause)

The tourism market is now flooded, and a bachelor's degree is just the starting point. (cause → consequence)

Negative to positive and vice versa

*Freya: "A standard degree is just the starting point. **You need more**."*

*Dan: "**It's not enough**."*

Freya: "Right."

---

4 IDENTIFY Read the following excerpt from the recording. Underline and identify where the speaker is referring (R), paraphrasing (P), or evaluating (E).

According to Morton, master's degrees are "the new normal," but his findings show that it's not the greater knowledge you get or the fact that employers might see a master's as evidence you're very motivated...his research focuses on the importance of networking. I'm not sure I agree with him, but I can see that it might be significant in certain contexts.

5 INTEGRATE Choose a topic you are interested in for which you will need to do a little research. Ensure that you refer to at least two different sources. Make notes and include the sources.

- Choosing to study a chosen subject in a university in the United States versus in another country (fees, length of degree, etc.)
- The benefits of having older employees
- The things that make employees remain in their job

6 EXPAND Prepare to give a presentation about your research. Refer to the Speaking box and include references for your research, paraphrasing in an appropriate way.

7 APPLY When you are ready, give your presentations in a small group. Those students who are listening should prepare to ask the speaker at least two questions about her or his findings or opinions.

8 WHAT'S YOUR ANGLE? Have you ever left a job or thought of leaving a job? If so, what were your reasons? Tell a partner.

Now go to page 149 for the Unit 3 Review.

4 Consequences

Do you think the boy understands the significance of the airplane?

How does this picture illustrate how history has consequences for younger generations?

BEHIND THE PHOTO

REAL-WORLD GOAL

Visit a place positively impacted by history or a scientific discovery

1 **Read the dilemma, and consider the consequences of each choice.**

You are the owner of an orphanage that is threatened with closure after 30 years due to lack of funding. Your home looks after 70 children aged three to six. You receive an anonymous donation one day of $350,000, enough to help support the orphanage for three years. However, you also discover that the donor, a former orphan himself, is a well-known criminal. What do you do?

2 **Consider the consequences of each choice. Then discuss in a small group.**

1 ACTIVATE Which of these would you find most stressful and why?

- doing a bungee jump
- being stuck in bad traffic when on the way to work or class
- going for a job interview
- giving a speech at an event, e.g., a wedding
- taking an important exam
- choosing what kind of vacation to go on
- taking on a large mortgage
- moving or leaving home

2 WHAT'S YOUR ANGLE? Working with a partner, add at least three more ideas to both the symptoms of stress (top) and the possible ways to fight stress (bottom).

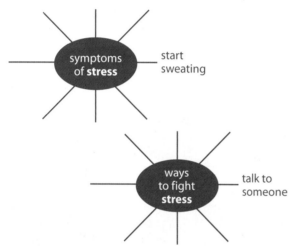

symptoms of **stress** — start sweating

ways to fight **stress** — talk to someone

3 IDENTIFY Read the magazine article about stress. What does the author think?

a   All stress is good
b   All stress is bad
c   Some stress is good
d   None of the above

STRESS IS DISTRESSING

The sensations are familiar. Your heart is pounding, your hands are sweaty, and your mouth is dry. You feel your blood racing around your body and your muscles tensing.

1   The physical symptoms of stress are easily recognizable, and it is common for most of us to react to these sensations negatively. Understandably, our attitude toward stress tends to be far from positive. However, findings from various studies suggest that stress is not all bad, and in fact, we should be thinking of it in a much more positive light.

2   There's no doubt that chronic stress, which usually continues for weeks or even years, has very negative effects on the body. It can lead to depression, digestion and back problems, insomnia, anxiety, and—both directly and indirectly—to a variety of other illnesses, such as heart disease. Although our understanding of the long-term effects of stress is still incomplete, it's widely accepted that it is related to low immunity, which makes our bodies less capable of combating disease and, therefore, increases our exposure to risks of all kinds.

3   Our reactions to stressful situations result in the same symptoms whether the situation is positive or negative and whether the stress is short-lived (acute) or chronic. This means, for example, that being followed down a dark, poorly lit road at night invites the same physical response in our bodies as when we are, let's say, publicly receiving an award for an incredible personal achievement.

4   Understanding why the response exists is key to learning how to manage stress itself. Our ancestors, when preparing to fight off an enemy or find food in dangerous or challenging situations, needed to react quickly to threats: the so-called fight-or-flight response. When we are stressed, we are in a high level of responsiveness; we are focused, motivated, and ready for action. Our bodies produce adrenalin, which accelerates our heart rate; the blood supply increases to the heart, lungs, and brain; and our muscles tense in preparation, so we feel alert.

5   Various studies have proved that exposure to this sort of short-term stress is actually beneficial to the body. It is the stress that allows us to study at the last minute before exams, to successfully meet an impossible deadline, to suddenly become wonderfully focused in an interview, or to somehow think clearly when experiencing extreme tension (provided panic does not set in!). These are **survival tactics**.

6   So, while long-term, chronic stress wears the body down and leaves us vulnerable to disease with our immune systems at risk, short-term stress actually has the opposite effect. Not only does it help our clarity of mind, according to psychologists such as Hans Selye (he called it a cognitive enhancer), it motivates us to do extraordinary things. It has also been shown to boost our immunity, at least temporarily, since our bodies are preparing for an attack or injury. This is why in tests comparing individuals with no stress and individuals with experience of short-term stress, the second group actually had a higher life expectancy. Furthermore, it seems that experiencing short-term stress will make us stronger when facing future stress, according to some studies.

7   Of course, having a life-changing experience, such as the death of a loved one or having no financial security, can damage our health. In these cases of chronic stress, the effects can be lessened using various strategies but are likely to be severe. However, it is important that we learn to understand stress and see it differently. Understanding that stress is primarily designed to protect us means we can embrace it and exploit it when the situation arises. Furthermore, knowing how to manage stress means that we will be able to keep it under control when necessary so that we do not collapse under pressure.

8   Dr. Hadley will be speaking on this topic on September 19 in The Oak Hall, Bradchester. Tickets will be available online starting August 1.

    ℞+ Oxford 5000™

4 IDENTIFY Match the paragraph headings to the first three paragraphs of the magazine article.

    __2__ The experience that triggers stress can be good or bad, but the symptoms do not change.

    __3__ We generally see stress as a bad thing, but this might not be fair.

    __1__ Long-term stress is harmful.

5 INTEGRATE Decide on useful paragraph headings for paragraphs 4 to 7. Compare with a partner and then select the best option in each case.

READING SKILL Highlighting and annotating

Highlighting and annotating key words in a text can help you focus on the main ideas and to process information, as well as to help find information later.

When **highlighting**, mark only the key words—avoid highlighting too many.

When **annotating**, be systematic and ensure your writing is legible. Use signs and simple abbreviations that you will understand later.

@	at	v	very
diff	different	w/	with
b/4	before	w/o	without
vs	versus/against	approx	approximately
e.g.	example	fr	From
etc.	etcetera, and so on	s/t	something
+	positive	∴	therefore
–	negative		

You can make up your own codes. The following is an example highlighted and annotated paragraph.

Our reaction to stressful situations causes the same symptoms whether the situation is positive or negative and whether the stress is short-lived (acute) or chronic. This means, for example, that if you are being followed down a dark, poorly lit road at night, then this invites the same physical response in our bodies as when we are, say, publicly receiving an award for an incredible personal achievement.

= symptoms:
Even if sit. is + / –,
dark alley vs getting award
Acute/chronic

6 APPLY Look at Paragraph 5 in the reading text. Highlight or underline a maximum of 15 words. Include any useful annotations at the side. Then compare your own ideas with a partner.

7 🔊 INTEGRATE Listen to two students briefly talking about the same article you read.

    1 How useful did they find it?

    2 What are they going to do in relation to this topic?

    3 Why is it particularly useful at the moment?

There are many different ways to talk about the future in English. They depend on things such as probability, time of decision-making, and the attitude of the speaker.

a I'm going to try to look at stress differently now.
b He finishes at 4 p.m.
c I plan to work on changing my attitude.
d I'm actually thinking of going to the talk he'll be giving.
e Tickets will be available online from August 1.
f I'm sure it'll help me. I think I'll go downtown now.
g We're just about to take our final exams.
h He's giving me a ride home!

See Grammar focus page 162.

8 IDENTIFY Match the statements with the examples in the Grammar box above. The first two have been done for you.

1 This form is used to talk about future events that are fixed since they are based on a schedule or calendar. _b_

2 This is a verb used to talk about intentions and ambitions. Other verbs like *hope, aim,* and *expect* can also be used. _c_

3 This form is used to make predictions and also to describe spontaneous decisions, including offers and promises. _f_ This same form also describes facts about the future in a neutral way. _e_

4 This form is used to talk about plans and intentions. It's also used to talk about predictions based on direct evidence. _A_

5 This expression is used to talk about something that will happen very soon and is fairly informal. It is similar to *on the verge / point of* + verb with *-ing.* _g_

6 This form is used to describe a future action that has already been fixed or decided for a specific time in the future. _d_

7 This form is used to describe fixed, personal arrangements for the near future that have been agreed upon. _h_

9 APPLY Choose the most appropriate future form. Then discuss why with a partner.

1 Oh, wait a moment. *I'm helping / I'll help* you with that heavy bag!

2 The professor *will be visiting / is about to visit* the department next month.

3 The number of people suffering from stress-related illnesses *is going to rise / will be rising.*

4 The man doesn't look well. I think he *'ll faint / 's going to faint.*

5 Look! The patient *leaves / is on the point of leaving.*

6 I promise I *'ll take / 'm taking* care of myself.

7 The lecture *'s just about to start / will start.* Quick, use that door at the back!

8 Jon *is on the verge of leaving / will be leaving* this afternoon because he has a flight to catch.

9 The new software *will probably be installed / is probably being installed* by the end of May.

10 EXPAND Respond to the statements in an appropriate way including the word given in parentheses.

1 I don't really want to travel all that way on my own. (come)
Reply: _You won't be on your own. I'll come with you!_

2 I can't seem to switch off this computer. (help)
Reply: _You can't switch off this computer. I'll will help you_

3 When does the presentation start exactly? (point)
Reply: _The presentation will start on point_

4 Bye for now, then. (tomorrow)
Reply: _Bye for now. I'll see you tomorrow_

5 Have you got your train ticket yet? (plane)
Reply: _____

6 When does your daughter take her final exams? (about)
Reply: _Your daughter_

7 Can we meet at 3:30 p.m. on Thursday, by any chance? (sorry)
Reply: _____

8 So, when will you next meet Mr. Antonelli? (seeing)
Reply: _____

11 VOCABULARY Match the two parts of the health-related collocations. The first two have been done for you.

1	feel	6	a	of mind
2	combat		b	a sensation
3	expose		c	disease
4	accelerate	9	d	stress
5	increase	8	e	under pressure
6	clarity	4	f	your heart rate
7	survival	10	g	your health
8	collapse	3	h	to risk
9	acute/chronic	5	i	the blood supply
10	damage	7	j	tactic

12 WHAT'S YOUR ANGLE? Work in groups. Discuss these questions, and find out how similar or different you are.

1 When was the last time your heart rate accelerated?

2 What do you do that may damage your health?

3 What is the simplest way to combat disease, in your opinion?

4 What kind of things help you to have clarity of mind when you most need it?

5 If you are feeling a little stressed, which sensations do you dislike the most?

6 Do you think chronic stress was as common in the past as it is nowadays? Why or why not?

1 ACTIVATE Complete the table with notes on your eating habits. Then compare your answers with a partner.

	Meat	Fish	Veggies	Fruit
What's your favorite kind?	chicken	salmon	cucumber	strawberries
How much/ many do you eat per week?	1x	1x	1x	5x
How do you usually prepare it/them?	Bake	Bake		

2 PREPARE You are going to hear a radio interview of the owner of a new insect restaurant in Bristol, UK. First look at the menu and try to identify at least five different insects. Before you listen, work with a partner to think of at least five questions you would like to ask the owner.

3 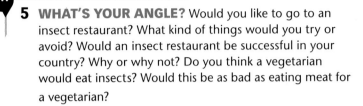 **IDENTIFY** Listen and note as many questions from the interview as you can. Did you predict any of the same questions?

4 🔊 **INTEGRATE** Listen again for the answers to the questions asked.

5 WHAT'S YOUR ANGLE? Would you like to go to an insect restaurant? What kind of things would you try or avoid? Would an insect restaurant be successful in your country? Why or why not? Do you think a vegetarian would eat insects? Would this be as bad as eating meat for a vegetarian?

6 IDENTIFY You are going to read an essay written in response to this statement: *It's time for people to stop eating meat.* Read it as quickly as you can to find out what these numbers refer to: 6,000, 10,000, 3 percent, 15,000, 10 billion, 18 percent, 50 percent.

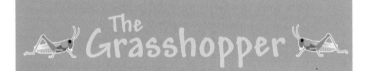

The Grasshopper

Evening menu
Mains

Black ant pancakes with wild mushrooms and root vegetables

Cricket chilli with salad and buffalo worm guacamole

Mealworm and grasshopper kebab with baked potatoes and bug pickle

Stir-fry with bambooworm and mealworm tofu, and cricket spring rolls

Meal burger (toasted mealworms and grasshoppers) with sweet potato fries

Goat cheese and locust salad with beets and cous-cous

Desserts

Caramel tart made with carrot and locusts

Buffalo worm and strawberry ice cream

Choco bug brownie

Scorpion toffees

By 2050, it is estimated that the world population will have reached around 10 billion people. As a result, future global problems are likely to center on issues such as food and water security, and environmental damage. Climate change is almost universally accepted as one of the severest problems of our time. Most people are aware of the connection between climate change and human activities that cause it: the use of fossil fuels and forest reduction. However, few people realize the enormous damage caused by our addiction to meat.

Most people consider meat to be both delicious and nutritious. On average, each of us consumes between 7,000 and 10,000 animals in our lives, including fish and shellfish. As countries such as India and China, which traditionally eat less meat, become richer, their meat consumption also rises. However, what about the cost to the planet? When digesting food, animals produce a huge amount of gas, called *methane*. This is significant because it contributes to the greenhouse effect, which in turn affects climate change. This gas, along with the other emissions involved in raising animals for meat, accounts for around 18 percent of all greenhouse gas emissions.

This means that animals produce more gas than all the emissions from transportation worldwide, including planes. If you include the related environmental costs, such as growing and treating animal feed, transportation, refrigeration, and cooking, the percentage is considerably higher (some sources estimate up to 50 percent of greenhouse gas emissions).

In addition, the amount of land and water needed to raise animals is huge. Around one third of the Earth's land not under ice is for animal use. This translates into millions of acres. To produce one kilo of beef requires about 15,000 liters of water. In contrast, for one kilo of potatoes, approximately 300 liters are needed, according to the Institute of Mechanical Engineers.

Be going to → intention

Present progressive → plans

Simple → clock time

will + verb — 1. Prediction

2. Instant, decision, offer, promise

With our growing population, more and more forests are being cut down either for animals or their food. Trees absorb carbon dioxide, which is one of the greenhouse gases, so we are creating yet another weak point in the fight against climate change.

What is more, factory farming also pollutes land and water directly. Animal waste runs off the land into streams and rivers, meaning that waters are directly affected. For example, it is widely accepted that the "dead zone," an area of 6,000 square miles in the Gulf of Mexico, is due to pollution from animal production. It is not simply animal waste, but the pesticides used on their feed and the antibiotics they are given that end up in streams and rivers, and ultimately the ocean.

It is true that humans have eaten meat for millennia and that the industry provides thousands of jobs, but it may be time to change. In many countries like the United States and the UK, the number of vegetarians is rising. In the United States, it is estimated that approximately 3 percent of the population are vegetarian (seven million people), with half a million being vegan. Although it seems most are motivated by concerns for their own health or animal welfare, in the future, people may consider alternatives to eating animals for environmental reasons.

7 **EXPAND** Read the essay again and find the four main reasons to support the argument for eating no or less meat. Then find the three arguments briefly mentioned to support eating meat.

8 **WHAT'S YOUR ANGLE?** Discuss these points with a partner. What do you think about the reasons given by the writer in support of vegetarianism?

1 How strong is the writer's argument?
2 Did anything surprise or interest you?
3 Do these environmental problems concern you? What do you think the solution is?
4 Why do you think the writer gives a counterargument at the start of the last paragraph?

GRAMMAR IN CONTEXT Noun phrases

A noun phrase always consists of a main noun or "head":
Forests are being cut down.

…but it can also be considerably longer than this. A noun can be pre-modified with elements before the head, for example, with an article, a number, a determiner, a possessive, an adjective, or another noun:
the future, 50 gallons, most people, our problems, environmental damage, world population

A noun can also be post-modified with elements that go after the head, for example, with a preposition + another noun or a relative clause:
the cost to the planet (preposition + another noun); antibiotics that they are fed on (relative clause)

A noun may be both pre-modified and post-modified:
It is one of the severest problems of our time.
  pre-modifier   head noun   post-modifier

See Grammar focus on page 162.

9 **IDENTIFY** Find the "head" noun in each sentence below. Then identify any pre- and post-modifiers that form part of a single noun phrase.

1 There were several unusual vegetables available.
  Head = *vegetables*. Pre-modified by *several unusual*; post-modified by *available*.
2 I bought some extremely fresh chicken the other day.
3 We are looking for a chef with experience and qualifications.
4 The butcher's shop where I went has only recently opened.
5 The roasted vegetables that I selected tasted delicious.
6 The five-course wedding meal at the hotel was entirely vegetarian.

Chef Joan Roca in Girona, Spain

10 **APPLY** Change these sentences so that you use the noun(s) provided instead of a verb. You may need to change or add other words in the sentence.

1   We now know a considerable amount about climate change. (knowledge)
    Our knowledge of climate change is considerable.
2   It is important that we reduce the amount of meat we consume. (reduction)
3   It's necessary to make people aware of the environmental impact that meat-eating has. (awareness)
4   When animals digest food, they release gases into the air. (digestion)
5   If toxic waste from farms enters the water, eventually river and sea life die. (death)
6   To produce meat protein for human beings seriously affects land and water resources (production, effect)
7   To survive, we may have to rely on plant-based food much more. (survival, reliance)

WRITING SKILL Explaining

When writing a formal text, full of information and facts, you may need to explain some of the more complicated points. This can be done through examples and also with the following grammar and punctuation.

With verbs:

This translates into millions of acres. Animal waste runs off the land…, meaning that waters are directly affected.

With signaling devices to show a result or cause, such as *so*, *because*, or *therefore*:

This is significant because…; Trees absorb carbon dioxide…, so we are creating yet another weak point.

With relative clauses:

Trees absorb carbon dioxide, which is one of the greenhouse gases…

With a colon:

Most people are aware of the connection between climate change and human activities that cause it: the use of fossil fuels and forest reduction.

---

11 **EXPAND** Work with a partner to complete these sentences appropriately with your own ideas. Start your clause with the first words and punctuation provided.

1   As countries get richer, people's diets change and this translates *into a huge rise in meat consumption.*
2   Animals may be the cause of up to 50 percent of greenhouse gas emissions. What this means is…
3   Pesticides are sprayed onto acres of crops for animal use, which…
4   Factory farms can hold several thousand animals, meaning…
5   Animals are fed growth hormones and antibiotics, and therefore…
6   The number of vegetarians is increasing in some countries but so is the number of vegans…

12 **PREPARE** Choose one of the following titles for an argument essay.

- It is a human right to eat and drink what we want to. Nobody should tell us what to do.
- Population growth is the biggest problem of our time. We need to act now.
- Rich countries need to help those countries without food by giving them money or food.

13 **PREPARE** Plan the essay. First, think of two to four strong arguments for your position. Include the following.

- An introduction stating what the issue is. Either present just your own argument here or both sides.
- Fact-based arguments in the main body. Use plenty of noun phrases and explaining language where relevant.
- Counterargument(s) should be acknowledged and detailed where appropriate, but keep your own position strong.
- Use a conclusion to repeat the main argument(s).

14 **WRITE** Write your essay, ensuring that you have at least four paragraphs. Write a minimum of 200 words.

15 **IMPROVE** Work with a partner. Review each other's essays. Check your partner's work for the following, and then implement your partner's suggestions.

- [ ] Logical paragraphing with a clear introduction and conclusion
- [ ] A clear argument with good supporting points
- [ ] Reference to counterargument(s)
- [ ] Accurate grammar, vocabulary, and spelling

4.3 Living with Robots

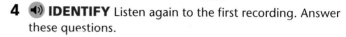

1 ► **ACTIVATE** Watch the video of friends talking. Circle the topics they mention.

⁻computers	⁻transportation	clothes
work	family life	ambitions
food	⁻ recycling	online shopping

2 **INTERACT** What's your opinion about the topics discussed? Do you agree or disagree with the friends' predictions? How is life going to be better in 20 years, and how will it be worse? Discuss in a small group.

Add your positive and negative ideas to the columns below.

👍   👎

LISTENING SKILL Understanding the speaker's audience and purpose

Speakers speak with different intentions: to explain, instruct, advertise, warn, describe, entertain, etc., depending on the genre, e.g., lecture, advertisement, chat. A speaker's purpose and audience affects *what* they say and *how* they say it.

Recognizing different genres can help comprehension because it allows you to apply what you have learned about the world and your existing knowledge of different genres or subgenres. For example, you can identify a radio advertisement from various clues: from the intonation and emphasis of the speaker, from their choice of words and the focus on the positive elements of the product, on the fact that there is a description of features, the use of comparatives and superlatives, and so on.

3 🔊 **APPLY** Listen to the four recordings, which are all about robots and artificial intelligence.

—adapted from the *Encyclopedia of Semiotics*, edited by Paul Bouissac

For each recording, identify the following:

a What the genre is, who is talking, and who the audience might be *people*   *woman, anyone*

b The purpose(s) of the speaker—choose one:
- [2] to inform
- [4] to explain and warn
- [1] to describe and entertain
- [3] to advertise

4 🔊 **IDENTIFY** Listen again to the first recording. Answer these questions.

1 Identify at least five special features of the high-tech hotel according to the guest.

2 What do the speakers say about the future at the end?

5 🔊 **IDENTIFY** Listen to the fourth recording again. Answer these questions.

1 According to the speaker, what's going to happen by 2045? What examples does he give? *job 84, AI, income*

2 What is the speaker concerned about? *education,*

GRAMMAR IN CONTEXT
The future continuous and the future perfect

The future continuous describes a future action that is already decided or fixed or an action that will be in progress at a specified time in the future.

We'll be living in houses like this before long.

It's also used to ask polite questions about someone's future plans.

Will you be joining us for dinner in our restaurant this evening?

The future perfect simple is used to refer to an event or activity that will be already completed before a definite time in the future (in bold).

***By 2045**, it's estimated that robots will have taken over 50 percent of the jobs in the global workforce.*

The future perfect continuous is similar to the future perfect simple but *also* focuses on the duration of the event or activity.

By December this year, our team will have been researching this area for precisely a decade.

See Grammar focus on page 162.

6 **ASSESS** Find the two statements that are grammatically incorrect. Restate or rewrite them to be correct.

1 By 2050, humanoid robots will be walking around with humans on the streets.

2 In 30 years, people will be enjoying a much better quality of life, thanks to robots.

3 In ten years, robots will have started to do many of the tasks that doctors and surgeons now do.

4 Driverless cars will have been becoming normal in five years' time in my country.

5 Over the next few years, young people will have been learning very different skills to prepare them for a different world of work.

6 In my country over the next decade, robots will be working in areas such as education.

7 WHAT'S YOUR ANGLE? Do you agree with the statements in Exercise 6? In a small group, discuss your opinions, giving reasons.

8 EXPAND Complete each sentence using either the future continuous, the future perfect simple, or future perfect continuous. Try to use a mixture of verb forms.

1 By the end of the lesson, we…(learn/study/practice)… (say what or for how long) *we had practiced for 2h*
2 In three hours' time, I…
3 This time tomorrow, I…
4 By the end of the year, I…
5 In the summer, I…
6 In 20 years' time, I…

VOCABULARY DEVELOPMENT
Approximating language

There are many different ways to make your language less specific.

With adjectives, particularly for ones related to color and size, it is common to add the suffix *-ish*.
reddish-pink, smallish

To describe a noun where the concept might be unfamiliar, use noun + *like* to compare it to something that is familiar.
a human-like robot, a machine with arm-like extensions

Some expressions modify the number and go before it.
approximately 5 million drivers; somewhere in the region of 150 robots; more or less 15 thousand visitors

Some give a loose period between two points.
Somewhere between 10 and 15 years' time; in 10–15 years' time (in 10 to 15 years' time)

Some expressions go after the number.
Two thousand years ago or more; 15 or so golf courses to choose from

Some act as a comment after the clause or noun phrase. These usually follow a comma and are more common in informal spoken English.
from the last five decades, or thereabouts
If you want to know what the future will look like in 30 years' time, give or take a few years, then now's your chance!

9 APPLY Read this description by a visitor to a robot exhibition. Rewrite it, making it more concise by changing the italicized words using *-ish* and *-like*.

The line for the exhibition was [1] *quite long*, and [2] *traveled down the steps a bit like a snake*. However, we were all entertained by my friend Jonathan, who [3] *behaved rather like a clown*. When we got to the entrance, a robot, [4] *which was fairly small* and [5] *resembled a girl*, took our tickets. Her hair [6] *reminded me a little of string* and was [7] *a kind of mixture of green and blue in color*. Anyway, she pointed us in the direction of the new museum elevators, which were [8] *a bit similar to bubbles in shape* and great fun to use!

10 INTEGRATE Look at these predictions for the year 2040. Make the figures sound less precise, using approximating language. Try to use expressions that you don't normally use.

1 I'll be earning double what I earn now!
2 The population of my country will have increased by 20 percent.
3 I think we'll be doing a 15-hour work week, or perhaps a little more.
4 People will retire at 55 since there will be less work to do.
5 The school graduation age will have been raised to 21.
6 About 75 percent of the working population will work from home.

11 WHAT'S YOUR ANGLE? Discuss these questions in a small group.

1 Which jobs in your country are or could be done by robots or AIs?
2 Will your own job and those jobs done currently by your family members change?
3 Is the future positive or negative, in terms of employment?
4 Will a future filled with AIs be safe? What steps should be taken?
5 Is it possible to produce truly "thinking" machines, which can weigh the consequences of important decisions, e.g., in medicine, the military?

4.4 Ticket Trouble

1 ACTIVATE Discuss the following questions with a partner.

1 Have you ever given a warning to someone? Why?
2 Have you ever received a warning from someone? Why?
3 Did you ever lose your temper? Why?

2 ▶ IDENTIFY Watch the video of Max and Dave at the train station, and decide if the following statements are true (T), false (F), or we don't know (DK).

1 Dave gives Max some good advice at the start.
2 Max has never used one of these machines before.
3 Dave is irritated even at the very beginning.
4 Max fails to stay calm when using the machine.
5 Max regrets listening to Dave's suggestion at the start.
6 Max misses his train.

3 NOTICE Write two adjectives to describe how Dave and Max feel by the end of the conversation.

Dave: _____ _____

Max: _____ _____

4 ASSESS At which point of the conversation do you think Max got irritated? Do you think he was irritated with Dave or the machine?

REAL-WORLD ENGLISH Warnings

Warnings can be made when there is a potentially negative outcome from performing or not performing certain actions.

I'm seriously going to lose it if you keep yelling.

The negative outcome is that you will lose your temper if this person doesn't change their tone.

Look, if you don't hurry, we'll miss the movie.

The negative outcome is potentially missing a scheduled film if this person wastes time.

Sometimes warnings are necessary or desirable because they can bring a positive outcome to a person.

Buy your ticket online. It's much faster.

The positive outcome is that this person will not have to wait.

5 ▶ **ANALYZE** Watch the video again. Can you find more warnings given by Max or Dave?

Max

_____

_____

Dave

_____

_____

6 **BUILD** Look at the following warnings and situations. What are the possible outcomes of each?

1 (driving instructor to learner) Drive slower, James.

_____

2 (boss to new employee) Always carry your security access pass with you.

_____

3 (neighbor to neighbor) I saw your dog crawl through the hole in your back fence.

_____

4 (waiter to customer) This plate is really hot.

_____

5 (mother to teenager) Call me when you get there.

_____

6 (child to parent) I flunked my spelling quiz.

_____

7 (teacher to student) You will not be able to graduate if you don't pass this class.

_____

7 **EXPAND** Who will experience the positive outcomes and negative outcomes in Exercise 6? Why?

	Positive Outcome	Negative Outcome
1	_____	_____
2	_____	_____
3	_____	_____
4	_____	_____
5	_____	_____
6	_____	_____
7	_____	_____

8 **ASSESS** Imagine that your parents are taking their first trip abroad. Their trip will last two weeks. They are packing for their early morning flight, which is tomorrow. What six warnings would you give them to ensure positive outcomes?

1 _____

2 _____

3 _____

4 _____

5 _____

6 _____

9 **BUILD** With a partner, prepare a one-minute role play based on the warnings you've given in Exercise 8.

10 **SHARE** Role-play your conversation for the class.

GO ONLINE to create your own version of the English For Real video.

4.5 The Consequence of Kindness

1 ACTIVATE Look at the pictures below. Can you think of something kind that you have done for a friend, a family member, or a stranger recently?

2 **IDENTIFY** Listen to three people discussing how someone they know helped a stranger. What did their old classmate do?

3 **IDENTIFY** Listen again, and complete the table with the information you hear.

Facts we find out about Joshua	Facts we find out about the woman	His reasons

4 WHAT'S YOUR ANGLE? Discuss these questions with a partner.

What's your opinion about what Joshua did? What do you think motivates people to do such extraordinary things, even when faced with negative consequences? Would you do anything like this? Do you know of any great acts of kindness?

PRONUNCIATION SKILL Consonant clusters

There are many words in English that have consonants together within the same syllable. When these are formed in different parts of the mouth, this can make the sounds hard to pronounce as one syllable.

For example, *consonants* has three syllables.

Avoid inserting an extra vowel and syllable between consonant sounds (*con son ant es*, four syllables). This can put a strain on your listener and can even be a barrier to communication.

5 **NOTICE** Decide on the number of syllables in these words taken from the recording. Then listen to check before relistening and repeating. Pay close attention to your pronunciation of the consonant clusters.

stranger	____	incredible	____	scratched	____
months	____	asked	____	kicked	____
risks	____	spring	____	twelve	____
changed	____	special	____		

6 APPLY Practice saying these two tricky sentences in your head. Then say them aloud to a partner. Who can say them more naturally?

1 Stuart kicked the stick at the stranger and then asked for it back.

2 The spring months passed swiftly, and the leaves of the twelve trees changed color.

SPEAKING Speculating and hypothesizing about causes and consequences

We can speculate about causes and consequences using different kinds of language, such as:

Modals, like *might, may,* or *could*
It could be that he just enjoys taking risks; he might regret it later.

Adverbs, like *perhaps*:
Perhaps there was someone in his family with a similar problem.

Questions:
What if he falls ill himself?

Verbs such as *wonder* and *suppose*:
I suppose it would have made him feel good.

7 PREPARE Prepare a role play between Joshua and one of his parents.

Imagine that you are Joshua Bentley's mother or father before the operation. He has just told you of his plans. You are very worried. Spend two to three minutes preparing arguments to dissuade him. Choose at least four different kinds of speculating language that you would like to use.

8 APPLY Work with a partner, and role play the conversation. Then trade roles.

Start like this:
Look, Joshua, I admire you for what you want to do, but what about the risks? I mean,...

Now go to page 150 for the Unit 4 Review.

5 Innovations

How much of innovation is based on tradition?

What prompts people to innovate?

Is innovation always better than tradition? Why?

BEHIND THE PHOTO

What might the solution be for the following puzzle?

A man needs to cross a river in a canoe. With him, he has a bag of grain, a chicken, and a fox. He can only carry one of the three at a time: if left alone together, the chicken will eat the grain and the fox will eat the chicken. How does he successfully cross the river with all three?

REAL-WORLD GOAL

Find out about an amazing new product or innovation, and try it if possible.

1 ACTIVATE Work in a small group. How many different types of clothing fabrics can you think of? If you don't know many words in English, note them down in your own language.

2 WHAT'S YOUR ANGLE? Work with a partner. Look at your own clothing, shoes, and accessories. What are they all made of? Discuss.

3 PREPARE You are going to read an article about fabrics made from milk, pineapple, banana, coconut, and fish. Discuss which parts of the product, plant, or animal might be used and how.

4 INTEGRATE Read the article, and find out what parts of the plants are used.

5 IDENTIFY Reread the article and find information for each of the images: Where is it made or found? What is it traditionally used for? What kind of fabric is it suited to? Write facts you find interesting about each.

6 WHAT'S YOUR ANGLE? How do you think the writer feels about these products overall? Which ones are interesting to you, and why? Discuss.

Milk, Fruit, and Fish Fabrics

In last month's edition of *What's New*, the article "Friendly Fabrics" highlighted unusual materials being used for **garments**. Natural products such as corn, coffee grounds, and recycled plastic drinking bottles can be exploited to produce fabrics that are comfortable, sustainable, and attractive.

This month, we look at some more unlikely sources, which are creating waves in the fashion industry and getting environmentalists excited.

Milk

Using milk to produce fabric is not an entirely new concept: milk protein was used for clothes in the 1930s. However, today's considerably simpler product is the creation of a young German entrepreneur named Anke Domaske, whose interest in fabrics developed when she was searching for a comfortable material that did not irritate her sick stepfather's skin. Qmilch fabric uses spoiled organic milk that would otherwise be wasted since millions of gallons of milk are thrown away every year.

Producing Qmilch is a simple process, involving the extraction of milk proteins to make a powder, which is then mixed with fluid and heated. Although it is currently nearly ten times more expensive to produce than cotton, it uses only a tiny proportion of water (about half a gallon per 2 pounds of milk fabric, instead of over 2,600 gallons for the same amount of cotton). The fabric produced is soft and silky in **texture**, easy to clean, and quick to dry. In addition to being hypoallergenic, it is also said to have antibacterial qualities and is ideal for dresses, underwear, and nightwear, as well as bed linen and car upholstery.

Tropical Fruits

The coconut, whose bristly "hair," or "coir," has been used for centuries in Asia to make brushes, to twist into ropes, or to **weave** into doormats, can also be used to produce fabric. The resulting material is quick drying and naturally absorbent, soaking up sweat and bad odors. It is, therefore, particularly well suited to sportswear and apparently offers UV protection, too. It is very durable, and since it is wrinkle resistant, there is no need for ironing.

And then there is the banana stem, which is usually burned when the fruit is removed, but which has also been traditionally used for blankets, Indian saris, and Japanese kimonos. Approximately one billion tons of these stems are wasted annually, and makers

upholstery– estofamento

Bristly – eriçado
doormats – capachos (tapete) doorway

READING SKILL Making an inference

Making an inference is sometimes called *reading between the lines*. It is where the reader decides on the underlying message that the writer has, which may not be obvious on first reading.

For example, we can infer from the article on fabrics that the writer supports sustainability and has regard for the environment, without the writer's opinion being stated explicitly. The example below suggests that pineapple plants are a potential source of material that is currently completely wasted. This is clear from the surrounding text yet is not spelled out.

Once again, this is a by-product of the pineapple harvest, as the leaves are usually left on the ground. The cotton-like fibers are scraped off the hard leaves…

Inference can also take place at the sentence level. This is when the reader's brain makes logical connections between ideas that are stated, and those that are not, to draw logical conclusions.

The boy climbed up the coconut palm and got out a sharp knife. We heard a dull thud as the coconut landed.

It can be inferred that the boy used the knife to cut down the coconut. This is not made explicit, but we draw on experience and knowledge to make sense of situations.

7 APPLY Read the last paragraph of the text, and think about the following questions.

Rebeca Coelho ♡

- Why does the writer feel cautious?
- Why does he or she refer to bamboo?
- What is the inference?

8 APPLY Read each sentence, and use inference to answer the question that follows it.

1 The young woman touched the elegant white dress in awe. Only three days to go before the big day. Question: What's going to happen soon?
   She's (probably) going to get married. It's her wedding dress.

2 The woman pushed the needle through the thick fabric. A drop of blood dropped from her finger onto the cotton layers. *What happened?*

3 Dara was deep in concentration at her sewing machine. It was dark now, and she suddenly felt very tired. *How long had she been there?*

4 She placed a small piece of pineapple in Lola's mouth. The little girl put her hand up immediately, licking her lips and smiling. *Why did the child raise her hand?*

5 The workers looked out of the window. The fruit was completely ripe, but there was no possibility of picking it today. *Why couldn't they work?*

6 Reggie got into the car, and the smell of brand-new upholstery and plastic hit him. He couldn't contain his excitement. *Why was he excited?*

claim that it is virtually carbon neutral. When mixed with other fibers, such as silk, the resulting material is soft, lightweight, and, interestingly, water-repellent. This makes the fabric very suitable for outdoor wear, such as raincoats.

Historically, the pineapple plant has also been used for clothing in the Philippines, where "piña" cloth is used to create luxury clothing like wedding dresses. Once again, this is a by-product of the pineapple harvest, as the leaves are usually left on the ground. The cotton-like fibers are scraped off the hard leaves, dried, and then spun into long, thin thread ready for production. The resulting fabric is washable, slightly transparent, and lightweight. It has a natural stiffness and also a slight shine, which means it is very appropriate for formal wear.

Fish

An ugly, snake-like fish that lives deep down on the ocean floor and that has survived for millions of years would seem an unlikely contributor to the clothing industry. The hagfish has special organs down its long body that produce a unique kind of milky glue or slime when it's attacked. This reacts with seawater, exploding in size and thereby protecting the hagfish from sharks and other predators, as the sticky slime interferes with other creatures' breathing.

The qualities of hagfish slime have fascinated scientists for years: it comprises millions of hair-like threads. Each fish carries hundreds of miles of these. Experts think these very strong and stretchy

threads can be used in clothing—sportswear or even bullet-proof vests—as an alternative to synthetic fabrics (nylon or lycra), which derive from oil. Unfortunately, scientists have not yet discovered how to breed hagfish in an artificial environment.

All of these natural products are environmentally friendly: sustainable, renewable, and biodegradable. Any such newly developed fabric tends to be met with great enthusiasm, although natural products such as these sometimes suffer when they reach large-scale production, as we have seen with fabrics such as bamboo. However, evidently the natural world has more secrets to reveal.

Next month, we'll be looking at self-repairing fabric that scientists have developed from squids' teeth, as well as fabric that can be made from tea.

＋ Oxford 5000™

Harvest – cosecha   garment – vestuario

thread – two

9 VOCABULARY Complete each sentence with one of the words in the box. You may need to change the words so they fit grammatically.

weave	harvest	thread	fiber
garment	texture	spin	

weave – tear

1 The __spinning__ wheel was invented in India more than a thousand years ago.

2 The shop was full of beautiful __garments__, ranging from everyday shirts to evening wear.

3 Around 50 billion coconuts are produced every year globally. The size of the __harvest__ partly depends on the weather.

4 On my trip, I saw local people sitting on the floor and __weaving__ baskets from thin pieces of bamboo.

5 Once the long __texture__ of the banana plant are mixed with silk, the resulting material is soft and silky.

6 By weaving the cotton __thread__ in certain ways, durable fabrics such as denim can be produced.

7 Cashmere comes from goats and is known for its warmth and beautiful, soft __fiber__.

10 WHAT'S YOUR ANGLE? Think about your own clothes. Think of three different items that you like and describe each one to a partner: sportswear, outdoor wear, nightwear, or anything else.

GRAMMAR IN CONTEXT Relative clauses

Defining relative clauses give essential information about the noun (underlined) that precedes it.

The fish has special <u>organs</u> down its long body *which / that produce a unique kind of milky glue or "slime."*

In these clauses the pronoun can be omitted if it refers to the object of the verb in the relative clause.

We'll be looking at <u>self-repairing fabric</u> (which/that/ø) *scientists have developed from squids' teeth.*

If followed by the verb *be*, we can leave out *be* and the pronoun. This is sometimes called a *reduced relative clause.*

The article "Friendly Fabrics" highlighted unusual <u>materials</u> *(that are) (being) used for clothing*

Non-defining relative clauses provide extra, nonessential information, marked by (a) comma(s).

This considerably simpler product is the creation of <u>a young German entrepreneur called Anke Domaske</u>, *whose interest developed when she was searching for a comfortable fabric…*

See Grammar focus on page 163.

---

11 IDENTIFY Decide if these sentences include defining or non-defining clauses. Then complete them using an appropriate relative pronoun. Where possible, omit the pronoun or the pronoun + *be* + verb.

1 Milk fabric is one solution _____ we can use in response to the problem of waste.

2 Qmilch fabric is odorless, _____ might surprise some people.

3 Domaske, _____ studied microbiology, launched Qmilch in 2011.

4 Some companies use coconut husk waste to make fabric and products _____ are very light and strong.

5 Coconuts can be blended with other materials to make fabrics, _____ last longer than other natural choices, such as cotton.

6 Three quarters of the cotton _____ is produced on large-scale farms in the U.S. is genetically modified.

7 Farmers in China and the U.S., _____ cotton is largely produced, need not worry yet about the rise in eco-friendly products.

8 The coconut, _____ shell, flesh, and milk are already widely used, is both a fruit and a nut, according to botanists.

12 NOTICE Listen to the recording, and check your answers to Exercise 11. Pay attention to the way the speaker's voice drops for a non-defining relative clause.

13 EXPAND Work with a partner. Take turns reading aloud a sentence from Exercise 11 to each other, paying close attention to your pronunciation.

14 APPLY Rewrite each pair of sentences as one longer sentence using a non-defining relative clause. Start with the noun phrase in bold.

1 **The leaves of the pineapple plant** are used to make soft fabric. They can also be used to make an alternative to leather. *which*

2 **The pineapple plant** is naturally shiny and hard. This lends a natural protective layer to the fabric as well. *which   which*

3 **In the Philippines**, there are nearly 60,000 hectares of pineapple plantations. It makes sense to use this resource more effectively. *where   that is*

4 **Banana fabric** is well suited to outerwear. It is also commonly used for cushions and blankets. *which*

5 **The hagfish** is practically blind. Scientists estimate that the species has been around for 300 million years. *which   practically blind*

6 **Hagfish slime threads** have been likened to spider silk in terms of strength. The fish produce threads around six inches in length.

54

5.2 Fun with Food

1 ACTIVATE Work with a partner to think of at least three objects designed or redesigned in the last ten years that you have used in the past 24 hours.

- Discuss some of the objects in terms of usefulness. What exactly do you like about them?
- How would it affect you if you didn't have each of the objects?

2 INTEGRATE Look at the advertisement for a special spaghetti fork. Would you like to buy one? How much would you pay for it? Discuss with a partner.

WHOEVER LIKES

Spaghetti

WILL LOVE THIS FORK!

Save effort and amuse yourself and others at the same time!

An easy-to-use gadget. Use whenever you have spaghetti, noodles, or spiralized vegetables!

Suitable for any age—adults or children.

FEATURES

- Available in different colors (green, purple, or red)
- Size: 8 in. x 1 in.
- Uses 2 AAA batteries (included)
- Detachable head for easy cleaning

★★★★ Well worth the money!

★★★★ It makes us laugh and also works like a dream!

3 ▶ ASSESS Watch the video without sound. Create a conversation with a partner that you will read out as the video plays.

4 ▶ ASSESS Watch the video with sound, and compare your versions with the original.

motif : design

high end – expensive

inspire – motivate, drive

Inextricably – impossible to separate

PRONUNCIATION SKILL Linking

In English, words flow smoothly. Where possible, words are contracted, e.g., *What's that?* In addition, words are joined wherever possible, such as where a word ends in a consonant sound and the next word begins with a vowel.

I hope you didn't spend a lot on that.

If a word ends in a vowel sound and the next word begins with a vowel, to help the flow, an extra sound can be added between the two:

My friend gave it to me /j/ as a joke gift.

Sometimes a /w/ sound is also added for the same reason.

I'm going to /w/ a cafe

If the same consonant ends one word and begins another, the two sounds start to blend into one.

My friend gave it to me

5 NOTICE Analyze the following sentences for linking.

1 First identify the stressed words in the sentence.
2 Identify any examples of consonant–vowel linking.
3 Identify any extra /w/ or /j/ sounds that are added to connect words or same-consonant-sound linking.

1 I've never seen anything like it.

2 It takes the work out of eating spaghetti, so it's a wonderful tool for lazy children!

3 Cheap at that price! I didn't regret it at all! We are planning to order another!

6 **APPLY** Practice saying the sentences in Exercise 5 aloud. Then listen to the recording, and compare with your own version.

7 **EXPAND** Work with a partner. Write two or three short and persuasive customer comments to be added to the Spaghetti Fork advertisement. Try to include at least one feature of linking in each one.

8 **ASSESS** Look at the product review of the Spaghetti Fork on the right. How satisfied is the customer?

9 **IDENTIFY** What happens in each of the main paragraphs in the review?

WRITING SKILL Language to praise and criticize

When praising something, we use positive words and phrases, particularly adjectives and adverbs:

useful, effortlessly

You can make your language more emphatic by adding adverbs to describe the degree or to emphasize:

***particularly** helpful*

When criticizing something, besides obviously negative words like *not* or *slow*, we also tend to use words like *too* and *enough*. If they follow praise, negative ideas are often introduced by words that show contrast, such as *but*, *however*, and *although*. To criticize politely, use softening devices like *rather*, and qualify the comment using *if* clauses.

This feels quite slow if you are in a hurry.

Giving reasons can also help to justify or soften a criticism.

It didn't work for her since she is left-handed.

---

10 **IDENTIFY** Look back through the advertisement, and see if you can find any of the following.

1 Positive adjectives and adverbs

2 Adverbs that describe adjectives or other adverbs to describe degree or to emphasize

3 Contrasting words at the start of a sentence or clause

4 Negative but polite criticism

11 **DEVELOP** Work with a partner. Make each sentence either more positive or less negative. You can add to the sentences, but keep all the original words.

1 The product is cheap and picks up your noodles well.

2 It's heavy for a child to lift.

3 I found it hard to remove the head.

4 Delivery was quick and efficient.

5 Customer service wasn't helpful.

Makes Eating Enjoyable!

◉◉◉◉◔ 4.5 out of 5

If you want to make eating spaghetti or noodles more enjoyable, whether it's for adults or children, this little gadget is absolutely ideal. I bought it for my kids three weeks ago, just for a bit of fun, but it's actually extremely useful.

This fork lets you avoid having to chop up the pasta or noodles into small pieces, so there's less mess. It works on batteries that can just be popped into the fork effortlessly. As soon as you remove your finger from the button, it immediately stops rotating. Some of the other reviews mentioned a short battery life, but we have used our fork a lot, and the batteries are still going strong.

The Spaghetti Fork is simple to handle, even for young children. I also found it particularly helpful as a distraction tool for my son, who tends to be a poor eater. (However grumpy he is, this fork cheers him up and distracts him from the food itself!) As a result, he eats far more than he normally would. In addition, the design is clearly robust and strong enough to withstand being dropped, even onto a tile floor. It cleans really easily, too, since you can simply twist off the fork end; this part is also dishwasher safe, which is extremely convenient. I've put it in there several times and it hasn't broken or even become discolored.

The fork certainly takes all the effort out of eating your own spaghetti! I don't mind the noise, though I do think some people might find it a little irritating. However, it twists about 20 times a minute, so this feels quite slow if you are in a hurry. We tried it with spiralized vegetables, too (zucchini and carrots), but it didn't seem to function as well: the vegetables kept slipping off, perhaps because of the turning speed. I think that, although this product is especially useful for children, the handle isn't small enough for most youngsters under seven. I let my daughter try it, too, but unfortunately, it didn't work for her since she is left-handed!

Overall, it's worth the money and is more than just a joke item, in my opinion! For any parent with a child who is a fussy eater, I think this is a must-buy, as long as they are right-handed. My son's enthusiasm has lasted, though I make sure we only have pasta or noodles once a week. That way, the novelty doesn't wear off!

😊 Pros	😞 Cons
• Very good at doing the job	• Noisy when in use
• Easy to use, with comfortable handle	• A little slow
• Makes eating pasta fun!	• Handle quite large for younger children
• Detachable fork end	• Difficult for left-handed people to use
• Batteries easy to access (slide open)	

12 WHAT'S YOUR ANGLE? Discuss in a small group.

1 When did you last read either official or customer reviews for a service or product?

2 Do you generally find reviews useful? How do they help you in the process of buying or selecting a product or service?

3 In your opinion is it OK for reviews to be openly negative?

4 Have you ever written an online review yourself? What for and why? How positive/negative was it?

GRAMMAR IN CONTEXT *Whoever, whatever, whichever, whenever, wherever,* and *however*

The suffix *-ever* can be added to question words to give it the meaning "it doesn't matter which, how, or when." These words can be used in different places in the sentences, such as the subject or as an adverbial.

Whoever likes spaghetti will love this fork!
However grumpy he is, this fork cheers him up.

Whenever can also have a meaning similar to "every time."

Use whenever you have spaghetti, noodles, or spiralized vegetables!

You can also use the *-ever* words to end a list, giving it a meaning similar to "and so on." This is generally informal.

Use it at home, at the office, wherever!

You can use the question word + *-ever* as a short response on its own. Polite intonation is essential here.

Can we talk this evening? Whenever.

See Grammar focus on page 163.

---

13 APPLY Complete each sentence by choosing the most appropriate *-ever* word.

1 <u>Whenever</u> you feel like a crunchy salad, just let the machine do the work for you!

2 <u>Whatever</u> vegetable you select, you'll see how simple it is in seconds.

3 Thanks to its robust design, <u>however</u> happens, you won't break it.

4 You can cut your cabbage <u>whenever</u> thickly or thinly as you want!

5 <u>Whoever</u> sees it in your kitchen will be green with envy! → *inveja*
jealous

14 🔊 **APPLY** Listen carefully, and respond to each sentence with a single-word *-ever* response. Be sure to sound polite.

15 PREPARE You are going to write a polite online review of a new gadget you have bought. Make notes on the following:

☐ Say what it is and when and where you bought it.
☐ Give the positives.
☐ Give the negatives.
☐ Write your overall recommendation or opinion.

16 WRITE Write your first draft of the review. Remember to add appropriate adjectives or adverbs to talk about the product's strengths, and be polite when commenting on any weaknesses.

17 IMPROVE Read through your review and correct any obvious errors. Then work with a partner and read each other's work. Rewrite your review based on your partner's feedback.

Ask your partner to check for:

■ Overall clarity and organization
■ Accuracy
■ A description of the product's strengths that is clear and positive sounding
■ A clear and polite account of the weaknesses
■ A useful summary

A toy store in Madrid, Spain

5.3 New Ink

1 ACTIVATE What do you know about 3-D printing? Do you know how it works? What can it be used for?

2 🔲 **PREPARE** Work with a partner to fill in the missing words.

dimensional	layers	other	physical process

3-D Printing *Noun*: the action or ¹_____ of making a ²_____ object from a three- ³_____ digital model, typically by laying down many thin ⁴_____ of a material, one after the ⁵_____.

—adapted from *New Oxford American Dictionary*, 3rd ed.

3 INTERACT Today, 3-D printing is used in many fields. Work with a partner to think of at least one thing that each of these groups of people might use 3-D printing for.

farmers	chefs	builders	surgeons
nutritionists	the military	engineers	
dentists	fashion designers	musicians	

4 INTEGRATE Which field from Exercise 3 does each of the following match?

1   Entire houses as well as parts of buildings
2   Equipment, such as watering systems or missing parts from machinery
3   Dresses made to fit individuals perfectly
4   Bridges
5   Cake decoration with a very high level of detail
6   Food that caters to an individual's health needs
7   Body parts, such as fingers, kidneys, and noses
8   Replacement teeth or crowns
9   Instruments, such as guitars
10   Parts of a plane or a gun

A participle clause is spoken with less emphasis than the main clause in a sentence, so participle clauses can be difficult to understand when listening.

🔊 *Hugo did what the printer instructions said, **reading the information slowly**.*

The subject is usually the same in both clauses. Therefore, in the above example, Hugo followed the instructions, *and* he read the information.

Notice that if the participle clause comes first, the participle clause has a slight rising tone at the end before the main clause begins.

🔊 ***Seeing the machine for the first time**, she tried to be open-minded about it.*

5 DEVELOP First say these sentences in your head, using appropriate intonation. Then read them aloud to a partner.

1   Wanting to be a dental nurse, Maria did the training as soon as she left school.
2   Being very interested in cooking, Marty pestered his parents to teach him to cook from a young age.
3   Traveling to work on a daily basis, she noticed that most people simply slept.
4   She said she would like to become the director, when questioned about her ambitions.
5   Having spoken at some length to the audience, the man sat down.

6 🔊 **NOTICE** Listen and repeat the sentences from Exercise 5. How similar was your intonation?

7 🔊 **IDENTIFY** You are going to listen to a talk show called *I Like Science*, a TV show where one expert explains a scientific innovation to the host and two celebrities. The topic this week is 3-D printing. Listen and find out which fields or jobs are mentioned from Exercise 3.

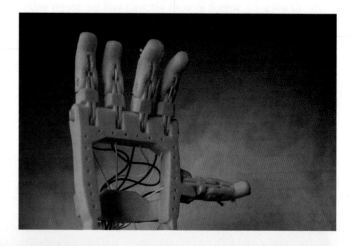

8 **IDENTIFY** Listen again. Take note of any details you hear about the following.

1 The printed house
2 The process of printing food
3 Reasons for printing food for the elderly

9 **WHAT'S YOUR ANGLE?** What have you learned about 3-D printing? Would you like to sample 3-D products? Will this innovation revolutionize our world?

GRAMMAR IN CONTEXT
Participle phrases and clauses

Participle phrases and clauses are often found in more formal writing and speaking. Because they require fewer words, they can be used to make writing or speaking more efficient. Three main participles are used in clauses:

The present participle:

***Not wanting to eat pureed meals all the time**, old people may lose interest in food.*
***Being in the world of TV**, nothing in my work has been 3-D printed.*

The past participle, which often expresses passive meaning:

***Established only a few years ago**, this project allowed food to be printed.*

The perfect participle:

***Having seen 3-D printing in action**, I am convinced this technology is going to revolutionize our world.*
***Having been 3-D printed**, it is earthquake safe.*

See Grammar focus on page 163.

10 **IDENTIFY** Look at these sentences. For each one decide if the participle clause indicates a reason (R), a condition (C), or a sequence of events or two simultaneous events (S).

1 Feeling tired, I stopped listening to the professor. ___
2 Putting down the instructions, I tried to get the machine to work. ___
3 Assuming you can't buy that part easily, you might be able to get it 3-D printed. ___
4 Given the chance, I'd definitely like to taste 3-D printed food. ___
5 Much loved, the professor always received lots of gifts at the end of the year. ___
6 Arriving at the TV center, the guests on the chat show all got to know one another. ___
7 Not knowing what to expect, he tasted the "printed" food with caution. ___

VOCABULARY DEVELOPMENT
Nouns formed from verbs

Many nouns are formed from verbs and often with some of the following suffixes: *-ment, -tion / -sion / -ion, -ence / -ance*.

If the verb ends in an *e*, remember to remove this first before adding the *-ion* suffix.

create → creation

11 **NOTICE** Mark the word stress on these verbs. Check in the dictionary, if necessary.

adapt	prefer	consider	establish
require	collaborate	avoid	amend
disturb	allow	adjust	distribute
replace	accept	appreciate	

12 **BUILD** What are the noun forms of the verbs in Exercise 11? Put them into the correct column.

-ance/-ence	(a)-tion/-ion	-ment

13 **INTEGRATE** Identify the stress on the nouns in Exercise 12. Then listen and repeat both the verbs and nouns. Can you form any generalizations about the word-stress patterns in the nouns?

14 **APPLY** Change these sentences, making each verb in italics into a noun. You will have to change other elements of the sentence.

1 Elderly people often *require* specific nutritional support.
   Specific nutritional support is often a requirement of elderly people.
2 It's important to *distribute* all the meals efficiently.
3 How to *avoid* tasteless and unattractive food is the motivation behind 3-D food printing for the elderly.
4 The software *adapts* the contents of each dish, meaning that every individual's needs can be catered to.
5 The levels of salt and fat, for example, can be *adjusted*.
6 People are now beginning to *accept* 3-D printing.

15 **WHAT'S YOUR ANGLE?** Complete the sentences so they are true for you. Then discuss them with a partner, paying attention to your pronunciation.

1 Having learned about 3-D printing, I…
2 After being helped to understand participle clauses, I…
3 Knowing a lot of vocabulary and grammar, I…
4 Being a student of English, I…
5 When doing my English homework, I (often)…

5.4 One More Thing...

1 ACTIVATE If you are successful at something, do you want to share it with other people? Do you want to tell it to your friends? How about strangers? Why?

2 IDENTIFY Max is working on a paper for his art class. His instructor, Professor Armstrong, has sent him an email giving feedback on his work so far. Read and find out (a) how well Max is doing and (b) what he needs to work on.

Hello Max,

I have read your first draft of your assignment on Matisse, and I want to let you know that I thoroughly enjoyed reading it. I've read a lot of assignments on this artist, and to be honest, yours was a really fresh and interesting approach. Well done! I can see that you've spent a long time researching but have also managed to successfully include your personal response to three of his paintings. The angle you take on his growth in style—especially in relation to his use of color—is relevant and insightful.

I'm very much looking forward to seeing the final draft. My only suggestion would be to cut back the biographical/background section—it's been done so many times before. It would be worth using the space to further develop your understanding of Matisse's three works.

Please don't hesitate to drop by my office if you have any queries.

Best,
Professor Armstrong

3 ▶ ANALYZE Andy wants to know how Max did on the assignment in Professor Armstrong's art class. Watch the video of their interaction. How would you describe (a) Max's and (b) Andy's attitude?

arrogant	embarrassed	confident	quiet
curious	amused	secretive	open
confused	pleased		

4 EXPAND Do you think Max wants to tell Andy his news? How can you tell?

60

Sometimes people don't willingly open up about certain topics because they are uncomfortable or embarrassed. We draw out information because we are encouraging someone to share. Encouraging someone to express their thoughts and feelings is an indication of your sincere interest. Relationship closeness, personality, and the topic of conversation can influence what you say when asking for more information. You can signal that you want more information directly by saying words like these:

Tell me more. (imperative) *What exactly did he say?* (direct question) *And?* (with an upward tone)

It would be awkward to push for more information if that person is not responding openly. Clues such as intonation, eye contact, and facial expression indicate to the listener whether it is alright to keep pressing for more details.

5 ▶ **NOTICE** Watch the video again, and listen for the intonation clues. Watch for the eye contact and facial expressions that indicate that Max is happy to give Andy more information.

6 **IDENTIFY** Look at these requests for additional information. Choose a number from 1–5 to show the closeness and familiarity. For example *no distance* is the language spoken between two best friends; whereas, a *great distance* would be between a young student and someone in a very important position.

Smaller Distance				Greater Distance
1	2	3	4	5

1   Can you elaborate on that? _4_
2   Tell me more! _3_
3   Could you expand a little? _3_
4   What do you mean, exactly? _3_
5   Could you give me a few more details? _4_
6   Can I ask a few questions about it, if that's OK? _3_
7   Is that it? Aren't you going to tell me anything else? _2_
8   It's still not clear. I need more information! _3_

7 **ASSESS** In your own language and culture, is it acceptable to ask for further questions in certain situations? Can you think of situations where it is and where it is not?

8 **ANALYZE** Read the conversations. What is the topic of each one? What does Speaker A say to get more information? Is Speaker B willing to provide more information? How can you tell?

Situation 1

A: So today's the big day. When will you get your results exactly?

B: I got them a few days ago.

A: Oh. Can I ask…?

B: How I did? Not too well.

A: In all of them?

B: Pretty much.

A: What, even after all that work?

B: Yeah.

A: Can you retake them?

B: Not sure. Did you hear from your brother about his visit?

Situation 2

A: So how are you doing? Feeling refreshed?

B: Oh yes. It was unforgettable. Blue sea, white sand… you know.

A: Wonderful. Got time for a coffee to tell me more?

B: Actually, I'd love to, but I've got about 600 emails to reply to. Can we meet after work, maybe, for a drink?

A: Let's do that. Can I just ask one thing?

B: Sure.

A: How were the accommodations? You were so worried…

B: They were perfect. No problems whatsoever. I'll tell you more later!

A: OK. See you then. I'll text you.

B: Great. Bye.

A: Yeah. Bye. See you.

9 **INTERACT** Work with a partner. Come up with one conversation where you draw out information successfully. Then come up with another conversation in which you can't draw out information because your partner is unwilling to provide it.

10 **SHARE** Role-play both conversations for your class. Have the class guess which conversation demonstrates drawing out information successfully and which one does not.

079619

GO ONLINE
to create your own version
of the English For Real video.

5.5 Appreciating Apps

1 ACTIVATE Define *innovation*, writing your definition in fewer than 16 words. Then compare with a partner.

2 WHAT'S YOUR ANGLE? In what ways do you believe the Internet has transformed our lives? Work with a partner to name at least five benefits.

3 INTEGRATE Using the numbers in the box, complete the text from the *Dictionary of Marketing* about the speed of development of the Internet.

40	70	4	100	20th	15	3.2

 Innovations in communications and media have spread much faster than those that drove the industrial economy of the [1] __20th__ century. For example, it took almost 50 years for electricity to be widely used in households and factories; it took [2] __40__ years for radio to gain 50 million listeners; television took [3] __15__ years to reach 50 million viewers. In contrast, the Internet reached 50 million users in [4] __4__ years once it had been opened to the general public in 1994. The population connected to the Internet has grown from [5] __70__ million in 1997 to an estimated [6] __3.2__ billion worldwide in 2015, which is more than 40 percent of the world population and is more than twice as many people as the population of the world's largest nation. Over this time, usage of the Internet has effectively been doubling, on average, every [7] __100__ days.
—adapted from *A Dictionary of Marketing*, 4th ed., by Charles Doyle

4 INTERACT Which three apps do you use most frequently and what for? Discuss in a small group.

5 ◀) **IDENTIFY** Listen to the audio. The speakers mention the following applications. With a partner, discuss and briefly describe what each app does.

- Be My Eyes
- ParkIt
- Spin Me Alarm
- Thief Catcher
- Word Lens

6 ◀) **IDENTIFY** List pros and cons of each app. Listen to the audio again if needed.

Thief Tracker _____

_____

Word Lens _____

_____

Spin Me Alarm _____

_____

ParkIt _____

_____

Be My Eyes _____

_____

SPEAKING Reaching a consensus

A consensus is an agreement on an idea, topic, or selection of options that is acceptable to everyone involved. In the process of reaching a consensus, ideas are discussed in a respectful way, and people openly talk about advantages and disadvantages and actively listen to others. There is typically a lot of checking, questioning, recapping, and summarizing of the discussion so far.

In the final analysis, even though you may partially disagree, you should be happy enough to give your consent in a final decision.

7 APPLY Match the phrases used in reaching a consensus.

1 Why don't we keep that one ___
2 Do we agree that ___
3 Right. Are we happy to discount, then, ___
4 So, that leaves us, so far, ___
5 Should we keep this one and perhaps ___
6 So, are we ___

a get rid of the language one?
b with the Park It and and the Word Lens apps.
c since we all like it?
d we all like this one, then?
e the Thief Tracker and the Spin Me alarm?
f agreed that we're left with…?

8 ◀) **IMPROVE** Listen and repeat the phrases from Exercise 7.

Now go to page 151 for the Unit 5 Review.

6 Rules

What rules are these people breaking?

What makes people follow rules?

What makes people break rules?

BEHIND THE PHOTO

REAL-WORLD GOAL

Find out some unusual laws or rules in your country that don't exist anymore

1 Think about these crimes. Individually, decide which three crimes are (a) most likely to happen in your country and (b) the most serious and why. Then discuss your answers in a small group.

burglary	murder	dangerous driving	drug dealing	corruption
terrorism	robbery	kidnapping	tax evasion	

2 Working in your group, add five or more crimes, using a dictionary if necessary.

6.1 Strange Laws Abroad

1 **ACTIVATE** Work with a partner. Take two minutes to think of seven laws relating to driving in your country (for example, *you have to wear a seat belt*).

2 **WHAT'S YOUR ANGLE?** Have you, or has someone you know, ever done something illegal when driving either at home or abroad? Were you caught? Tell your partner what happened.

READING SKILL Recognizing and understanding mood and atmosphere

Writers convey mood and atmosphere through the details that they include and the language they use.

For a lighter mood, the writer might include extra, humorous details that are not essential to the story. In addition, the writer might use:

- A chatty style, perhaps with exclamation marks
  Have a great time!

- Conversely, perhaps a serious tone describing things that are not serious
  We'd managed to skillfully avoid any major family disagreements. (meaning, in simple terms, we hadn't had any big arguments)

- Amusing vocabulary
  gobbled up the cookies

- Positive vocabulary
  enjoyable

- Comment adverbs
  thankfully

A darker mood can be created by a frightening setting. In terms of language, the writer might use:

- Short sentences to convey tension
- Repetition of some words or phrases or of sentence structure
- Descriptive adjectives, adverbs, and verbs to convey emotion (such as *anxious*) or to describe the effect on the senses (such as *deafening*)

3 **IDENTIFY** Read the two extracts from travel blogs where people unknowingly broke the law when driving abroad. What did each person do wrong?

| Home | About | Search 🔍 |

Rules of the road abroad

I've just come back from a really enjoyable trip around Germany. Our last day was spoiled, however, by a small problem on the autobahn (the freeway). We were happily traveling along from Cologne to the Frankfurt airport, munching chocolate cookies and listening to the last installment of a play on the radio. It was the final day of a fabulous three-week vacation, in which we'd managed to skillfully avoid any major family disagreements and generally have a great time!

It was 6 p.m., and thankfully, we were on time for our long flight home. The kids were fast asleep with their mouths open, and my wife and I were totally absorbed in the play. I was, ironically, also enjoying the last moments of the wonderful German roads. Suddenly, our rental car started to shake, and our **vehicle** slowed quickly to a halt. After a moment's panic, I realized that we had run out of gas. (I'd been semi-aware about 15 minutes earlier of an orange light shining brightly from the dashboard…)

Fortunately, we'd stopped less than a mile from the next gas station. After the initial panic, my wife and I congratulated each other on our good fortune. We quickly calculated that there was still plenty of time to make our flight. In my relief, I gobbled up the remaining cookies.

Just as I undid my seat belt to walk to the station, however, I noticed some more bright lights: the traffic **police** had pulled up. I thought nothing of it and smiled cheerfully, my mouth full, as I rolled my window down. They requested my documents, then asked what the problem was. I was informed that I had committed an **offense**.

Apparently you're not allowed to run out of gas on the autobahn, so we had to **pay** a **fine** of around $100. It's the driver's responsibility to be aware of the fuel situation. You aren't supposed to walk on the autobahn, either, which is another **criminal** offense! Thankfully, we still made it to the airport on time. The kids slept through the entire incident!

Check the rules before you go!

We encountered a similarly unexpected law when we were on our honeymoon in northern Spain.

We'd spent the day at the beach. We were heading back to our hotel in Barcelona, along some quiet country roads. It was just before the main summer season, and we'd driven a long way to find a particularly beautiful beach mentioned in our guidebook. It was around 9:30 p.m. We left in the evening light, but within about 15 minutes, everything suddenly changed.

The clouds became black, low, and threatening; you could see practically nothing. Then the storm started: balls of ice, the size of golf balls, started crashing down from the sky. The noise on the metal of the car roof was deafeningly loud. We had to stop completely. We couldn't hear ourselves think, let alone talk. Then, from nowhere, two large, shapeless figures in black passed by. We saw them briefly in the headlights. One of them seemed to fall against the hood for a second. Perhaps we should have let them shelter in the car, but at that moment, we were simply terrified. Without thinking, we sped off in silence.

The storm passed, and within a few minutes, we felt less anxious. Then, as we were nearing the outskirts of the city, we were stopped at a police checkpoint. We were ordered out of the car by the armed police, who then inspected the vehicle carefully for nearly 20 minutes, with few words and no search warrant. They were searching for stolen goods, and as they finished, one officer shone his flashlight over us, pausing at the sight of our feet. He explained that you can't wear flip-flops in Spain when driving (strong footwear is obligatory). Without realizing it, we'd broken the law! Fortunately for us, they just gave us a warning and told us we could go; we didn't even have to pay a fine. They obviously had more serious laws to enforce that night. We found out later that a criminal ring was trafficking luxury goods across Europe.

We learned that you should always check out the rules of the road before traveling abroad.

꘎+ Oxford 5000™

4 INTEGRATE Work with a partner. Without rereading the texts, decide whether each element comes from the first or the second story.

radio play	shapeless figures
flashlight	beautiful beach
terrible noise	bright lights
vehicle check	flight home
pay a fine	initial panic
gas station	black clouds

5 ASSESS Check your answers to Exercise 4 against the texts.

6 IDENTIFY Reread the texts and answer these questions.

1 In the first story, why had it been a good family vacation?

2 Had the driver been completely unaware of the gas situation?

3 Why was the driver's mouth full when speaking to the police?

4 In what ways were they lucky and unlucky?

5 In the second story, what do you think the figures in black were doing?

6 Were the dark figures and the police check connected?

7 Why were they stopped the second time?

8 Why didn't the couple get fined?

9 What are the similarities between these two stories?

10 Are the moods the same or different in the two texts? In what way?

7 INTEGRATE Look at the two blog entries again. What examples can you find of the features mentioned in the Reading Skill box?

GRAMMAR IN CONTEXT
Expressing obligation, prohibition, and advice

To express obligation, prohibition, and advice, we can use modals and semimodals.

1 We _had to_ pay a fine of around $100. (obligation)

2 We _didn't_ even _have to_ pay a fine. (lack of obligation)

3 You _should_ always check out the rules of the road before traveling abroad. (advice)

4 They just gave us a warning and told us we _could_ go. (permission)

5 You _can't_ wear flip-flops in Spain when driving. (prohibition)

See Grammar focus on page 164.

8 IDENTIFY Read these sentences, which use modals and some other phrases. Decide which functions they express. You may need to use one function more than once.

obligation	permission	lack of obligation
prohibition	advice	

1 Strong footwear is _obligatory_ when driving in many countries.

2 If driving, it _isn't necessary_ to have your passport with you.

3 After looking at our documents, the police said we _were allowed to go_.

4 You're _not allowed to_ run out of gas on the autobahn.

5 I remember my father _telling_ me, "You _must_ take out insurance if you're traveling abroad."

6 I think _we'd better_ use the GPS since we don't know this area very well.

7 You _aren't supposed_ to walk on the autobahn, either!

9 **INTEGRATE** Read about these laws taken from a website called Strange Laws Abroad. Do you have any similar laws in your own country?

| Home | About | Search | 🔍 |

Peculiar Laws around the World

(Your Guide to a Running List of Weird Rules)

Did you know...

1 It is illegal in Thailand to step on bank notes.
2 It is against the law in the UK to carry a plank of wood along a London sidewalk (unless you are unloading from a vehicle).
3 In China, there is a law that states you must visit your parents "often."
4 In Greece, you can't wear high heels if you are visiting ancient historic sites.
5 In France, you can marry someone who has died as long as you can prove that you had both intended to get married beforehand.
6 On the Pacific island of Samoa, it is against the law to forget your wife's birthday.
7 In Montana, in the United States, weddings can take place where both the bride and groom are absent. Friends can stand in for the couple.
8 In Japan, it's forbidden to be obese: companies and local governments have to measure people's waists (waists should not exceed 33.5 inches [85 cm] for men and 35.4 inches [90 cm] for women).

10 **WHAT'S YOUR ANGLE?** Which of the above laws do you find the most surprising? Discuss what the possible reason or logic is behind each law. Which of these laws would or wouldn't work in your country?

11 **APPLY** Rewrite six of the rules from Exercise 9, choosing one of the words and phrases below. Do not use the same word more than once.

| allowed | not allowed | supposed |
| not supposed | isn't necessary | obligatory |

It's illegal in Thailand to step on bank notes. → In Thailand, you're <u>not allowed to</u> step on bank notes.

🅠 **VOCABULARY DEVELOPMENT** Collocations

Collocations are natural pairings or groupings of two or more words. Some collocations are stronger than others, e.g., *carry out* and *commit* are verbs that collocate with the noun *crime*. However, *commit* is a stronger collocation, that is, it is more frequently used. When you are a student, it is helpful to record words in collocations, not as single words, where appropriate. Strong collocations can be found in some modern dictionaries.

Different word class elements can combine to form collocations.

Verb + noun:	*commit a crime*
Adjective + noun:	*a serious crime*
Noun + noun:	*crime scene*

12 **IDENTIFY** Match the parts of the collocations.

1	enforce	a	offense
2	break	b	warrant
3	stolen	c	checkpoint
4	pay	d	a warning
5	criminal	e	goods
6	search/**arrest**	f	a law
7	give (someone)	g	the law
8	armed	h	a vehicle
9	inspect	i	police
10	police	j	a fine

🔧+ Oxford 5000™

13 **USE** Complete each sentence with a collocation from Exercise 12. You may have to change some words slightly so they fit grammatically.

1 It's more and more common to see _____ on the streets these days since some criminals themselves have weapons.
2 Someone I know was suspected of cybercrime, so the police turned up one day with a _____ to inspect his computer.
3 The trunk of the man's car was full of _____, such as designer watches and sunglasses.
4 If someone has _____ by committing a minor crime, then judges will try to give community work instead of a prison sentence.
5 The problem of my neighbor's late-night parties has improved since he was _____ by local police.
6 I think it's important that traffic police _____ by giving out speeding tickets, for example, since this reduces road accidents.

6.2 The Trick of Trust

1 ACTIVATE Carefully read this definition of a crime. Do you know what the crime is even if you don't know the English word? Can you think of an example?

X is an offense under the X Act 2006, punishable with imprisonment or a fine. The offense is committed when the offender intends to benefit him or herself or another person, or to cause loss to another person, or to expose someone else to risk of loss. The offense can be committed in three ways (as described in the Act). It can be committed if the offender dishonestly makes a false description of a situation, fails to provide information that he or she has a legal duty to tell, or abuses a position of trust to protect the financial interests of another.

—adapted from *A Dictionary of Law Enforcement*, 2nd ed., by Graham Gooch and Michael Williams

2 IDENTIFY Read about the same type of crime described in Exercise 1. What is this crime?

There's a crime that is becoming a major problem. It involves the theft of personal identification information such as digital certificates, passwords, and PINs in order to use them for some criminal purpose. There is an extensive amount of research being carried out on biometric identification systems, which are intended to provide nearly foolproof identification schemes.

—adapted from *A Dictionary of the Internet*, 3rd ed., by Darrel Ince

3 IDENTIFY Find out more about biometric identification systems by reading the following text. Complete each sentence using a word from the box below.

pattern	errors	physical	speed
properties	face	shape	

Biometric Identification System

A system that uses some ¹ _____ human characteristic to determine the identity of the user of a computer system. Typical characteristics that have been used include: typing characteristics, such as the ² _____ of typing or the number of ³ _____ made; the image of a ⁴ _____; fingerprints; hand ⁵ _____; handwriting characteristics; voice ⁶ _____; DNA patterns; and eye characteristics, such as the ⁷ _____ of blood vessels in the retina. Often this technique is used with some other form of identification, such as a password.

—adapted from *A Dictionary of the Internet*, 3rd ed., by Darrel Ince

4 INTERACT Work with a partner and find out whether he or she has experienced any biometric checks. If so, describe what happened.

5 WHAT'S YOUR ANGLE? Complete each sentence with one of the following adverbs so that it is true for you. Then discuss in a small group. Find out if anyone has been the victim of fraud.

never	occasionally	sometimes
often	usually	always

1 I _____ destroy letters containing my personal information, such as name, address, or personal details, before putting them in the garbage.

2 I _____ avoid social media sites where there is no privacy setting.

3 I _____ use the same password on the Internet for different sites.

4 I _____ use a strong password, so it includes random words, symbols, or numbers.

5 I _____ give my bank details over the phone if I believe the caller is official.

6 I _____ access my online bank account from a public Wi-Fi zone.

7 I _____ check that I have the latest security software on my devices.

8 I _____ leave bills lying around.

6 IDENTIFY You are going to hear part of a presentation to college students on identity theft given by a policewoman. Read the statements. Then listen and decide if they are true (T) or false (F).

1 The speaker says people are careful with their physical belongings but not with personal information.

2 If your personal information is stolen, the main type of crime is credit card fraud.

3 The policeman's colleague was a victim of identity theft and is no longer a policewoman.

4 You generally find out within hours if you are a victim.

5 If you are a victim of identity theft, you may not actually lose any money directly.

6 The biggest problem, if you are an innocent victim, is the length of time it can take to sort it out.

7 If someone has your details, there are around five crimes they could then commit.

8 This type of crime is falling as people become more aware.

7 WHAT'S YOUR ANGLE? What information surprised you from the policewoman's talk? Did you learn anything? Which groups of people might benefit from hearing such presentations, and why?

8 EXPAND Look at the pictures, which show some of the events in a personal story about identity fraud. Work with a partner to figure out what happened.

9 ASSESS Read about the incident, and see if your predictions were right. This example of identity theft was published in a college magazine as part of a campaign to warn young people of the dangers.

This happened in early September, last year. I'd been living in Boston for two years. Although I am a newly qualified accountant, I'd been making ends meet by doing waitressing jobs. I had applied for countless jobs but rarely got a response, which was very demotivating.

Then I saw an online ad by a job agency advertising various positions. After contacting them, I was asked to attend an interview downtown, with my résumé, a reference letter, and ID.

I arrived at the offices on time, feeling nervous but excited. The place was professional looking, and a receptionist greeted me and around 30 other candidates. Posters of the agency, Flying High, decorated the walls, and several of the staff had badges with this logo on them. The job that particularly interested me was as a housekeeper for wealthy homeowners based in the Boston suburbs who were often away on business.

I was interviewed by two men in suits, who were friendly and knowledgeable. It was challenging, but after nearly an hour, they gave me positive feedback, suggesting I was a strong candidate. The salary and conditions were good, and the benefits package sounded attractive. I was asked to wait outside with nine other applicants. We, the lucky candidates, were invited to start the process for a criminal background check, necessary in any job that might involve contact with children. The agency staff explained they were happy to help start this process to save time. As there was a small charge, we needed to give our bank and personal details, including a copy of our passports. We should have been suspicious at this point, but everyone was simply excited. We were told to expect a call from the agency within ten days. As we left, they gave us a Flying High bag with various company products: a mug, pens, and a key ring.

After nine working days, I hadn't heard anything, and feeling impatient, I decided to contact the company. The line was dead; my emails bounced back. Realizing something was wrong, I revisited the original offices that afternoon. The people were unfamiliar to me, and the receptionists had never heard of Flying High. And there were no CCTV cameras in sight.

The full realization of what had happened hit me in the face. I called the police and they listened without emotion, saying that such so-called scams were common. I was advised to contact the passport office and the bank immediately because they were concerned about identity theft. I found that $700 had been withdrawn from my account to pay for goods in my name. The police suspected there would be several more victims but warned me that the offenders move quickly and skillfully from place to place, so they were almost impossible to catch.

Since then, I have experienced great difficulties trying to do simple things, such as getting a loan for a motorcycle and starting a new cell phone contract. The incident has had a huge impact on my life. I find it difficult to trust people now, and I avoid going online whenever possible. I live in fear of being tricked again.

Anna P., Boston

10 **WHAT'S YOUR ANGLE?** Do you think that you could have become a victim in a similar situation? At which point might you have become suspicious? What would you have done?

GRAMMAR IN CONTEXT Retrospection

We use *should have* or *ought to have* to express regret or to criticize things we ourselves did in the past or things other people did. It is used to express a better alternative to the reality.

We should have been / ought to have been suspicious at this point, but everyone was simply excited.

See Grammar focus on page 164.

11 **APPLY** Write three things that Anna should (not) have or ought (not) to have done in this case.

12 **INTERACT** Think about three things that you regret, and why. They can be large or small things, recent or far in the past. Then tell a partner, asking each other at least one question about each point.

WRITING SKILL Reporting a real event

Reporting an event or incident typically requires some or all of the following features.

• Background information about the main character or event:
This happened in early September last year…, I had applied for countless jobs…

• Details of what happened, usually in chronological order:
Then…, After…, in the end…

• The details leading up to the discovery or climax:
I decided to…, I realized…

• What happened as a consequence:
I called the police…, I was advised to…

• A brief reflection or summary of the impact or value of the event:
Since then…, as a result…, it's had a huge impact…

13 **IDENTIFY** Identify which elements of the Writing Skill are included in Anna's story and at which point.

14 **PREPARE** You are going to write a story about being a victim of identity fraud for display in the classroom to raise awareness of the crime. Use the story of someone you know or research examples online. Include the elements mentioned in the Writing Skill box. Plan your story, using paragraph headings and notes. Then tell a partner what happened, using your plan to guide you.

15 **WRITE** Write your story, using between 200 and 300 words.

16 **IMPROVE** Ask your partner to read your work. Ask him or her to check your grammar and word choice and that the following details are clear.

☐ The background to the incident
☐ The events
☐ The result and the victim's reaction to what happened
☐ The impact on the victim

17 **DEVELOP** Rewrite your story, using the feedback from your partner.

Technology security expert Luigi Auriemma in his office in Malta

6.3 One More Job

1 ACTIVATE What kinds of things are typically taken in burglaries?

2 PREPARE Look at the picture below. What do you think was kept in these safe-deposit boxes that were in a safe-deposit center in London?

3 SHARE Look at these elements from the story of one of the largest burglaries in legal history in the UK. With a partner, discuss what might have happened.

- gang of elderly men
- cash, jewelry, diamonds, sapphires, gold, watches
- £14 million ($18 million)
- £25 million ($32 million)
- problem
- "Basil"
- 50-cm (1.5-foot) thick concrete wall
- 73 boxes
- special tools
- dustbins (garbage cans)
- elevator shaft
- returned next day with equipment
- one third in a cemetery
- 59–77

4 🔊 INTEGRATE Listen to a news report from the day of the men's arrest. Check your predictions.

5 🔊 NOTICE Listen again, then with a partner, complete a timeline (below) of the main events in this story.

6 VOCABULARY Complete the sentences based on what you heard, using the words below. Compare your answers with a partner. Check a dictionary, if necessary, at the end.

prosecuted	under surveillance	in custody
cooperate	imprisoned	assault
accused	**be heard**	**recovered**
bug		

🖥+ Oxford 5000™

CCTV and digital tracking enabled the police to identify and then put the men [1] _____, although the criminals remained unaware. The police also managed to [2] _____ one of the suspects' cars. The gang are now [3] _____, and their case will [4] _____ in court next year. There was no violence, and no weapons or [5] _____ were involved. The [6] _____ are expected to be [7] _____ for around ten years. However, the men could also be [8] _____ in a later court hearing when additional sentences will be given if they do not [9] _____ with police. Only around one third or less of the gold and jewels have been [10] _____ so far.

7 🔊 ASSESS Listen and check your answers to Exercise 6.

> ## LISTENING SKILL
> ### Understanding metaphors and idioms
>
> When talking, speakers often use metaphors and idioms in a range of genres and styles. They are often said quickly, and as a listener, you may not be able to listen a second or third time. Coping with unfamiliar metaphors and idioms can add to the level of challenge.
>
> A good strategy, in many listening situations, is to ignore unknown language and to aim to understand the gist. You can try to do this from the context, from known language, and from clues such as the speaker's intonation and stress. If possible, make a note of the metaphor or idiom, which will give you more time to reflect, research, and process. In some cases, you may be able to ask for clarification from the speakers themselves.

Bank Holiday weekend March 2015 Burglars approach building in workmen's clothes.

8 IDENTIFY Identify and highlight the idioms and metaphors in these sentences. Do you know what they mean? If not, can you guess from the context? How do they translate into your first language? Discuss with a partner.

1 If people commit a crime, they have to pay for it.
2 The detective listened to the victim's account with a stony expression on her face.
3 The woman's face lit up when she discovered her gold ring had been found.
4 The men claimed to be innocent, but they didn't have a leg to stand on in court because of the evidence.
5 It seems the burglar had a change of heart because he left most of the valuables behind.
6 His daughter was the apple of his eye. When she moved away to New Zealand, he turned to a life of crime.

9 **ASSESS** Listen to three students discussing the case. Which of these topics do they discuss in relation to the Hatton Garden burglars?

details of what they stole	details of the criminals'
their victims	backgrounds
their mistakes	their punishment
their reasons	

10 **BUILD** Listen again and say *Stop!* every time you hear an idiom or metaphor. Tell your teacher what the sentence or expression is, so it can be recorded. Then work with a partner to figure out the meaning.

GRAMMAR IN CONTEXT Modals of speculation

A variety of modal verbs are used to speculate about the present and future:

But who uses safe-deposit boxes anyway? They <u>have to be</u> criminals, surely!

These hunts <u>can take</u> years, and he <u>could</u> even get away with it.

Do you think the stuff <u>might be</u> recovered?

Should (not) is used to show that something is or will be true:

They <u>should</u> find out in the next year or so.

For speculation about the past, modals are followed by a perfect infinitive and can be in the continuous or passive form:

The judge <u>must have been</u> quite impressed with them.

People <u>who may not have been</u> able to afford the insurance, for example…

They <u>can't have been</u> thinking very carefully.

They <u>might have been</u> given a different kind of sentence.

See Grammar focus on page 164.

---

11 **NOTICE** How are the *past* modals in the Grammar box pronounced when said fluently? Think about contractions and weak forms. Say the sentences to a partner. Then listen and repeat.

12 APPLY Change these sentences so that they mean the same thing, but use the given modal in either past or present form. Then take turns saying them aloud to a partner.

1 There's no way the thieves will get away with this! (*can't*)
   They can't get away with this.
2 Maybe they didn't have enough time to steal more valuables. (*might*)
3 It's certainly true that they knew exactly which safe to open. (*must*)
4 I think they heard the police arrive, and so they left in a hurry. (*could*)
5 That piece by Picasso is worth at least $20 million, I'm sure. (*has to*)
6 At the moment, it's impossible to state the value of the missing goods. (*can't*)
7 It's possible that the thieves realized that the piece was a fake but took it anyway. (*may*)
8 The police are likely to find them soon, according to reports. (*should*)

13 EXPAND What do you think the Hatton Garden burglars did with the stolen goods that were not found? Finish the sentences.

1 They must have…
2 They might have…
3 They could have…
4 They can't have…

14 WHAT'S YOUR ANGLE? Work in a small group. Speculate on the following questions.

1 Why do you think these elderly burglars decided to commit this crime at this point in their lives?
2 What do you think a more suitable sentence for these men might have been?
3 Where's the best place to keep valuable items safe these days?

6.4 Look on the Bright Side

1 **ACTIVATE** Imagine that you tell a friend that you are feeling down because you failed your driving test and you only have one opportunity left to pass. What responses would you want to hear? Talk with a partner about why you would or would not want to hear the following responses. You can use the chart to rate how you feel about each response.

No		Neutral		Yes
1	2	3	4	5

1 Whatever. Don't worry about it.
2 You're not the first person this has happened to, and you certainly won't be the last.
3 I'm really sorry to hear about that. Is there anything I can do to help?
4 Have you ever heard of the cabbage soup diet? It's amazing! You should try it.
5 You are really, really good at so many things. I'm sure they didn't have a good reason to fail you. Don't worry about it. I bet you will pass next time.

2 ▶ **IDENTIFY** Watch the video, and find out what went wrong for Kevin and how Andy reacted.

REAL-WORLD ENGLISH Redirecting a negative conversation

When you redirect a negative conversation, you are showing the speaker that you care by both actively listening and helping them look at the bright side of a bad situation. You can cast the issue in a different light and say words in a less negative way.

It's only one out of 20 experiments you have to do this semester. This won't count against you that badly.

You can also use an earlier success to redefine the current failure and change the priority of the issues.

In all of your other experiments and exams, you've gotten nearly perfect grades. You'll still be ranked the top student in class, and this experience will help you in the long run.

Make sure that whatever you say is balanced. Overly positive responses can come off as fake, which might suggest you can't empathize with what your friend is going through.

3 ▶ **ANALYZE** Watch the video again. Which of the things detailed in the Real-World English box does Andy do? Write any specific examples you hear him use. Compare your notes with your partner.

A Say words in a less negative way

_____

B Use an earlier success

_____

C Show you are actively listening

_____

4 **EXPAND** Would you respond similarly to Andy in this situation? Why or why not? If your behavior would differ, is that because of a personal or a cultural difference?

5 **IDENTIFY** Read the examples. Which is not a strategy of redirecting a negative conversation?

1 This is just one opportunity out of many that you will have. Trust me, you'll have your chance to shine.

2 If I was in your shoes, I think I'd take the matter further.

3 But just think about the other stuff you handed in. You've been a star student.

4 Ah. You must feel really annoyed. I'm sorry.

6 **APPLY** Imagine your friend is feeling negative because he or she has gone on five job interviews in the past few weeks and has not been called back with an offer. How would you employ each of the following strategies?

Show you are actively listening

_____

Say words in a less negative way

_____

Use an earlier success

_____

7 **EXPAND** Work with a partner, and read the following situations. Write down what you would say.

A: Your friend has just found out that she won't pass her English class and this will have a domino effect on her academic plans. She is feeling really bad about this. What do you say to your friend?

B: Your friend doesn't like his new job of six months and feels trapped. He initially thought this would be his dream job where he could showcase his talents and experience, but he feels stifled. What do you say to your friend?

8 **BUILD** With your partner, choose one of the situations from Exercise 7 and prepare a role play.

9 **SHARE** Role-play your conversation for the class.

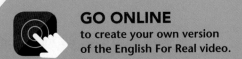

GO ONLINE
to create your own version
of the English For Real video.

6.5 Fair Is Fair

1 ACTIVATE Look at the following newspaper headlines, which are true stories. What do you think might have happened in each case?

> **Woman Charged with Theft for Keeping $50 Bill Found on Shop Floor**

> **Family Man Who Escaped Sentence Due to Admin Error Arrested 13 Years Later**

> Judge Says $300,000 Fine for Speeding in Ferrari

2 ▶ INTEGRATE Watch the video of two friends discussing the last headline from above. What happened exactly?

3 WHAT'S YOUR ANGLE? Do you think this punishment is too severe? Do you think it is acceptable to give different fines depending on the situation? What circumstances might influence you if you were a judge?

4 ◀ IDENTIFY Listen to two people discussing this case. What additional facts do you learn about the driver and situation?

● PRONUNCIATION SKILL Assimilation

◀ Assimilation is when a consonant sound at the end of a word is adjusted because of where the next sound, the one at the start of the next word, is formed in the mouth. Listen to some examples:

fast cars: /t/ changes to /k/ before /k/
fine people: /n/ changes to /m/ before /p/
nice shoes: /s/ changes to /ʃ/ before /ʃ/
I'd come: /d/ changes to /g/ before /k/

---

5 NOTICE Work with a partner and look at the words in italics. How does the sound at the end of the first word change? Some of the changes mentioned are in addition to those in the Pronunciation Skill box.

1 They're the *secret police*.
2 The criminals were based in *Great Britain*.
3 They stole a *handbag*.
4 The offender was a *good man*.
5 The victim was a *foreign man*.
6 My *credit card* was taken.
7 *Both sides* have a case.
8 The fine was *quite big*.
9 He's been driving a *red car*.

6 NOTICE Listen and compare your ideas from Exercise 5.

● SPEAKING Conceding a point

In a discussion or argument, if you acknowledge a point to be true or right, then you *concede*, even if you initially disagreed. This is seen as an acceptance of the other speaker's argument. Typically, conceding a point is preceded by questions to find out precise details.

When you concede, you can use language like:
OK, I can see (now) where you are coming from.

---

7 ◀ PREPARE Listen again to the conversation in Exercise 4. At which point does (a) Rose concede a point and (b) James concede a point? What words do they use to do this?

8 SHARE Work in a small group. Select a statement that you have different views on. Think for two minutes about what to say, then discuss. If you change your mind even partly during the discussion, then concede appropriately.

- Policemen and women deserve to be very well paid.
- Nowadays, no police should be armed.
- People who commit crimes have usually been mistreated by their family or by society. They deserve pity, not punishment.

Now go to page 152 for the Unit 6 Review.

7 Inspiration

Who famously was inspired while sitting in the bath?

Where do you get inspiration?

What can inspiration achieve?

BEHIND THE PHOTO

Check the things that inspire you. Discuss your answers with a partner.

- [ ] Your favorite book or poem
- [ ] A concert, play, or dance performance
- [ ] A natural scene like a waterfall or sunset
- [ ] An athletic challenge
- [ ] Important public figures
- [ ] Interesting family members

- [ ] Loyal friends
- [ ] Learning to do something new
- [ ] Stories people tell
- [ ] Historical places
- [ ] An unforgettable event, experience, or trip

REAL-WORLD GOAL

Go for a walk in a park or other natural setting, and write about it

7.1 Get Inspired

1 ACTIVATE Look at the photos of possible sources of inspiration. What might be inspiring about each of them?

2 WHAT'S YOUR ANGLE? Which source in Exercise 1 do you find most inspiring? What other things inspire you?

> **READING SKILL**
> **Working out meaning from context**
>
> You can often guess the meaning of unfamiliar words or expressions from the context. Sometimes we give the definition after the new word, and it's often set apart by commas, dashes, or parentheses. You can also look for examples that explain the word or read the sentences before and after it for other clues.
>
> *Second, this inspiration transcends, or goes beyond, the ordinary or usual approach.*
>
> (*Transcend* means "to go beyond something.")

3 IDENTIFY Read the article about inspiration on the next page. Pay attention to the underlined words as you read. How is inspiration connected to creativity?

4 ASSESS Read the article again. Use context to work out the meaning of the underlined words. Write the correct word next to its definition.

1 _____ to cause a feeling in someone, to bring something to mind
2 _____ new
3 _____ an attempt to do something that involves hard work
4 _____ a reason for doing something
5 _____ to force

5 INTEGRATE Complete each sentence with the correct form of an underlined word in the article.

1 The speech provided me with the _____.
2 It's a beautiful painting, but it _____ sadness in me.
3 I appreciate that the idea is _____, but I don't think it will work. It's just too strange.
4 Writing a book takes a lot of _____ and a lot of time.
5 Our supervisor encourages us to take classes, but she doesn't _____ us to do so.

6 EXPAND Read the article again. Complete the sentences.

1 Thomas Edison thought that _____ was the most important part of genius.
2 Thrash and Elliott believe that inspiration comes from _____ the person.
3 When you are inspired, you feel that you _____ to take action.
4 When you make something new, that is _____.
5 More inspired writers write _____ overall, but they write _____ paragraphs and use _____ vocabulary.
6 People who are often inspired tend to be open to _____.

7 WHAT'S YOUR ANGLE? Do you usually feel inspiration when you write? Or do you need to think carefully and work hard when you write? Is the process different in different languages?

The Power of Inspiration

"Genius is one percent inspiration, ninety-nine percent perspiration,"
—Thomas Edison, ca.1903, *Harper's Monthly Magazine*, September 1932

Is hard work the only key to success? Or do we need inspiration, too? Over the last 20 years, researchers have studied the importance of inspiration, identifying its characteristics, its association with creativity, its sources, and its variability across individuals. Recently, these researchers have learned that inspiration spreads easily. The more inspired we are, the more we inspire others.

What is inspiration? Research conducted in 2003 and 2004 by Todd M. Thrash and Andrew J. Elliott identified three core characteristics. First, inspiration comes from outside the person who is inspired. We cannot decide on our own to be inspired, but instead something—an idea, nature, art, music, or even another person—<u>evokes</u> inspiration, causes us to feel it. Second, this inspiration transcends, or goes beyond, the ordinary or usual in our lives. When inspired, we see new possibilities, ones that we didn't realize existed before. And finally, inspiration <u>compels</u> us to take action in order to make the idea real.

The researchers also described two aspects of inspiration. One is passive: we are inspired by something, which means we appreciate the source of the inspiration. The other aspect is active: we are inspired to do something. For example, if a beautiful landscape inspires you, you may paint it, or if a person inspires you, you may try to take on some of his or her qualities. Being inspired motivates us to transmit the idea to others.

Although creativity and inspiration are linked, they are not the same thing. Creativity involves being both <u>novel</u> and useful, and it results in some kind of product. Basically, we're making something new that has some purpose even if it's only beauty. Inspiration provides the <u>motive</u>, or reason, to do something, and that can lead to creativity. Although hard work—Edison's "perspiration"—is necessary for creativity, inspiration is important, too. The relationship between inspiration and <u>effort</u> is a positive one: the more we are inspired, the harder we tend to work.

In a later study, the researchers looked specifically at writers, analyzing the effects of both inspiration and effort. First, they assessed writers' level of inspiration, and then the researchers gave them a writing task. If the writers had a high level of inspiration, their writing showed greater creativity. They wrote more, although in shorter paragraphs, wrote without pausing, and revised their work less. When writers felt less inspired and had to rely more on effort, their writing was technically better. They used more difficult vocabulary, but they took more time, wrote less overall, and deleted more.

Another study suggests that people who are inspired also inspire others. Thrash and his colleagues explored how inspiration could be transmitted through poetry. They found that inspiration could be spread easily to others. If the writer felt a great deal of inspiration, the reader was also more inspired, even though their only connection was through the poems. In general, readers responded more to the insight expressed than to how original something was. The researchers concluded that an inspired writer enlightens and sends chills through future generations of thinkers.

If inspiration is important to the creative process, how can we get more of it? Research suggests that some people naturally feel more inspiration than others. People who often report a state of inspiration are by nature more open to new experiences. They are also more motivated to achieve mastery of their work. Other personality traits that are often found along with inspiration are creativity, **healthy self-esteem**, **optimism**, and **competence**. People who are often inspired tend to be less **competitive** and more **tolerant** than others. If you try to cultivate these traits, you may open yourself up to inspiration.

Another thing you can do is surround yourself with things or people that inspire you. Inspirational people often share certain characteristics. They tend to be focused on others rather than themselves. They usually have a clear vision of their path forward. They are often good communicators, who listen well and tell compelling stories.

Although hard work may be necessary for success, we probably need inspiration to fuel our creativity. Our best ideas may come from sources outside of ourselves, including other inspired people, that cause us to think in a new way and imagine other possibilities and solutions. If Edison hadn't been inspired, all his hard work wouldn't have mattered.

ᵵ⁺ Oxford 5000™

Conditionals have an *if* clause and a main clause. We use the **zero conditional** to talk about a real situation with a result that is always true or is a fact. Zero conditionals can refer to the past, present, or future.

If the writers had a high level of inspiration, their writing showed greater creativity.

For example, if a beautiful landscape inspires you, you may paint it.

You'll write more if you're inspired.

We use the **first conditional** to talk about a present or future condition that is possible or probable.

If you try to cultivate these traits, you may open yourself up to inspiration.

We use the **second conditional** to talk about a present or future situation that is unreal or improbable.

If I had musical talent, I could / would compose an opera.

We use the **third conditional** to talk about a hypothetical situation in the past with a past outcome.

If Edison hadn't been inspired, his hard work wouldn't have mattered.

See Grammar focus on page 165.

8 IDENTIFY Choose the correct form of the verb in parentheses to complete each conditional sentence.

1   If I listen to music, I _____ (*feel*) more inspired.

2   People are more likely to feel inspiration if they _____ (*be*) open to new experiences.

3   We _____ (*excel*) at something if we practiced for 10,000 hours.

4   If you work hard at something, you _____ (*improve*).

5   If I _____ (*be*) more inspired, I would have written more.

9 WHAT'S YOUR ANGLE? Discuss the questions below with a partner.

1   If you want to feel inspired, what can you do?

2   If you need to write a paper for class, what do you do to prepare?

3   What will you do in the future if you have to solve a difficult problem?

4   If you want to learn more about a topic, what can you do?

5   How would you explain inspiration if someone asked you about it?

10 VOCABULARY Match the characteristics with the description.

1   able to do something well ___

2   make you better able to challenge or succeed ___

3   a feeling that good things will happen ___

4   confidence in one's abilities ___

5   the ability to form new ideas about things not present ___

6   introduction or use of new ideas ___

7   ability to accept what other people say or do even if you don't agree ___

a   **innovative** approach

b   **sense** of optimism

c   **demonstrate** competence

d   become competitive

e   tolerant **attitude**

f   healthy self-esteem

g   **active imagination**

⚡+ Oxford 5000™

11 ◀) BUILD Use the phrases in Exercise 10 to complete the sentences. Then listen and check your answers.

1   A good résumé can really help you _____ in the job market.

2   The company took an _____ to solving the problem.

3   Finishing the project on time is one way to _____.

4   I think everything will turn out well. I have a strong _____.

5   Someone with a _____ can get along with different kinds of people.

6   If a child has a _____, she usually does better in school because she is confident.

7   I always picture the worst happening. I have an _____.

12 WHAT'S YOUR ANGLE? Which of the characteristics in Exercise 10 do you think you have? Which do you think are linked to inspiration? Share your ideas in a small group. Which characteristic do you think is most important for success?

7.2 The Importance of Heroes

1 ACTIVATE Look at the photos. Who are the people? What do they have in common? Why are they important?

2 IDENTIFY Match the descriptions to the photos.

1 ___ an environmental political activist who founded the Green Belt Movement in Kenya, which focuses on planting trees, conservation, and women's rights
2 ___ a Jamaican sprinter and the fastest human ever
3 ___ Pakistani activist for education of girls and youngest-ever recipient of the Nobel Peace Prize
4 ___ led India to independence from Great Britain

3 WHAT'S YOUR ANGLE? Which of the people in Exercise 1 do you find most inspiring? Why? Share your ideas with a partner.

b

c

a

d

4 ASSESS Read the essay. Why does the writer admire this person?

Jimmy Carter, An Inspirational Failure

1   Inspiration has many sources. Some people are inspired by a vivid blue sky, others by music, still others by experiences. But most of us can point to at least one person who inspires us. Often it's an important person like a famous soccer player, an actor, or even a world leader. Jimmy Carter is perhaps the only U.S. president who is more appreciated for his work after he left office than for his actual administration. He is admirable for how much he accomplished, especially to improve the lives of others, after the failures of his presidency.

2   Throughout his life, Jimmy Carter was serious and determined. He grew up in rural Georgia, the son of a hard-working peanut farmer. He was the first one in his father's family to attend college, and he went to the highly competitive U.S. Naval Academy. Had his father not died, Carter might have stayed in the navy. Instead, he returned home to run the farm. He became active in local politics, rising through the ranks in the 1950s and 1960s. He was elected governor of Georgia in 1970 and president of the United States in 1976.

3   Carter had two major handicaps when he began his presidency. First, he lacked experience dealing with Congress and didn't want to make deals that would compromise his integrity. Second, he wanted to limit government and make it more efficient. However, he did have some successes in the areas of civil rights at home and human rights abroad. He also negotiated treaties and avoided wars. His mediocre record turned disastrous in his last year. The economy worsened with oil shortages and rising fuel prices. Relationships with other countries, including the Soviet Union and Iran, collapsed, and Carter lost the 1980 election to Ronald Reagan.

4   Carter's presidency was considered a spectacular failure. Upon his return to Georgia, he was briefly depressed and uncertain about his future. But he didn't remain discouraged, instead devoting himself to humanitarian causes. He established the Carter Center and continued to mediate conflicts, supervise elections abroad, and focus attention on disease and poverty around the world. He also became involved with Habitat for Humanity, an organization that builds homes for poor people. Although some still criticize him, his reputation has been largely restored since he left the presidency. In 2002, Carter was awarded the Nobel Peace Prize for his decades of work to find peaceful solutions to conflicts and to promote human rights.

5   In 2015, at 90, Carter found out that he had cancer that had spread to his liver and his brain. When asked if he had any regrets, Carter said he wished he had done some things differently, so he would have been re-elected. But after writing 29 books, building thousands of homes, and monitoring a hundred elections worldwide, he has helped many through his compassion, hard work, and commitment. He'd probably rather his presidency had gone well, but he's an inspirational figure nonetheless. If only we could all be such successful failures!

—adapted from *The Oxford Companion to United States History* by Paul S. Boyer

5 IDENTIFY Write the number of the paragraph next to the topic.

____ His presidency

____ His early life

____ Regrets and accomplishments

____ An active postpresidency

____ A source of inspiration

6 INTEGRATE Read the essay again and complete the phrases.

1 vivid _____

2 famous _____

3 attend _____

4 negotiate _____

5 devoting (himself) to _____

6 became involved with _____

7 promote _____

7 EXPAND Work in a small group. Brainstorm other words that could be used to complete each phrase in Exercise 6. Share your ideas with the class.

 GRAMMAR IN CONTEXT
Structures for unreal situations

We use *wish, if only*, and other terms to talk about things we would like to change now or in the future and to express regret about past actions and situations.

Carter said he wished he had done things differently, so he would have been re-elected.

He'd probably rather his presidency had gone well, but he's an inspirational figure nonetheless.

If only we could all be such successful failures!

See Grammar focus on page 165.

8 ASSESS How do you express the ideas in the Grammar box in your first language? Discuss with a partner.

9 INTEGRATE Complete the sentences with information from the essay and your own ideas.

1 Had he not been elected governor, Carter probably wouldn't _____.

2 The writer of the essay probably wishes that Carter _____.

3 If only Carter didn't have cancer, _____.

4 If only he hadn't made mistakes as president, _____.

5 Many leaders would probably rather _____.

10 INTERACT Work in a small group. Share your ideas from Exercise 9.

WRITING SKILL Selecting appropriate vocabulary

Your vocabulary choice is affected by genre, audience, and purpose. Selecting appropriate vocabulary will make your writing stronger. More specific words are usually better than general or vague vocabulary.

Some people are inspired by ~~beautiful things~~ a vivid sunset. (*sunset* is more specific and visual than *things* and *vivid* is less commonly used than *beautiful*)

You should also consider connotation since words can convey a particular attitude or meaning.

His mediocre record ~~was worse~~ turned disastrous in his last year. (*disastrous* is much stronger than *worse*)

Remember that some words are better in certain settings than in others. Consider your genre (e.g., an essay versus an email), your audience, and your purpose.

But most of us can point to at least one ~~guy~~ person who inspires us. (*guy* is too informal for an essay)

---

11 ASSESS Choose the best words to complete the text.

One of the ¹ *guys / people* who inspires me the most is my father. He grew up in a small rural town but left at a young age because he wanted to travel the world. He studied history and found a job working for the government. His career took him to more than 60 ² *countries / places* as well as both the North and South Poles! His love of traveling was something he shared with my mother, and after he ³ *stopped working / retired*, they continued their ⁴ *foreign adventures / trips*—riding camels in Egypt, hiking to Machu Picchu in Peru, and walking the Great Wall in China. My father's ⁵ *wonderful / good* sense of humor, his optimism, and his openness to new ⁶ *stuff / experiences* draws people to him.

12 INTEGRATE Read paragraphs 3 and 4 in the essay about Jimmy Carter again. Which paragraph is more negative and which more positive? Find the words in each paragraph that have a positive or negative connotation. Discuss with a partner.

13 APPLY Write the words the writer uses to describe Jimmy Carter. Are they positive or negative? Write + or –.

Descriptive words	Positive or negative?

14 PREPARE To prepare to write about a person who inspires you, fill in the chart with words and phrases to describe that person.

Descriptive words	Positive or negative?

15 WRITE Write a first draft of a paragraph about a person who inspires you. Select appropriate vocabulary to describe the person.

An employee of an architecture firm in his office in Ho Chi Minh City, Vietnam

16 SHARE Read your description and correct any grammar and spelling mistakes. Check for examples of what you have learned. Then exchange your paragraph with a partner and give feedback.

Check for the correct use of:

☐ Conditionals
☐ Vocabulary for personal qualities
☐ Appropriate vocabulary

17 IMPROVE Rewrite your paragraph to incorporate your partner's feedback.

7.3 Are You Psyched?

1 ACTIVATE Read the caption and look at the picture. What emotions might this man be feeling, and do you think they help to inspire him?

In this podcast, we'll talk about the effect of emotions on inspiration.

VOCABULARY DEVELOPMENT
Literal and figurative meaning

Every word and phrase has a **literal** meaning, which is the most basic meaning of the word or phrase, not an extended or poetic meaning. However, we often use **figurative language**, including metaphors, to express ideas in a nonliteral way, so they create a particular mental picture. Figurative language can also have a greater impact on listeners and be more persuasive.

To determine if an expression has a literal or figurative meaning, think about the context. Has the speaker or writer already been talking about that topic? Or is the use of the expression surprising?

Literal: *The children **blew** bubbles at the party.* (*blow* means "to expel air")

Figurative: *It **blew my mind**.* (*to blow someone's mind* means "to affect very strongly")

2 BUILD Read the pairs of sentences. Decide if the meaning of the bold phrase is literal (L) or figurative (F).

1 Listeners like to stay **ahead of the curve** on topics that can help them in their relationships at home and at work. ___
2 The car was going too fast **ahead of the curve**. ___
3 The pilot **brought** the plane **up to speed** as soon as she reached the correct altitude. ___
4 Our manager **brought** us **up to speed** on the new rules. ___
5 The explorers were in **uncharted territory**, and didn't expect to find the village. ___
6 In the early 1990s, the Internet was basically **uncharted territory**, and no one knew exactly how it worked. ___
7 My best friend is **cut from a different cloth** than I am. She's outgoing, and I'm very shy. ___
8 His pants were **cut from a different cloth** than his jacket. ___
9 The dominant wolf ran **ahead of the pack**. ___
10 Creative people are often **ahead of the pack**. ___

3 USE Complete each sentence with the correct expression from Exercise 2.

1 My brother is _____. His reactions are almost always the opposite of mine.
2 The company president is going to _____ on the latest marketing plan.
3 Those researchers are _____. They are doing some very creative work.
4 No one had ever performed that surgery before. They were in _____.
5 Apple was _____ on music technology with its iPod.

LISTENING SKILL Recognizing word boundaries

Speakers often link words, so knowing where one word ends and the next begins will help listeners with comprehension. Note that the following phrases sound similar when spoken. Listen to the context to make sure you clearly understand what is being said.

🔊 *A way to find inspiration*
A way to define inspiration
A waiter finds inspiration

4 IDENTIFY Read one of the sentences in each pair below to a partner. Looking at the text, can your partner identify which one you said?

1 a Is Jean around?
  b Is Gina around?

2 a I just saw this guy fall.
  b I just saw the sky fall.

3 a Why tease her?
  b A white T-shirt?

4 a My aunts are in Spain.
  b My answer is Spain.

5 a F-I-N-D
  b If I end it.

5 ASSESS You are going to hear about how negative emotions affect inspiration and creativity. Read the sentences below, and choose the ones you think are true.

1 Positive emotions, like happiness and joy, inspire us more than negative ones.
2 Emotions that are stable or consistent over time are more helpful to creativity.
3 If your emotions change from negative to positive, you will be more creative.
4 You are better able to see relationships between ideas if you have mixed emotions (both positive and negative).
5 If you feel rejected by others, it may help you be more creative.

6 🔊 **ASSESS** Listen to the podcast, and check your answers to Exercise 5.

7 🔊 **INTEGRATE** Listen again, and complete the notes.

Speaker: _____ Field: _____

Positive emotions: _____, _____, and _____.

Negative emotions: _____, _____, and _____.

Study of employees: Most productive started _____ and ended _____.

Study of 80 students: thought about _____ event → more creative

People with mixed emotions → see _____

Creativity = ability to _____ + ability to _____

8 **WHAT'S YOUR ANGLE?** Does the research surprise you? What emotions make you more creative or feel inspired?

9 🔊 **EXPAND** Listen to the excerpts from the podcast. Complete each sentence with the words you hear.

1 Are you saying that _____?

2 It was _____.

3 It means we're _____ but _____.

4 What _____?

10 🔊 **APPLY** Listen again and repeat the sentences in Exercise 9.

GRAMMAR IN CONTEXT Alternatives to *if*

We use the expressions *unless, provided that, as long as, imagine, suppose,* and *assuming* as alternatives to *if*. *Unless* means "except if."

You can't go unless you have an invitation. = You can go if you have an invitation.

We can also use inversions. The words Elisa uses in the podcast as alternatives to *if* are in bold.

*But **unless** you have some negative emotions, too, you might not be so creative.*

*It's important, **provided that** they started out with negative emotions.*

***Suppose** you went to Japan for the first time; you might pay more attention, noticing signs for the train, or smells from a restaurant.*

See Grammar focus on page 165.

---

11 **IDENTIFY** Read the sentences and choose the correct word or phrase to complete each one.

1 I can write *only if / suppose* I'm listening to music.

2 *Had they felt / They felt* positive emotions first, they wouldn't have been as productive.

3 It's difficult to be creative *if / unless* you feel inspired.

4 I will finish the project *suppose / assuming* I get started early enough.

5 The students would write creatively *provided that / unless* they felt inspired.

6 *Were you / You were* to brainstorm first, you might be able to come up with more innovative solutions.

12 **INTEGRATE** Complete the text with alternatives to *if*.

no matter	provided	suppose	unless	were

Is it impossible to be creative [1] _____ we are in a negative mood? Of course not! There are other ways to become inspired. One psychologist looked at the role of exercise. [2] _____ a person exercised regularly, would that affect creativity? She gave thinking tasks to two groups. Participants did better on the tasks [3] _____ that they exercised at least four times a week. Another study found that certain kinds of meditation could help generate ideas [4] _____ how experienced the person was at meditation. [5] _____ you to try these techniques, you might get inspired, too.

13 **EXPAND** Choose one of the sentences in Exercise 12 to write a paragraph about. Exchange with a partner.

14 **WHAT'S YOUR ANGLE?** Complete the sentences with your ideas. Work in a group to compare answers.

1 I can't write a paper unless _____.

2 Suppose I had to solve a problem at work. I would _____.

3 New technology will continue to improve our lives provided that _____.

4 Anyone can be creative assuming _____.

5 I would have been more successful had I known _____.

7.4 You Can Do It

1 **ACTIVATE** Imagine that someone you don't know very well has been assigned a project and says to you, "This'll be interesting, but I've never done anything like this." Choose how you would respond.

   a No response, just shrug your shoulders and walk away.

   b Tell this person about all of the difficult things you've overcome without anyone else's help.

   c Say, "Sorry to hear about that," and then continue doing your own work.

   d Instruct this person on how to start the project without acknowledging what they said.

   e Say something showing you recognize their difficulty, and then say something supportive.

2 **ASSESS** Look at the pictures. What is happening? Why do you think Andy is upset? How could Phil and Sam help? What could you say to encourage Andy?

3 ▶ **IDENTIFY** Watch the video and find out what happened. Answer these questions.

   1 What does Cathy ask Andy to do?

   2 How does Andy feel about the task?

   3 Why do Phil and Sam come to talk to Andy?

   4 Do Phil and Sam help Andy? How?

   5 Does Andy get the job done?

4 **ASSESS** Choose the true statements.

   1 Andy wants to please Cathy.

   2 Andy is a whiz at computers.

   3 Andy is nervous about the task Cathy's asked him to do.

   4 It doesn't matter how quickly Andy finishes.

ENGLISH FOR REAL

We give encouragement when someone is about to begin or is in the process of trying to complete a task that may be difficult. The type of encouragement you give depends on the relationship between the people involved, the degree of difficulty of the task, and/or the setting.

First, identify what the person's difficulty is. Then respond based on how well you know that person.

A: *I've never written anything like this before. I don't think I can finish this paper before tomorrow's class!*

1B: *Come on, you can do it!* (friend or family member)
Or

2B: *I have confidence in you.* (someone you don't know very well)

The setting or who you are speaking to may determine how or if you respond.

A: *This is a challenging project.*

1B: *I know. Keep up the good work.*
Or

2B: *Give it your best shot.*

It might be fine for a teacher to respond to Speaker A as a student in front of others or in private, but it may not be appropriate to respond to Speaker A as a co-worker in front of your boss.

5 ▶ **ASSESS** Watch the video again, and answer the following questions. Explain your choices to a partner.

1 Cathy says to Andy: "Well, do your best. I have confidence in you." Would it be appropriate for Andy to say this to Cathy if she needed encouragement?

2 Andy says to Sam: "Ok, Sam! Give it your best shot!" Would it be appropriate for Andy to say this in front of Cathy?

3 Would it be appropriate for Cathy to say to Andy: "Ok, Andy! Give it your best shot!"? Why or why not?

6 🔊 **IDENTIFY** Listen to the expressions. Decide if you would use each phrase for a friend or family member (F) or someone you don't know well (S). Some phrases can be used for both.

1 What have you got to lose? ___

2 I have confidence in you. ___

3 You're on the right track. ___

4 Just do your best. ___

5 That was a nice try. ___

6 It's worth a shot. ___

7 Come on, you can do it. ___

8 Give it your best shot. ___

9 You've almost got it. ___

10 Good effort. ___

11 Keep up the good work. ___

12 Don't give up. ___

13 You're just about there. ___

14 Go for it. ___

7 **INTERACT** Work with a partner. Take turns role-playing each of the two different scenarios, and give appropriate encouragement. Think about whether you use different expressions when your roles change.

1 I have a test tomorrow, and I'm just not ready.
   a two classmates
   b a student and a teacher

2 I tried a new recipe, but it didn't turn out very well.
   a a husband and wife
   b a caller and a chef on a cooking show

3 Do you think I should interview for the new position?
   a an employee and supervisor
   b two friends

4 I'm thinking about taking a drawing class.
   a two sisters
   b a student and a counselor at school

5 I've been working on this for hours!
   a child to parent
   b two co-workers who know each other slightly

GO ONLINE
to create your own version
of the English For Real video.

7.5 What You Need to Create

1 ACTIVATE Answer the questions. Then discuss your ideas with a partner.

1 What have you created recently? Why did you create it?

2 Did something specific inspire you? If so, what was it?

2 ◆)) IDENTIFY Listen to a conversation about inspiration. Then answer the questions.

1 What is the name of the writer from South America?

2 What inspired her memoir?

3 Who is the playwright?

4 What inspired him?

5 When do creative people often solve problems?

3 ◆)) NOTICE Listen and mark the pauses between thought groups. Decide if the speaker sounds excited or calm. Then listen again and repeat.

1 Her best-known works are novels, but she also wrote a powerful memoir inspired by a personal tragedy.

2 If you ask me, I'd rather be inspired by something more positive.

3 Did you know that Lin-Manuel Miranda got his inspiration on vacation?

4 According to him, he was only able to write his hit play because he was reading a book on vacation.

5 In my psychology class, we learned that creative people often solve problems when they're daydreaming.

4 BUILD Work with a partner. Partner A will mark the thought groups in sentences 1 to 3. Partner B will mark the thought groups in sentences 4 to 6. Read your sentences to each other. As you listen, mark where your partner pauses.

1 The writer's daughter, Paula, became seriously ill, so she wrote a letter to Paula that formed the basis of the memoir.

2 I'm more inspired by people who help others than by people who make a lot of money.

3 Anita Roddick founded a company called The Body Shop that is environmentally friendly and even uses recycled containers.

4 In my opinion, creative people like artists and musicians are more easily inspired than the rest of us.

5 One of the most inspirational places I've ever visited was Macchu Pichu in Peru.

6 Some of my best ideas have come to me when I've been walking through the woods.

5 PREPARE Complete the sentences below with your own opinions.

I feel inspired by _____.

I am most creative when _____.

The best way to become more creative is to _____.

I believe that creative people are _____.

6 DEVELOP For each idea in Exercise 5, think of at least one reason that supports it.

I feel inspired by nature. When I walk in a park, I feel relaxed and calm, and I get a lot of good ideas.

7 INTERACT Work with a partner. Express your opinions and reasons from Exercises 5 and 6, or express new ideas. Do you and your partner agree?

8 WHAT'S YOUR ANGLE? Which reasons are the strongest? Did you change your mind about anything?

Now go to page 153 for the Unit 7 Review.

8 Feelings

▼ **What feelings does this image evoke?**

▼ **What expresses emotions better: words or images?**

▼ **Why do we feel emotion?**

BEHIND THE PHOTO

Read the list of emotions. Rank them (1–8) according to how easily you can express them to other people. Discuss them with a partner.

___ amusement   ___ happiness

___ anger   ___ irritation

___ boredom   ___ sadness

___ fear   ___ worry

REAL-WORLD GOAL

Try something new that makes you a little nervous

8.1 A Happy Life

1 ACTIVATE Look at the pictures. What makes you happy? Are there different kinds of happiness? Discuss with a partner.

LISTENING SKILL
Recognizing features of connected speech

Speakers often change individual sounds when they connect words together. They add, delete, or modify specific sounds of consonants and vowels. You will comprehend more when you recognize the changes speakers make when they connect speech.

Insertions of /j/ and /w/:

We add /j/ and /w/ sounds between consonants and vowels and between two vowels, so the words "glide" through the mouth. The /j/ sound comes after /iː/, /ei/, /ai/, and /ɔi/ vowel sounds. The /w/ sound comes after /uːw/, /oʊ/, and /ɔː/ sounds.

he is [hiːjɪz] (vowel-vowel)
accumulation [əˌkjuːmjəˈleɪʃən]
view of [vjuːwəv]

Catenation:

We also join a consonant at the end of one word with a vowel beginning the next word.

second of　　*lead an*　　*can only*　　*look at*

Assimilation:

Sometimes a sound will change because of a neighboring sound.

looked (**d** sounds like **t** because of the unvoiced consonant **k**)
have to (**v** sounds like **f** because of the unvoiced **t** of **to**)
chocolate cake (the **t** sound isn't heard because of the hard **c** sound in **cake**)

2 🔊 **NOTICE** Listen to the sentences. Mark the sentences to show where a /j/ or /w/ sound has been inserted, where a consonant connects to a vowel in the next word, and where a consonant sound has changed or been deleted.

1　Remember that we are exploring what it means to lead an ethical, or good, life.
2　Bentham and Mill's view of happiness focuses on the consequences.
3　Mill is aware that Bentham's view is too simple.
4　These are some of the "ingredients" that make up a life of happiness.

3 🔊 **APPLY** Listen and repeat the sentences in Exercise 2.

4 WHAT'S YOUR ANGLE? Answer the questions. Then discuss your ideas with a partner.

1　What are two things you need to have a life of happiness?
2　Which is more important, being good or being happy?
3　How are you trying to live a good life? Has this changed over time?
4　How would you advise a younger person to live a good life?

5 IDENTIFY Read the summaries. Which do you agree with the most? Why?

1　If something causes happiness, then it's good. Happiness equals the amount of pleasure you experience minus the amount of pain.
2　If you are a good person, then you will do good, and this will make you happy. However, you will only know if you are truly happy at the end of your life when you can see all you have achieved.
3　Happiness is not a simple equation. Although something that causes pleasure to many people and little pain can be considered good, some pleasures are more important than others.

6 🔊 📑 **ASSESS** Listen to the lecture. Write the number of the summary in Exercise 5 next to the philosopher.

—adapted from *The Oxford Companion to Philosophy*, edited by Ted Honderich

Aristotle ____

Jeremy Bentham ____

John Stuart Mill ____

7 🔊 **INTEGRATE** Listen to the lecture again. Choose the statements that are true.

1 Aristotle lived in the eighteenth century.

2 Aristotle believed that single actions could determine your happiness.

3 The Utilitarians thought something was good if it made people happy.

4 Jeremy Bentham believed that happiness and goodness were based on the amount of pleasure experienced minus the amount of pain.

5 Mills' view of happiness and a good life was a combination of Aristotle's and Bentham's views.

GRAMMAR IN CONTEXT Ellipsis with nouns

We can leave out words to avoid repetition in a sentence with nouns and noun phrases. We often leave out several words in a sentence because we want to be more efficient with our language and the person we are speaking to already understands the context or the ideas we are talking about.

The following words can be left out to avoid repetition if the meaning is clear without them:

- nouns after a number (*three individuals*)
- a quantifier such as *any, some, loads* (*some feelings*)
- a superlative adjective (*the worst day*)
- this/that/these/those (*these ideas*).

You're at a birthday party and experience two units of **appreciation** *for a thoughtful gift, plus one unit for an* **enthusiastic** *greeting from an old friend, minus one unit of* **embarrassment** *at forgetting someone's name or* **guilt** *that you broke an expensive plate.*

People can pursue happiness as well as pursue more specific goals, such as knowledge or artistic and cultural activity or moral goodness, and they pursue these things for their own sake. These things are some of the "ingredients" that go to make up a life of happiness.

👂+ Oxford 5000™

See Grammar focus on page 166.

8 **APPLY** Change the sentences to avoid repetition. Use ellipsis.

1 Both Bentham and Mill were Utilitarian philosophers, but Mill was the more famous Utilitarian philosopher.

2 In theory, an action that brought happiness to two individuals would not be as morally good as an action that brought happiness to three individuals.

3 According to the lecturer, there are four major moral theories, but he only mentioned two major moral theories.

4 A number of philosophers have thought about happiness, but the earliest philosopher who thought about happiness may have been Aristotle.

9 **VOCABULARY** Read the sentences. Choose the best definition for the word in bold.

1 I go to bed very late, so waking up early is **torture**.
   a a pleasant experience
   b something that causes anguish and pain

2 His **guilt** was written all over his face. I knew he had eaten my last cookie.
   a a feeling of having done wrong
   b a feeling of great pleasure

3 We were **eager** to see the show. We had heard wonderful things about it.
   a strongly wanting to do something
   b not very interested

4 The **enthusiastic** crowd applauded for several minutes.
   a showing hesitation
   b showing intense enjoyment

5 The runner raised his hands in **triumph** after winning.
   a nervousness or distress
   b joy resulting from success

6 She threw her phone down in **frustration**.
   a feeling upset or annoyed at not being able to do something
   b feeling a sense of satisfaction

7 I couldn't hide my **embarrassment** at making the mistake. My face was burning.
   a the state of feeling foolish
   b the state of feeling confused

8 My boss showed her **appreciation** for our hard work by giving us a day off.
   a gratitude
   b irritation or anger

9 I applied for a scholarship. It's not a sure thing, but I'm **hopeful**.
   a feeling sadness
   b feeling optimism

👂+ Oxford 5000™

10 🔊 **BUILD** Choose the best words to complete the paragraph. Then listen and check your answers.

Do you want to be happier? If so, you can practice habits that will help. Cultivate a(n) [1] *appreciation / frustration* for everyday pleasures, such as a beautiful sunset or fresh-baked bread. Surround yourself with people who are filled with [2] *frustration / optimism* rather than those who have a gloomy outlook on life. And don't sweat the small stuff. So you forgot someone's name at work—let go of your [3] *embarrassment / triumph*. Remember that everyone makes mistakes, so feel less [4] *guilt / appreciation*. If you think your job is [5] *hopeful / torture*, find another one. It's as simple as doing more things that give you pleasure and fewer things that cause you pain.

8.2 Thrilled to Bits

1 ACTIVATE Look at the icons or emoji below. What emotions do they represent? Discuss with a partner.

2 WHAT'S YOUR ANGLE? Answer the questions. Then discuss your answers with a partner.

1 Do you use emoji? Why or why not?
2 Why do you think emoji are popular?
3 In what ways is using emoji similar to speaking a language?

3 IDENTIFY Read the online article. Then review your answers to Exercise 2.

| Home | About |

Search 🔍

Speaking Emoji

Have you ever been so happy that mere words failed you? If so, you are not alone. Sometimes an adjective such as *happy* or *glad* is not quite enough to convey what we are truly feeling. Perhaps that is why we default to idioms like *walking on air* or *tickled pink* to express similar states that vary by degree. Now we may have a new communicative tool that is especially good at describing our feelings.

 Did you know that the fastest growing language in the UK is *emoji*? At least, that's what Professor Vyv Evans of Bangor University says. The word *emoji* comes from Japanese and is a combination of *e* (picture) and *moji* (character). In 2015, the Oxford dictionary announced that its word of the year was, well, not a word at all but an emoji—a picture of eyebrows, eyes, big tears, and a huge grin—laughing with tears of joy.

It should not be surprising that the most popular emoji express an emotion. In a recent survey in the UK, nearly three-quarters of people aged 18 to 25 found it easier to express their feelings in emoji than in text. Six billion emoji are sent worldwide every day. Eighty to ninety percent of adults with smart phones in the UK use emoji. The most popular is the face with tears of joy accounting for 20 percent of the emoji sent in the UK and 17 percent in the United States.

A quick review of the history of emoji shows not only how they were created but also why. The first emoji were developed in the 1990s and were very simple. They were inspired by manga, the Japanese art form, and Chinese characters. Before smartphones came on the market, companies wanted to entice teenagers into using pagers and thought the icons would appeal to them. Over the next decade, the use of emoji became very popular in Japan but didn't spread to other countries until the release of the first Apple iPhone in 2007, which allowed access to an emoji keyboard. Now, most people with smartphones around the world use emoji as part of their daily communication.

Like all language, emoji perform two essential functions: to convey ideas and to influence the attitudes and behaviors of others. As the young adults in the survey indicated, emoji are useful in expressing emotions in writing. Current emoji reflect a range of emotional states, including astonished, worried, relieved, confused, anguished, pensive, and furious. You can use emoji in text as you would intonation in speech. This allows your audience to better understand your tone, particularly when the emotion might be different from the literal meaning of the written words. For example, you might add the emoji for nail polish to signal your complete indifference to this boast: *I had my best 10k time in the race today*.

According to Professor Evans, 60 to 70 percent of our **communication** comes from nonverbal cues, such as **facial expressions** and gestures. Text alone can't fill in the missing information, but emoji often can. Another reason that emoji may be so appealing is because they help us bridge the gap between literal and figurative language. Idioms often paint a vivid mental picture. Just as we can say "tears of joy" with a single emoji, we could combine emoji to express other states of happiness, such as **"on cloud nine,"** **"thrilled to bits,"** or **"over the moon."**

Can emoji replace traditional written language? No, although the BBC offers news headlines in emoji each week and people have begun to translate complete books such as *Moby Dick* and *Alice in Wonderland* into emoji. What emoji offer us is a way to transmit our ideas and emotions quickly and vividly with an appreciation of nuance.

4 ASSESS Read the article again. Choose the statements that are true.

1 Emoji are especially good at expressing complicated ideas.

2 The most popular emoji express an emotion.

3 Most young adults find it easier to express their feelings in emoji than in text.

4 Emoji were invented in 2007.

5 Emoji can be used in text the way intonation is used in speech.

6 Emoji can take the place of facial expressions.

7 Experts predict that emoji will take the place of written language.

READING SKILL
Subjective versus objective information

Effective writing uses objective information in the form of factual observations, as well as subjective statements that make value judgments based on the facts. Subjective information in addition to facts can make your argument more persuasive.

Objective information is verifiable and not based on personal feelings. Examples of objective information include scientific facts, historical dates, and research results.

When a writer uses expressions of opinion (*I think*), hedging words (*perhaps*), modals (*should, ought to*), and certain adjectives and adverbs (*the best, amazingly*), it indicates subjective information.

According to Professor Evans, 60 to 70 percent of our communication comes from nonverbal cues, such as facial expressions and gestures. (objective)
Emoji can convey those quickly and effectively. (subjective)

5 IDENTIFY Read the statements. Decide if the information is subjective (S) or objective (O).

1 Sometimes an adjective, such as *happy* or *glad,* is not quite enough to convey what we are truly feeling. ___

2 Now we may have a new communicative tool that is especially good at describing our feelings. ___

3 In 2015, the Oxford dictionary announced that its word of the year was, well, not a word at all but an emoji—a picture of eyebrows, eyes, big tears, and a huge grin— laughing with tears of joy. ___

4 Eighty to ninety percent of adults with smartphones in the UK use emoji. ___

5 The most popular is the face with tears of joy, and it accounts for 20 percent of the emoji sent in the UK and 17 percent in the U.S. ___

6 Over the next decade, the use of emoji became very popular in Japan but didn't spread to other countries until the release of the first Apple iPhone in 2007, which allowed access to an emoji keyboard. ___

7 Another reason that emoji may be so appealing is because they help us bridge the gap between literal and figurative language. ___

6 ASSESS Read the objective information below. Which of these facts would you use to argue for or against the use of emoji? Why?

1 Emoji look different on different smartphone platforms.

2 According to one study, in 25 percent of the cases involving the same emoji, participants couldn't agree if it was positive, neutral, or negative.

3 People in the study didn't all think the tears-of-joy emoji was positive.

4 Only 4.5 percent of emoji are interpreted consistently by all participants.

7 INTEGRATE Write four sentences with subjective information to support the objective information in Exercise 6.

Emoji can be very confusing.

_____

_____

_____

_____

8 EXPAND Form a group of two or three students. Share your ideas from Exercise 7. Whose subjective support is more persuasive?

GRAMMAR IN CONTEXT Ellipsis after modals, auxiliaries, question words, and *if* clauses

We can leave out words to avoid repetition in a sentence after auxiliaries (*be, do, have*), modal verbs, question words (such as *how, where, who, why*), and *if* clauses.

You can use emoji in text as you <u>would</u> use intonation in speech.
Text alone can't fill in the missing information, but emoji often <u>can</u> fill in missing information.
A quick review of the history of emoji shows not only how they were created but <u>why</u> they were created.
Have you ever been so happy that mere words failed you? If you have ever been so happy that mere words failed you, you are not alone.

See Grammar focus on page 166.

9 APPLY Rewrite the sentences. Use ellipsis where possible.

1 Do you like to use emoji? If you like to use emoji, you're not alone.

_____

2 Young adults find it easy to use emoji. Older adults sometimes don't find it easy to use emoji.

_____

3 I read a study about emoji use. I don't remember where I read a study about emoji use.

_____

4 My sister uses emoji often when she texts. I don't think my brother uses emoji often when he texts.

_____

VOCABULARY DEVELOPMENT
Idioms for expressing joy

Using figurative language such as idioms can help you express your feelings by creating a vivid mental picture. Many idioms for expressing joy relate to being in a high place.

walking on air   on cloud 9   over the moon

---

10 IDENTIFY Match the idiom to the image below that best illustrates it.

1 walking on air _____
2 on cloud nine _____
3 over the moon _____
4 tickled pink _____
5 thrilled to bits _____
6 **music to one's ears** _____
7 **jump for joy** _____
8 **on top of the world** _____

11 🔊 **BUILD** Listen and repeat the idioms from Exercise 10.

12 USE Complete the sentences with idioms from Exercise 10.

1 Wendy and Peter are getting married. They're over _____.

2 Hector was accepted to his first choice of college. He's on top _____.

3 I'm going to be a grandmother. I'm thrilled _____.

4 The news makes me want to _____.

5 Marisol got a part in a movie. She's walking _____.

6 Reiko was invited to the wedding. She's tickled _____.

7 Ben just got a promotion. He's on _____.

8 I heard our company got an important contract. That's _____.

13 APPLY Think about the idioms for joy and the ways they are similar. Look at the idioms below. Choose the ones you think express happiness and the ones that could express sadness. Compare your ideas with a partner.

1 down in the dumps
2 stars in your eyes
3 have a sinking feeling
4 in seventh heaven
5 coming up roses
6 feeling blue

14 WHAT'S YOUR ANGLE? Answer the questions.

1 What kind of news would be music to your ears?
2 Have you ever seen anyone literally jump for joy? What was the situation?
3 What makes you feel like you're on top of the world?

a

b

c

d

e

f

g

h

8.3 The Worst Ever

1 ACTIVATE Read the list below. Choose one idea, and describe it to a partner.

- Most embarrassing situation
- What you find frustrating
- A time you felt pure delight
- Something that gives you satisfaction or fulfillment
- What you're most frightened by

2 IDENTIFY Read the email. What kinds of feelings does the writer describe?

Hi Henry,

How was your game last Saturday? Did you win? I looked for the results on the school's website, but they weren't posted yet.

I didn't get any exercise this weekend even though I had planned to. I was supposed to go to the mountains with a friend, and we were going to hike a lot. You know the expression "best laid plans"? Well, my best laid plans were completely disrupted.

Remember my friend Ben? I've told you about him before. Sometimes maintaining our friendship is difficult. He's always wanted to be a singer. He's a good singer, but not great, and I try to support him. When he's singing somewhere, I usually go and give him encouragement. Friday night, he was performing at a café in the next town. I didn't plan to go because I was leaving early the next morning, but he really wanted me to. So, against my better judgment, I drove the ten miles to the dinky little café in a bad neighborhood.

I was glad I did because almost no one was in the audience. I was sort of embarrassed for him. Ben was playing a song on his guitar, and someone in the café started coughing. He'd stop for a minute and then start back up. Every time he started again, Ben would make a face and lose his concentration. I could tell he was getting very frustrated. My own discomfort increased with every interruption. Although Ben wants to be a singer, he gets really stressed out when he performs. I knew this experience could make his anxiety worse. And it did.

He had finally lost it, by which I mean he yelled at the poor sick man (who probably had pneumonia or some other potentially fatal disease), and then put his head down on a table. He was devastated. The staff at the café brought him cake. I patted his back and told him to breathe slowly, in, 2, 3, 4 and out, 2, 3, 4.

I finally got Ben in his car and safely on his way home. I wish I could say the same thing. When I got to my own car, it had a flat tire. I didn't have a spare, so I spent hours waiting for a tow truck and finding a ride home. Needless to say, I couldn't drive up to the mountains the next morning. What a disappointment! And Ben hasn't even said thanks! It was the worst ever.

Hope to see you soon.

Jamal

3 ASSESS Complete the sentences.

1 Jamal and Ben are _____.

2 Ben wants to be a _____.

3 Jamal planned to go to _____ last weekend.

4 On Friday night, Ben was going to sing at _____.

5 During his performance, a man started to _____.

6 Jamal had to wait for _____.

4 INTEGRATE Answer the questions.

1 Why was Jamal disappointed about the weekend?

2 How did Jamal feel when he saw the small audience?

3 Why did Ben become frustrated?

4 What made Jamal's level of discomfort increase?

5 What problem does Ben have when he performs?

GRAMMAR IN CONTEXT Ellipsis with infinitives

We can also avoid repetition when we are using infinitives after other verbs. When we use ellipsis in this case, we stop after the word *to*.

I didn't get any exercise this weekend even though I had planned to ~~get exercise~~.

I didn't plan to go because I was leaving early the next morning, but he really wanted me to ~~go~~.

See Grammar focus on page 166.

5 ASSESS Use ellipsis to rewrite and shorten the sentences.

1 Many people check their email on vacation even if they don't plan to check their email.

2 I've never tried meditation, but I've often wanted to try meditation.

3 Jamal went to the performance because Ben asked him to go to the performance.

4 My advice is don't do anything on the weekend that you don't have to do on the weekend.

6 INTEGRATE Combine the ideas. Use ellipsis if possible.

1 I went to the event. I didn't want to go to the event. (*although*)

_____

2 Many people came. They didn't plan to come. (*although*)

_____

3 Ana didn't help me with the project. I asked her to help me with the project. (*even though*)

_____

4 We didn't get a ticket to the concert. We hope to get a ticket to the concert. (*but*)

_____

7 WHAT'S YOUR ANGLE? Answer the questions. Then discuss your ideas with a partner.

1 Do you make time to do the things you want to?

2 How do you feel when you can't do what you planned to?

3 In emails, are you able to express the feelings you'd like to?

PRONUNCIATION SKILL
Intonation to show surprise and certainty

Intonation gives English its musical quality. It is used to highlight important meanings in speech and to communicate the speaker's feelings or attitude. If a speaker is using a rising tone at the end of a thought group, it might mean he or she is unsure or surprised about something. If a speaker's tone rises and falls at the end of a thought group, he or she might be communicating certainty or the completion of an idea.

🔊 *Your vacation starts next week.*
Your vacation starts next week.

8 🔊 **NOTICE** Listen to the sentences. Decide if the intonation pattern is rising (R) or rising-falling (RF).

1 We won our game.

2 He's a good singer, but not very confident.

3 Maria got a promotion to department manager.

4 I can't find the file I was working on.

5 Using emoji is similar to speaking a language.

9 INTERACT Work with a partner. Take turns saying the sentences in Exercise 8 using different intonation. Tell your partner what intonation you hear.

10 WHAT'S YOUR ANGLE? Think about something you'll never forget that made you feel joy or sorrow. Answer the questions. Then discuss with a partner.

1 What happened?

2 When did it happen?

3 Who was with you?

4 Where did it happen?

5 How did you feel?

6 Who did you want to tell?

> Conveying feelings effectively in writing helps the reader connect with the writer. Because they cannot see your facial expressions or body language, your readers must rely on your words alone to interpret your emotions. Using precise vocabulary is one way to be effective.
>
> *She was ~~sad~~ devastated.* (*devastated* is much stronger than *sad*)
>
> However, sometimes you may want to soften your language to be more polite or tactful.
>
> *Sometimes maintaining our friendship is ~~impossible~~ difficult.* (*difficult* is more polite than *impossible*)

11 PREPARE Complete each sentence with the best word or phrase for the situation given in parentheses.

1 I had to give a presentation in class today. I was *nervous / terrified*. (email to a friend)

2 The little girl's face was filled with *happiness / delight*. (news report)

3 The change in schedule made me *a little uncomfortable / very upset*. (email to a supervisor)

4 If you're looking for *personal satisfaction / a good feeling*, you should pursue a meaningful career. (essay)

5 I got tickets to the final match of the World Cup. I'm *glad / thrilled*. (text to your brother)

12 WRITE Write an informal email to someone you want to tell about an experience. Use the model email in Exercise 2 and your answers to Exercise 10.

13 DEVELOP Read your email. Check that it follows these guidelines.

☐ Does it start with a question to the recipient?
☐ Does it describe something that happened in detail?
☐ Does it use ellipsis when appropriate?
☐ Does it convey feelings effectively?

14 SHARE Exchange emails with a partner. Check each other's work with respect to the guidelines in Exercise 13.

15 IMPROVE Rewrite your email to incorporate feedback.

High school students in Johannesburg, South Africa

1 **ACTIVATE** imagine that someone you see every day looks a little down. He or she reveals to you feelings of insecurity regarding the quality of his or her work in a new job or on a school project. What would you say to this person?

2 **ASSESS** Look at the pictures. Which response fits each situation?

"What's up? You seem down."

"That's...wow! Amazing. Good for you."

3 ▶ **IDENTIFY** Watch the video, and find out what happened.

1 How does Andy feel? What happened?

2 How does Kevin feel? Why?

3 Why is Max surprised?

REAL-WORLD ENGLISH Expressing empathy

When you empathize with someone, the nature of the emotions they express can affect your response. Daily problems compared to more serious situations can affect the degree of empathy you demonstrate.

If a person is expressing sadness or disappointment, truly listen and be present. Show you are paying attention by being able to look them in the eye while facing them. Communicate that you **notice the other person's emotions** with a question.

You seem upset. What happened?   *What's wrong?*

Once you find out what's on that person's mind, show you understand by **asking for clarification or state any prior knowledge you have** about the situation.

I understand.   *I know what you mean.*   *I realize that...*
I hear what you're saying. How bad is it?   *I get that, especially since you prepared for so long.*

You can also **validate the other person's feelings**.

That must be hard.   *I'd be upset, too.*   *I can imagine how disappointing that is.*
No wonder you're upset.   *Too bad.*   *Really?*

Gently offer a suggestion on how the other person can resolve his or her difficulty.

Sorry. Maybe you could talk to your boss and find out what went wrong.

Take your time, and remember to withhold judgment as you listen.

4 ▶ **ANALYZE** Watch the video again. Refer to the Real-World English box, and identify how Max expresses empathy as Andy tells his story.

1 Max: Hey Andy. What's up? You seem…down.

    _____

    Andy: Yeah, I got my exam results. I'm not too thrilled because I got a 76.

2 Max: I get that, especially since you studied so hard for that exam.

    _____

    Andy: Professor Jackson said she was disappointed because I didn't finish the last five questions.

3 Max: No wonder you look so upset.

    _____

    Andy: Yeah. I didn't sleep and then during the test…my brain froze.

4 Max: Sorry, Andy. Maybe you could talk to Professor Jackson. _____

5 **BUILD** Complete the conversations. Think about how you would show empathy to the following people.

1 *Your roommate who you hang out with all the time looks sad.*

(Notice his or her emotions):

    _____

Your roommate: I just failed my final exam.

(Respond to show you understand, and ask for clarification): _____

Your roommate: It was worth 25% of my total grade in the class.

(Validate your roommate's feelings):

    _____

Your roommate: This'll really bring down my GPA.

(Gently offer a suggestion): _____

2 *You are at your professor's office for an appointment, and he has a concerned look on his face.*

(Notice his emotions): _____

Your professor: Someone ran into my car in the parking lot.

(Respond to show you understand, and ask for clarification): _____

Your professor: I'm a little shaken.

(Validate your professor's feelings): _____

Your professor: It's also just so much to deal with at a really crazy time of the semester.

(Gently offer a suggestion): _____

6 **DEVELOP** Share your answers with a partner. Do you notice any differences between how you express empathy between the two people? With which person do you feel you could continue making more moves to demonstrate your empathy?

7 **INTERACT** Work with a partner. Role-play the conversation you chose from Exercise 5 together, then role-play it for the class.

8 **ANALYZE** Think about the strategies discussed in the Real-World English box. How would you express empathy in the following situations? Complete the conversations.

1 You are on a beach vacation with your close friend who is expecting an important phone text. Your friend says to you, "I want to sit in the sun, but if I do it is difficult to see my cell phone screen."

2 You are at the movies with another close friend. After you've found your seats, your friend suddenly realizes that his cell phone is missing and he never backed up photos from a recent vacation.

9 **SHARE** With your class, discuss how you would express empathy in the conversations in Exercise 8.

 GO ONLINE to create your own version of the English For Real video.

97

8.5 Forget about It!

1 ACTIVATE Look at the photos. What are the people feeling? How do you know?

2 WHAT'S YOUR ANGLE? Look at the photos again. In which of the situations would it be easier for you to express your feelings? Why? Discuss your ideas with a partner.

3 ◀)) **IDENTIFY** Listen to a conversation about expressing feelings. Then choose the true statements.

1 Leila works with Peter and Mr. Gutierrez.
2 Leila's supervisor presented her idea as his own.
3 Allie knows Peter well.
4 Allie wants to know how Leila is feeling.
5 Allie doesn't give Leila advice.
6 Leila plans to talk to Peter tomorrow.

4 ◀)) **ASSESS** Work with a partner. Discuss the questions. Listen again if necessary.

1 What's the relationship between Allie and Leila? Why do you think so?
2 How does Leila feel? Why?
3 Why didn't Leila say anything at work?
4 How are Allie and Leila's communication styles different?
5 What do you think Leila will do now?

SPEAKING Expressing attitudes and feelings

We can express a feeling directly by saying *I feel*. We can also express an attitude by using certain adverbs and adverbial phrases:

actually	*hopefully*	*generally*	*obviously*
to be honest	*of course*	*apparently*	

Actually, I do feel a little stressed.
To be honest, I thought Mr. Gutierrez might think I was being competitive or whiny.

5 DEVELOP Read the statements below. Which do you agree with? Give reasons to support your opinion.

1 Other people should know what we're feeling without needing to be told.
2 Expressing negative feelings is never a good idea.
3 People should always express whatever they are feeling. You have a right to your emotions.
4 People will think you're weak if you feel depressed or anxious.
5 It's better to stay silent than to say something directly.
6 You should be able to solve your own problems, so talking about feelings isn't helpful.

6 SHARE Form a group with two or three other students. Discuss your ideas in Exercise 5. Use expressions to show your feelings and attitudes.

Now go to page 154 for the Unit 8 Review.

9 Development

▼ What kinds of development does the image show?

▼ Is development always a good thing?

▼ What can we do to develop our careers?

BEHIND THE PHOTO ▶

Work with a partner. Imagine that you had the power to change the world.

1 What would you change?
2 What technology would you need?
3 How will people need to change to help you reach your goal?

REAL-WORLD GOAL

Practice a new skill every day for a week

9.1 You Too Can Be an Expert!

1 ACTIVATE Look at the photos below. What does it take to excel at each activity? Discuss with a partner.

2 IDENTIFY Read the statements. Choose the ones you think are true. Discuss your ideas with a partner.

1 An expert is someone who knows a lot about something.
2 To be an expert, you must be able to produce excellent results that are measurable.
3 Experts need to begin with a natural talent.
4 Preparation is more important than talent in developing expertise.
5 Anyone can become an expert.

3 ◀» ASSESS Listen to the podcast. Check your answers to Exercise 2.

4 ◀» EXPAND Listen to the podcast again. Complete the notes.

Speaker: _____, grad. Psych.
Expert, 3 things:
1 Performs demons. & consist. better
2 Actions produce _____.
3 _____ results
Can measure both objective and _____ fields
Ex: _____
Talent helps, but _____ more imp., ~ _____ hrs, _____ years
Anders Ericsson stud. Ppl who memorized _____.
_____ → super memorizers
Practice necessary
Have to _____ → keep imprv
Deliberate practice: _____ + _____ → revise
Ex: _____

5 ◀» BUILD Choose the best word to complete each sentence. Then listen and check your answers.

1 Through practice, they were able to *transform / adjust* into super-memorizers.
2 You can become much better, providing you *revolutionize / adjust* your practice.
3 They had to keep *converting / modifying* their techniques.
4 Deliberate practice involves using feedback to *adjust / transition* your technique or strategy accordingly.
5 Your technique will continue to *modify / evolve*, and you'll reach a new level of performance.

6 WHAT'S YOUR ANGLE? Answer the questions. Then discuss them in a group.

1 After listening to the podcast, have you modified your ideas about expertise? Why or why not?
2 What methods do coaches usually use to help people develop their skills?
3 Think about a new situation you have been in recently. How did you adapt?

GRAMMAR IN CONTEXT Passive voice

We use passive voice when we want to focus on the action rather than the performer of the action. We form the passive with the verb *be* + past participle. We can use the passive in all tenses, with modal verbs, and in the infinitive.

*I can see how athletes' performances **can be evaluated**.*
*Of course, the paintings **have to be judged**.*
*But some of the participants in the study **were trained** to remember many more numbers after hearing them only once.*
*Deliberate practice involves **being coached** and using feedback to revise your technique or strategy.*
*When you **are being coached**, you **are forced** to look at your performance in a new way.*

See Grammar focus on page 167.

7 IDENTIFY Read the text about the development of musical ability. Choose the active or passive voice.

8 INTEGRATE Rewrite the sentences in passive voice.

1 People can develop expertise through deliberate practice.
_____ through deliberate practice.
2 Someone will give awards to the winning athletes.
_____ to the winning athletes.
3 People often acquire musical skills through early training.
_____ through early training.
4 Scientists have done research on memorization techniques.
_____ on memorization techniques.

9 ASSESS Listen and check your answers to Exercise 8.

10 WHAT'S YOUR ANGLE? Answer the questions. Then discuss your ideas in a group.

1 Do you think any skill can be developed into expertise? Why or why not?
2 What is something you have spent a lot of time practicing? How did you practice?

Children and Music

The developmental psychology of music focuses on change in musical skills as children age. Change due to growth or development [1] *may distinguish / may be distinguished* from that due to training, but there is evidence that training may be more effective at particular stages or ages.

By the time children go to school they already have some experience with music. Infants [2] *expose / are exposed* to music (and music-like sounds) in the home (for example, through recordings, radio, and television), speech, and play songs and lullabies sung by adults. Adult speech and song [3] *provide / are provided* infants with pleasurable musical interaction and a possible basis for their later engagement with music.

The main method researchers use to study infants [4] *involves / is involved* observation of head turning, in which the infant [5] *shows / is shown* awareness of something new or interesting. Such studies [6] *indicate / is indicated* that infants are sensitive to many aspects of music; these results [7] *have led / have been led* some investigators to conclude that biology rather than culture-specific learning is the main factor in infant music perception.

Research beyond infancy focuses on changes in musical ability acquired through training and environment, rather than age. Within western culture, high levels of performance skill [8] *commonly attribute / are commonly attributed* to innate talents, even though there's no strong evidence of a genetic basis for musical ability. One of the best predictors of musical skill is the amount and type of instrumental practice in which a performer [9] *engages / is engaged*. Estimates of practice time and biographical accounts suggest that highly skilled performers [10] *have practiced / have been practiced* 10,000 hours by the age of 21; this highlights the role that motivation plays.

Assessment of musical ability [11] *has shown / has been shown* to be unreliable: for example, musically expert judges [12] *influence / are influenced* by such factors as gender and attractiveness. Objective measures of musical ability [13] *have attempted / have been attempted*, but the use of standardized tests to predict musical aptitude has been largely unsuccessful.

—adapted from *The Oxford Companion to Music*, by Alison Latham

9.2 The Powers of a Superhero

1 ACTIVATE Look at the photos. What superpowers does each character possess? Discuss in a small group.

2 WHAT'S YOUR ANGLE? Which of the powers in Exercise 1 would you most like to have and why? Discuss with a partner.

3 VOCABULARY Read the sentences. Choose the best definition for the word or phrase in bold.

1 Glasses are one way to **enhance** vision.
   a increase or further improve
   b control or restrict

2 Deliberate practice **facilitates** the development of expertise.
   a makes possible or easier
   b leads a discussion

3 The surgery will improve the heart's **ability** to **function**.
   a to grow or develop
   b to work in the correct way

4 Biomedical **interventions** are sometimes necessary to save a life.
   a the act of interrupting
   b action taken to improve a situation or condition

5 Completely driverless cars are **on the** **horizon**.
   a able to lift off the ground
   b likely to happen soon

6 The city should **devise** a better system to control traffic.
   a invent a new way of doing something
   b behave in a dishonest way

7 Firefighters need breathing **apparatus** to enter the burning building.
   a equipment needed for a task
   b the structure of an organization

8 If you are a surgeon, you have **specialized** skills.
   a developed for a particular purpose
   b different from normal

🕮+ Oxford 5000™

4 IDENTIFY Read the article. What kind of abilities are currently being enhanced? Discuss your ideas with a partner.

5 BUILD Complete each sentence with the correct form of a word from Exercise 3.

1 With the help of biomedical _____, people can _____ beyond what is necessary to live.

2 Eating certain things can _____ someone's ability to see at night.

3 One technology _____ is a prosthetic limb that can feel.

4 Engineers work with doctors to _____ equipment that can help patients in new ways.

5 The cost of a cutting-edge _____, like the one that helps people carry heavy loads, can be high.

6 USE Answer the questions. Then discuss your ideas in a group.

1 How is human enhancement different from other medical interventions?

2 What are some ways that the medical field can help people with physical disabilities function more independently?

3 What kinds of apparatuses can help people perform their jobs more effectively?

4 Scientists are devising a variety of solutions in the area of human enhancement. How might they improve your life?

5 In what ways does technology facilitate better performance (e.g., at work, on teams)?

READING SKILL Recognizing and understanding rhetorical questions

Writers use rhetorical questions in order to make a point without the expectation of a reply. These questions often act to engage the reader's interest and to present the writer's main ideas.

Have you ever wanted the powers of a superhero? (The writer is engaging the reader's interest.)
What is human enhancement? (The answer is one of the writer's main ideas.)

You can use rhetorical questions to assert or rebut an argument, to obtain agreement, or to effect a response.

It sounds scary, doesn't it? (The writer goes on to argue against this.)
You remember the movie Iron Man, *right?* (The writer is obtaining agreement.)

7 ASSESS Find the rhetorical questions in the article. Why is the writer using each one? Discuss your ideas with a partner.

THE AGE OF
SUPERHEROES

Have you ever wanted the powers of a superhero? <u>Most people would like to fly, wouldn't they?</u>
Or climb buildings or lift cars? Maybe to see through walls or hear in color?
What used to be considered science fiction or fantasy is now within reach.
The era of human enhancement is upon us.

What is human enhancement? It is <u>generally considered to be</u> any biomedical intervention that is used to improve someone's functioning and condition beyond what is required for health and survival. A biomedical intervention could include implanting sensors in a prosthetic limb to facilitate the sense of touch, attaching electrodes to your brain to stimulate learning, introducing beneficial bacteria into the gut, or even changing your diet to enhance night vision.

Professor Maciej Henneberg and Dr. Aurthur Saniotis, both at the University of Adelaide, maintain that human adaptation, including methods of enhancement, is an ongoing process, part of a complex system that is continuously changing. These enhancement methods themselves are complex and ever changing.

Take the topic of brain–computer interfaces. <u>It sounds scary, doesn't it?</u> But it may solve some difficult problems. Using such an interface, a monkey in the United States can move an object on a computer in Japan. The same kind of brain–computer connection has been used by a paralyzed woman to feed herself chocolate. The uses for this kind of technology are impressive, particularly for people with locked-in syndrome. If you have this syndrome, you are aware of everything going on around you but completely unable to move anything except your eyes. Imagine if these patients could use their brains to not only communicate with other people but to control technology that might help them be more self-sufficient.

You remember the movie *Iron Man*, right? With the scientist in a special robotic suit? Robotics are another way we can enhance human performance. Robotic exoskeletons are already helping people with paralysis. For example, a paraplegic woman walked the London Marathon in a robotic exoskeleton. However, the same kind of technology is being used in other situations. Scientists are devising equipment that would allow someone to carry 200 pounds for several hours without fatiguing. This kind

of apparatus could be used by the military, construction workers, recreational climbers, or rescue personnel. A body-extender robot has also been used by rescue workers in Italy to lift walls off earthquake survivors.

Such robotics are a logical extension of the technology developed first for prosthetics. Prosthetic devices have been around for centuries. They take the place of a missing body part. The first time someone strapped on a wooden stick in place of an amputated leg, he wore a prosthetic. The field of prosthetics has come a long way since then. Take the case of Josef Metelka, an exceptional athlete with 13 legs, 12 of them specialized for specific sports such as snowboarding and biking. Each is tailored to the environment (e.g., snow) and task (e.g., twisting and landing).

What is on the horizon for these replacement body parts? <u>It is hoped</u> that soon they may be able to feel. A Danish man recently underwent surgery to test out a new technology. A team of robotics experts, engineers, neuroscientists, and surgeons from Italy, Switzerland, and Germany implanted electrodes into nerves in the man's upper arm. These were connected to artificial sensors in a prosthetic hand. Through electronics and software, touch and pressure feedback was delivered to the man's brain, allowing the patient to "feel"—at least, to tell the shape and stiffness of an object through touch.

How else might a person take advantage of enhancement technology? One area of research that seems to have practical application for almost anyone is *transcranial direct current stimulation* (TDCS). TDCS changes the way the neurons in our brains send signals. Electrodes are attached to the head to stimulate the brain. Almost everyone shows improvement in learning and reduction in anxiety. And if you had access to Ce6, a compound found in deep-sea fish, you could do what Gabriel Licina did—he added it to eyedrops to improve his ability to see in the dark.

We may be at the very beginning of the era of human enhancement. There's no way to predict how far we can go, is there?

8 IDENTIFY Match the rhetorical question to the idea.

1 Have you ever wanted the powers of a superhero? ___
2 What is human enhancement? ___
3 It sounds scary, doesn't it? ___
4 You remember the movie *Iron Man*, right? ___
5 What is on the horizon for these replacement parts? ___
6 How might the average person take advantage of advancement technology? ___

a Robotics are another way we can enhance human performance.
b But it may solve some difficult problems.
c The era of human enhancement is upon us.
d Soon they may be able to feel.
e It's a biomedical intervention that improves a person's functioning and condition.
f One way is TDCS, which can improve learning.

GRAMMAR IN CONTEXT Tag questions

We usually put a tag question at the end of a statement. If the main verb in the statement is positive, the tag question is usually negative; if the main verb in the statement is negative, the tag question is usually positive. This is true for all verb tenses.

It sounds scary, doesn't it?

When we use negative words such as *no, no one, hardly, nothing, never,* and *nobody,* the main verb and the tag question are both positive. When the subject is *everyone, no one, someone,* etc., we use a plural verb in the tag question.

There's no way to predict how far we can go, is there?

In conversations, we use tag questions to check information or to find out if someone agrees with us. We also use tag questions to show we are paying attention and to encourage more conversation.

See Grammar focus on page 167.

9 APPLY Complete each tag question using the correct auxiliary.

1 This article is very interesting, _____?
2 You haven't seen the movie, _____?
3 No one currently has one of those prosthetic hands that can feel, _____?
4 There are a lot of different kinds of prosthetics, _____?
5 They had to perform surgery, _____?

PRONUNCIATION SKILL
Intonation in tag questions

There are two intonation patterns for tag questions. In tag questions that elicit agreement, the speaker is requesting confirmation from the other person. The speaker is certain, or fairly certain of the listener's agreement. In these tag questions, the intonation falls in a way that is similar to the falling intonation of statements.

It sounds scary, doesn't it?

However, in other tag questions, the speaker is unsure of the listener's response. The rising intonation pattern signals uncertainty, as in true *yes/no* questions.

Superman has X-ray vision, doesn't he?

Be careful! If the rising intonation is too extreme, it can sound like the speaker doesn't believe something or is making an accusation.

10 NOTICE Listen to the questions. Decide if the intonation pattern you hear is expressing uncertainty (EU) or requesting confirmation (RC). Then listen again and repeat.

1 You read the article, didn't you?
2 He can't see in the dark, can he?
3 They don't really feel with prosthetic limbs, do they?
4 It's amazing what technology can do, isn't it?
5 You understand my point, right?

11 ASSESS Read the exchanges. Which would you use falling intonation in? Listen and check your answers.

1 A: The exam was much harder than I expected!
   B: You passed, didn't you?
2 A: The game was completely one-sided. I felt sorry for the other team.
   B: You won, didn't you?
3 A: Halima has gone to the main office to check lost and found.
   B: She didn't find her keys, did she?
4 A: I'm going to submit my application tomorrow.
   B: Really? We can't submit applications after midnight, can we?

12 WHAT'S YOUR ANGLE? Answer the questions about yourself. Then practice asking and answering with a partner.

1 You would like a superpower, wouldn't you?
2 You don't read a lot of superhero comics, do you?
3 You understood the purpose of rhetorical questions, didn't you?

1 ACTIVATE Look at the photos and answer the questions.

1 Why might people like to go on each of these vacations?
2 Which do you think looks most relaxing?
3 Which looks like the most fun?

2 WHAT'S YOUR ANGLE? Which of the vacations in Exercise 1 would you like to do and why? Discuss your ideas with a partner.

3 IDENTIFY Read the email. What is the writer's purpose?

From: Anna Scott [mailto:a.scott@speedstermail.com]

Sent: Wednesday, August 3, 2018 1:09 PM

To: Fatima Sanders

Subject: Concerns about my vacation

Dear Ms. Sanders,

I am writing to express my dissatisfaction with my recent Personal and Planetary Productivity Retreat. While many aspects of the retreat were enjoyable, I don't feel it lived up to its description on your website. I have undergone a series of setbacks in my personal and professional life in the last few years, and I was looking for a way to help myself and to become more aware of my role in the global community.

According to the testimonials on your website, your service is considered to be one of the best in this field. The typical morning schedule showed a progression of activities: a sunrise yoga and meditation session followed by listening to nature, a cleansing vegan snack, and then purposeful movement. It all sounds lovely, doesn't it?

However, the reality didn't live up to the description exactly. It's true that the day started at sunrise with yoga. While the poses themselves could be considered yoga, or yoga-like, I've never done yoga in a drenching monsoon. Evidently, the yoga studio was undergoing renovation, so we practiced in an outdoor parking lot. It is very difficult, if not impossible, to meditate with water streaming down one's face. Also, we had to move when the director needed our parking space.

Once we had toweled off, we proceeded to the nature-listening exercise. I was still a little damp, and after the experience in the parking lot, I was beginning to wonder what sort of nature we might be able to access. The location was much more urban than expected. I shouldn't have worried. We were each given a small houseplant to hold and listen to. As you might expect, houseplants are rather quiet. A few people shook theirs, which did rustle the leaves a bit, but my plant hadn't been watered regularly, and the leaves began to fall off. We remembered it was raining, though, so we put all the houseplants out in the parking lot.

The cleansing snack turned out to be prune juice. I'm allergic, but our facilitator gave me some water instead. The day went downhill from there, if you can imagine. Purposeful movement turned out to be a ten-mile run! The other participants and the instructor were very pleasant and helpful.

It is said that "what doesn't kill you makes you stronger," and that may be true, but it's not what I'm looking for in a vacation. I expect that you will refund the entire cost of this trip.

Best regards,
Anna Scott

—adapted from *Oxford Dictionary of Proverbs,* by Jennifer Speake

105

4 INTEGRATE Answer the questions.

1 Why did Anna go on the retreat?
2 What was she hoping to do?
3 In what ways was she disappointed?
4 What did she like about the retreat?
5 What does she want the company to do?

5 INTERACT Ask and answer the questions with a partner.

1 Would you go on a retreat like this one? Why or why not?
2 What aspects of a vacation are most important to you?
3 From the email, do you think you would get along with the writer? Why or why not?

 GRAMMAR IN CONTEXT
Use of the passive in impersonal reporting

We use the passive to create a more impersonal or objective style, especially in business or academic contexts. One way we do this is with reporting verbs such as *say, think, suggest, recommend, consider, report, hope, expect,* and *understand.*

The structure with reporting verbs is:

subject + passive verb + infinitive/*that* clause
*According to the testimonials on your website, **your service is considered to be** one of the best in this field.*
***It is said** that "what doesn't kill you makes you stronger," and that may be true, but it's not what I'm looking for in a vacation.*

See Grammar focus on page 167.

6 APPLY Rewrite the following sentences in the passive to be more impersonal and objective. Use infinitives or *that* clauses with the reporting verbs.

1 Commenters on the website, including Jane Hamilton and Audrey Price, mentioned that the food was excellent.

_____

2 Mark Jones and Berta Santiago said that the accommodations were unattractive.

_____

3 Most people believe the retreat center provides a good experience.

_____

4 I have suggested before that the website provide more accurate information.

_____

 7 WHAT'S YOUR ANGLE? Complete the sentences with your own ideas about vacation destinations. Then discuss them with a partner.

1 It has been said that _____, but I disagree.
2 _____ is considered to be a great place to go on vacation.
3 I've always wanted to try _____ because it has been described as life changing.
4 Vacations are believed to _____.

WRITING SKILL Using formal email language

In many situations, email has taken the place of the formal business letter. Although emails can be informal when between friends and family, in formal contexts you must use formal language and conventions.

1 Begin the body of the email with a formal greeting or salutation:
Dear Mr. / Ms. Sanders,

2 Explain your reason for writing:
I'm writing to express my dissatisfaction with my recent Personal and Planetary Productivity Retreat.

3 Use appropriate vocabulary:
While many aspects of the retreat were enjoyable, I don't feel it lived up to its description on your website.

4 Conclude with a closing and your name (your full name if you are strangers):
Sincerely,   Best regards,

8 IDENTIFY Find each example of formal email language in the email on page 105.

9 PREPARE Answer the questions about your own experiences. Discuss in a group.

1 Have you ever gone on a self-help vacation or a trip that was supposed to improve you in some way? If so, what was it?

2 Describe a vacation or trip you went on that did not turn out as expected. What happened?

3 What would bother you or disappoint you the most about a vacation?

10 WRITE Write a formal email or letter of complaint to the travel agency for your self-help vacation. You can write about an actual experience using your ideas or the ideas below. Use the model email in Exercise 3 and your answers to Exercise 9.

• The accommodations and food were of poor quality.
• The activities were not as described.
• The staff was rude, untrained, or unhelpful.

11 DEVELOP Read your email. Check that it follows these guidelines.

☐ Does it start with a salutation or greeting?
☐ Does it explain the reason for writing?
☐ Does it describe problems?
☐ Does it use appropriate vocabulary?
☐ Does it use a closing?

12 SHARE Exchange emails with a partner. Check each other's work with respect to the guidelines in Exercise 11.

13 IMPROVE Rewrite the email to incorporate feedback.

9.4 If You Ask Me

1 ACTIVATE In which situation(s) do you feel most comfortable talking about your beliefs? Discuss with a partner.

- With a friend at a coffee shop
- With a colleague at work while working on a project
- With a fellow student at a library
- With a fellow passenger on the subway
- With your boss outside of work
- With your professor during his or her office hours

2 EXPAND Do you agree that everyone should eat with chopsticks all the time? How would you respond to the following people if they said this to you?

	Colleague/Classmate	Professor/Boss
1. Don't say anything	☐	☐
2. "That's the worst idea I've ever heard."	☐	☐
3. "NO!"	☐	☐
4. "I don't agree, but sure."	☐	☐
5. "Hmm…I guess."	☐	☐
6. "I'll consider trying it."	☐	☐
7. "I agree with you 100%!"	☐	☐
8. "I don't want to talk about this."	☐	☐

3 ▶ IDENTIFY Watch the video, and find out what happened.

1 What are Kevin, Phil, and Andy discussing?
2 Do they all agree? How do you know?
3 Do you think Andy changes his opinion? Why or why not?

ENGLISH FOR REAL

Whenever you propose an idea you believe in, some people may either not understand it or dislike the idea. You can defend your belief without getting caught up in criticizing naysayers.

After introducing your belief, demonstrate experience that establishes your reasoning.

Eating with chopsticks for the entire month I was traveling through Japan last year really helped me develop an appreciation for taking my time while eating because I had to concentrate on my meal rather than doing a million things at once.

You may need to clarify your purpose if someone disagrees with the validity of your experience.

A: There's nothing wrong with multitasking while eating. Not everyone has the luxury of taking long lunches.

B: It's not about doing as much as you can within a given timeframe. It's about enjoying a meal and taking a little time out.

If asked, you can list more reasons for your belief.

Well, I'm a huge believer in not overeating, and eating with chopsticks prevents that from happening a lot more than if I had shoveled food in my mouth with a fork. I was forced to eat slower, AND I ate way less than I normally would have because I felt fuller faster.

When it appears that the conversation is ending, sometimes you can get the last word in by providing a big takeaway.

A: Sounds like you're overthinking this.

B: Yeah, well using chopsticks meant a smaller pant size and a happier stomach for me.

However, be sensitive about other people's beliefs. Sometimes, insisting on your opinion can lead to a conflict. In such situations, it may be better to acknowledge that people's opinions vary and that it is not your goal to convince the other person that you are right.

Well, personally, I prefer to eat with chopsticks, but I understand that other people may prefer a fork and a knife.

4 NOTICE During a conversation, if someone states a belief and you disagree with it, do you normally let it go, or do you talk about it?

5 ▶ ANALYZE Watch the video again. Write which function of defending a belief is used.

providing a takeaway	clarify your purpose
introduce your belief	demonstrate experience
list reasons for your belief	

1 I wore one from kindergarten through high school.

   _____

2 Choosing what to wear can be stressful and a big waste of time! _____

3 When you wear a uniform, you don't have to think about what to wear! _____

4 Fewer items of clothing means less maintenance!

   _____

5 I think there are more benefits to wearing uniforms than there are to being trendy. _____

6 ASSESS Do you think Phil would defend his belief to a professor the same way he did with Andy and Kevin? Why or why not?

7 BUILD Choose one of the topics. Prepare to defend it using the strategies from the Real-World English box.

- We are becoming too dependent on computers.
- Teachers should earn more money.
- Homework isn't helpful.
- Public transportation should be free.
- Your choice

8 INTEGRATE Work with a partner, and take turns defending your beliefs from Exercise 7 in an active conversation.

9 SHARE With your partner, role-play your conversation.

GO ONLINE
to create your own version
of the English For Real video.

9.5 I'm Not Sure about That

1 ACTIVATE Look at the robots below. What do you think each is used for? Discuss your ideas with a partner.

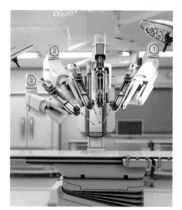 

2 🔊 **IDENTIFY** Listen to the conversation. Then decide if each expression expresses certainty (C) or uncertainty (U).

1	absolutely	___	5	I'm sure	___
2	I'm not sure	___	6	Probably not	___
3	I have my doubts	___	7	It's possible that	___
4	I'm quite certain	___	8	It's likely you're right	___

3 🔊 **INTEGRATE** Answer the questions. Listen to the conversation again if needed.

1 What is the first speaker reading an article about?
2 What does the second speaker think about this technology?
3 Who is more excited about it?
4 According to research, what kind of robots do people prefer?
5 Do the speakers agree?

SPEAKING
Expressing shades of opinion and uncertainty

Sometimes we are completely confident about something, but often we have doubts to varying degrees. When you express your opinion, you should let your listener know about your degree of certainty. When you express something in absolute terms, it is sometimes harder to receive than if you express it with less certainty. Less certainty often seems more polite.

More certain	Less certain
Of course	*It's likely / probable*
Of course not	*It could / may / might (not)*
I'm sure / certain / positive	*It's possible / conceivable*
	I'm not sure / certain / positive
	It's unlikely / improbable
	I doubt / It's doubtful

Be careful! *Of course* and *of course not* can sound like the other person has made an unnecessary or obvious point.

---

4 ▶ **PREPARE** Watch the video. Complete the sentences.

1 Remote presence robots are controlled by _____. They have a _____ that lets the patient see the physician. The robots have a sensitive high-tech _____ system that helps them avoid collisions with people and other equipment. There is a _____ in the room.
2 A robot courier _____ tools and equipment. It responds to voice _____.
3 Some robots are _____. They are actually able to do a better job than humans because they can kill _____. Some studies show they have reduced infections by _____.
4 Surgical robots assist with _____. They are taught the _____ for each operation. They use _____ software.

5 ▶ **DEVELOP** Watch the video again. Complete the sentences with the expressions for certainty and uncertainty that you hear.

1 If a doctor is far from the hospital, _____, he or she can control a robot that moves around the hospital checking on patients and even inspecting them.
2 And _____, there is a nurse in the room as well.
3 Some doctors say it's a great system, but others _____.
4 _____, Lynn, that's something I thought about as well.
5 That's _____.
6 I _____ I'd want a robot operating on me. _____ if the information is available, but would you tell us about their performance?

6 ▶ **SPEAK** Read the questions. Watch the video again. Then discuss your ideas in a group. Use expressions for certainty and uncertainty.

1 How do you feel about talking to your doctor through a robot?
2 What do you think robots should do in a hospital?
3 How might robots be better or worse than human staff in a hospital?

7 WHAT'S YOUR ANGLE? Answer the questions. Then discuss them with a partner.

1 What other kinds of robots do you know about?
2 What kind of robot would you want?

Now go to page 155 for the Unit 9 Review.

10 News

Why are disasters like this news?

What social benefit does news have?

Who decides what is news?

BEHIND THE PHOTO

Work with a partner. Brainstorm four important news stories in the last year.
Identify reasons the events were in the news.

News Story	Reason
The California wildfires	It affected a large area and many people lost their homes

REAL-WORLD GOAL

Read a news article
to determine if it's
trustworthy or fake news

1 ACTIVATE Look at the photos. What does each represent? Do you recognize these events? Why are they news?

2 WHAT'S YOUR ANGLE? Answer the questions. Then discuss them with a partner.

1 Have you ever experienced a natural disaster? What was it?

2 What is the worst disaster your country has experienced in the last decade? What happened? What damage did it cause?

VOCABULARY DEVELOPMENT
Phrases for giving estimates

When you are not sure of precise numbers, you should give a guess or an estimate. Use these expressions to let your audience know you are giving an estimate.

Off the top of my head,…
Knowing…will…
If I had to take a guess,…
It's difficult to say, but I think…
I wouldn't be surprised if…
We're talking about maybe…
It's somewhere in the ballpark of…

3 ◄)) BUILD Complete the phrases for giving estimates. Compare answers with a partner. Then listen and check your answers.

1 If _____, I'd say 100,000 homes lost power.

2 How much oil was spilled? It's _____ of 20,000 gallons.

3 I _____ if a dozen people were injured in the accident.

4 We're _____ 20 towns.

5 It's _____, but I think there were between 150 and 200 passengers.

6 _____ the current levels, the water will rise two meters or more.

4 USE Read the details below about an event that involved both an earthquake and a tsunami. Work with a partner. Take turns asking and answering questions to give estimates.

- Location: Indian Ocean
- Wave height of tsunami: 30 meters
- Dead: 225,000
- Magnitude of earthquake: 9.1
- Countries affected: 14
- Duration of earthquake: 8–10 minutes

5 ◄)) IDENTIFY Listen to the news report. Choose the statements that are true.

1 The meteorologist is in Haiti.
2 She is talking about an earthquake.
3 Haiti has experienced other recent natural disasters.
4 Fortunately, the situation is not going to get worse.
5 A "storm of the century" is something that happens every 100 years.

6 🔊 **ASSESS** Listen again. Choose the correct information to complete each sentence.

1　The meteorologist is reporting from *Florida / Haiti*.
2　Hurricane Helena is following a path similar to Hurricane Matthew in *2016 / 2006*.
3　Matthew killed *a thousand / ten thousand* people.
4　After Matthew, *17,000 / 175,000* lived in shelters.
5　Rebuilding will take more than *$120 million / $210 million*.
6　Marie thinks the wave height may reach *20–25 feet / 30–35 feet*.
7　The storm may cause *tornadoes / blizzards* as it heads north.

LISTENING SKILL
Understanding the use of attitude adverbs

Speakers often signal their attitudes with certain adverbs or adverb phrases. These adverbs usually come at the beginning of the sentence, and they refer to the entire sentence or clause to follow.

Attitude adverbs:

frankly, clearly, obviously, naturally, fortunately, hopefully, really, confidentially, surprisingly, sadly, astonishingly, apparently

Adverbial phrases:

to be honest, to be blunt, to be completely frank, to tell the truth, for what it's worth

Surprisingly, *most of the aid organizations seem to be underprepared.* (The speaker is giving surprising information.)

7 🔊 **ASSESS** Listen to the excerpts from the news report. Choose the speaker's attitude or stance.

1　a　This information should be easy to confirm.
　　b　This information is unexpected.
2　a　It seems that this is the case.
　　b　This information is very surprising.
3　a　This information is good news.
　　b　This is what I hope will happen.
4　a　This information is bad news.
　　b　This information is a secret.

8 🔊 **APPLY** Listen to the speaker. Put the sentences in order of the stance expressed.

___ The speaker thinks the news is lucky.
___ The speaker is surprised by the information.
___ The speaker thinks the news is unfortunate.
___ The speaker thinks the information is clear.
___ The speaker is being honest.
___ The speaker is optimistic.

GRAMMAR IN CONTEXT
***It* as introductory subject**

We often start a sentence with *it* as an introductory or "empty" subject, followed by the verb *be*. Using *it* in this way makes a statement more objective.

Common structures begin with *it + be +* adjective/noun, often followed by infinitives or *that* clauses.

It's possible, but that may not be a good thing.

Other structures include:

• *It +* adjective + *for / of +* object + infinitive
　It's somewhat common for these storms to bounce back out to sea.

• *It's + time +* infinitive,
　It's time to leave.

• *It's + high time / about time +* pronoun + verb in past form
　It's about time we all began to prepare for what could truly be the storm of the century.

• *It's +* adjective + question word
　It's impressive how high the waves already are.

See Grammar focus on page 168.

9 **INTEGRATE** Put the following words in order to make sentences. Then compare answers with a partner.

1　make landfall / the storm / it / in Bali / looks like / will
2　for the waves / unusual / to reach / it's / that height
3　time / other options / to / it's / consider
4　about / leave / it's / time / we
5　how / tragic / so many / people / it's / died

10 🔊 **ASSESS** Listen and check your answers to Exercise 9.

11 🔊 **EXPAND** Match the sentence halves to give information about the news report. Compare your answers with a partner. Then listen and check your answers.

1　It's highly likely the hurricane ___
2　It's terrible how much ___
3　It's not the first time ___
4　It's time for people ___
5　It's possible the storm ___

a　will get stronger if it goes back out to sea.
b　of Haiti was destroyed by Matthew.
c　will hit Haiti.
d　this has happened to the country.
e　to get ready for the storm.

10.2 Fake News

1 ACTIVATE Look at the list below. Are they all equally important in a news story? Discuss your ideas with a partner.

number of people
affected

amount of damage
or injury

surprise

location

fame of people involved

emotional content

2 WHAT'S YOUR ANGLE? Answer the questions. Then discuss your answers with a partner.

1 What kind of news do you like to read?

2 Where do you get your news?

3 How do you decide whether you can trust a news source?

3 VOCABULARY Read the sentences. Choose the best synonym for each word in bold.

deceive	discover	fair	pass from
observe	funny	prove	person to
reference	reliable	remove	person

1 I love **humorous** stories. They make me laugh. _____

2 I **monitor** the weather forecasts. I like to be prepared. _____

3 I think news organizations should be **neutral**. I like to form my own opinions. _____

4 Basically I think social media is a **trustworthy source** of information. I believe most of it. _____

5 I can usually **detect** fake news stories. There are often clues. _____

6 Most news organizations **misinform** their readers. You can't believe anything they say. _____

7 I wish my newsfeed would **exclude** all stories about celebrities. I don't find them interesting. _____

8 I try not to **circulate** rumors. They may not be true, and telling other people isn't helpful. _____

9 When I read something online, I try to **verify** that it's accurate. Some information is obviously wrong. _____

ȶ⁺ Oxford 5000™

4 BUILD Which of the statements in Exercise 3 are true for you? Discuss your ideas with a partner.

5 USE Complete the paragraphs with the correct form of the bold words from Exercise 3.

What is news? Traditional news has always included information about recent events judged to be interesting, important, or unusual enough to be newsworthy, which are then published in media ranging from newspapers to blogs. Although news emphasizes that which is new and surprising, much of it follows a cycle and is predictable. Whether it is concerned with producing hard news or soft news, journalism depends on sourcing and ¹_____ facts and providing the sources of information. In most news organizations, news may be required to be ²_____ rather than to show preferences. Even in those newsrooms that sometimes pursue their organization's media agenda, most items of news are typically reported with balance, giving both sides of any story and separating fact from opinion. The more ³_____ or reliable media show this balance, and they never ⁴_____ their audience.

Only a tiny proportion of events happening in the world every day becomes news. Only a few of the events that journalists ⁵_____ make the news. To help them decide which ones to select, journalists include or ⁶_____ news items according to criteria that are known as *news values*. News might be general in orientation (as in a major newspaper), more narrowly focused, or aimed at a special-interest audience (as in trade rags, music magazines, and even on ⁷_____ websites designed to make light of the news).

—adapted from *A Dictionary of Journalism* by Tony Harcup

6 IDENTIFY Read the article on the next page. Choose the best main idea.

____ Fake news is an advertising tool.

____ Fake news deceives many readers.

____ Fake news has been made possible because of the Internet.

7 ASSESS Read the article again. Identify the true statements.

1 College students are much better at detecting fake news than younger students are.

2 Social media allows information to be spread very quickly.

3 More fake news gets produced because readers pay for it.

4 Fake news can actually create real problems.

5 Humorous stories are often remembered better than serious stories.

6 Unlike fake news, most real stories are neutral.

7 Unfortunately, fake news websites look just like real news sites.

8 Technology may be able to help readers filter out fake news.

Fake News

Just how gullible is the public when it comes to fake news? How much made-up news will people find credible? Recent research suggests that a small percentage of people will believe just about anything they read, but the majority are more selective. More disturbingly, some study results show students from middle school through college may be <u>particularly</u> bad at detecting fake news.

Fake news is the deliberate attempt to misinform. For a long time, less reliable sources of news have provided accounts of two-headed babies, alien spacecraft, and strange creatures that attack farm animals. However, in the last few years, more believable, but <u>still</u> false, stories have appeared on both social media platforms and in traditional media. These reports range from stories about a successful head transplant to an Ebola quarantine in Texas to chariot wheels at the bottom of the Red Sea to a prehistoric shark in Pakistan.

Many of these fake stories owe their spread to social media. In one survey, 62 percent of the respondents said they get news from social media, and the Internet makes it easy to distribute the news more <u>widely</u>. Like an infection, a false story can pass from one reader to the next; with a few clicks here and there, the contagion <u>rapidly</u> multiplies. In the past, people read newspapers or watched television and through word of mouth relayed the news to a few other people. Now, each reader can circulate to thousands more. That is why such content is called *viral*—because it acts like a virus. The virus may be more like a deadly flu than like a cold, however. In 2017, a man threatened people in a pizza parlor in Washington, DC, because of an online story. Perhaps not surprisingly, when researchers looked at how fake news compared to real news on social media, fake news stories got more engagement, meaning more people read and shared them.

The sources of fake news are varied. Some people generate stories for political reasons, others as a joke, still others for financial gain. When people click and share fake news stories, advertisers make money. These advertisers pay the websites that produce such viral stories.

Teenagers in the poor town of Veles, Macedonia, have little opportunity for regular employment. Now they can make a good income creating websites with stories for readers in countries far away. Trending stories are successful in something known as the "attention economy." <u>Basically</u>, if people pay attention to a topic, through clicks and shares, more content on that topic will be commissioned and produced.

People usually share these stories because they think they are real. In a Stanford University study, students at all levels failed to detect false news. College students hardly ever tried to verify the facts in the story or find out if the source was trustworthy. Eighty percent of middle school students thought an advertisement was news, and 30 percent of high school students thought a fake news account was more trustworthy than the real news story. And it's not just students who are fooled—another study found that 75 percent of American readers thought that fake news headlines were accurate. Even when the story is not meant to deceive, such as satire, it is often misunderstood. Unfortunately, being humorous makes something easier to recall, even if the specific facts are <u>highly</u> unlikely.

How can we avoid the trap of false news? Now, more than ever, people need to be savvy consumers and read articles critically. Real news stories are often neutral and avoid expressing opinions. They refer to information from multiple reliable sources. They use quotes and precise numbers. Their facts can be verified. Readers can also pay attention to the website when reading online. Sites ending in *.lo, .com., or .co,* or that use odd names should be regarded with suspicion. The use of ALL CAPS, unusual grammar, or bad web design can also be warning signs.

Just as technology has made the abundance of fake news possible, it may also be coming to our aid. Computer algorithms can find and exclude 86 percent of satirical posts. Such humorous pieces often use <u>excessively</u> long sentences and random juxtapositions of people, events, and places, which the software detects. Another project monitors news articles for their sentiment and tone. But until technology can do the job well, readers will just have to work hard to find the truth.

@ ▶ READING SKILL Identifying and understanding analogy

Writers often use analogies, or comparisons, to explain or clarify ideas. Analogies are often used to explain complex concepts by likening them to something familiar. They can also be used to strengthen an argument. Analogies are sometimes more extended than metaphors and similes. When you read an analogy, identify the two things being compared. Then think about the familiar idea: What are its characteristics? How does it function? Is there a process it follows?

Like an infection, a false story can pass from one reader to the next.

What two things are being compared? (an infection and a false story)

What is an infection? (a sickness caused by something outside the body)

What is the process? (an infection spreads, worsens)

8 INTEGRATE Reread paragraph 3. What does the use of analogy tell you about fake news? Check the statements.

1 ___ A false story can multiply quickly online.

2 ___ False stories are spread mostly by mouth.

3 ___ Fake news stories are spread from person to person.

4 ___ Some stories may be a bother, but others are actually dangerous.

9 EXPAND Read the analogies. What do they tell you about media or news? Discuss your ideas with a partner.

1 Being on social media is like being in a beehive.

2 The news spread like a wildfire.

3 Good news consumers are detectives.

4 Social media networks keep us in our own bubbles.

5 For a news story to be credible, the reader has to be able to follow the breadcrumbs back to the sources.

 GRAMMAR IN CONTEXT Adverbs

Adverbs can have different positions in the sentence. As a general rule, single-word adverbs generally go in the middle of a clause, and longer adverbial phrases generally go at the beginning or at the end.

*People are **usually** sharing these stories because they think they are real.*

Adverbs of degree generally go immediately before the word they modify.

***Unfortunately**, being humorous makes something easier to recall, even if the specific facts are highly unlikely.*

Adverbs of manner generally go after the verb they modify and the object.

*The Internet makes it easy to distribute the news more **widely**.*

Adverbs that comment on the whole sentence or clause usually go before but can sometimes go after the sentence or clause.

***Basically**, if people pay attention to a topic through clicks and shares, more content on that topic will be commissioned and produced.*

Certain adverbs often form collocations with certain verbs or adjectives (*fatally injured, deeply regret, apologize profusely, highly motivated*).

*Their facts can be verified and their sources are **perfectly clear**.*

Some adverbs have two spelling forms, with and without the *-ly* ending. These adverbs have different meanings and can be easily confused.

*College students **hardly** ever tried to verify the facts in the story or find out if the source was trustworthy.*
*Until technology can do the job well, readers will just have to work **hard** to find the truth.*

See Grammar focus on page 168.

10 IDENTIFY Decide where the adverb should go in each sentence below.

1 I looked at social media last week. (*hardly*)

2 She avoids social media. (*generally*)

3 We worked on the website but had some problems with implementation. (*hard*)

4 News organizations are motivated to increase traffic (the number of users) to their websites. (*highly*)

5 If someone is injured in an accident, it may be on the local news. (*fatally*)

6 People don't always recognize fake news. (*unfortunately*)

11 ASSESS What kind of adverb is it? Write *Frequency, Degree, Manner,* or *Attitude* for each adverb in Exercise 10.

12 INTEGRATE Put the words and phrases in the correct order to make sentences with adverbs.

1 gave / the article / regarding sources / perfectly clear / guidelines

2 should / sources / basically / by name / you / always / cite

3 totally / on social media / articles / some / are misleading

4 stories / widely / some ridiculous / believed / are

5 moved / all / hardly / the reporters / afternoon

6 some / very / spread / quickly / stories

7 that / extremely / unreliable / is / website

8 the / journalists / best / highly motivated / are written / stories / by

13 🔊 **ASSESS** Listen and check your answers to Exercise 12.

A technology conference is recorded and streamed live from Boston, United States.

10.3 Then It Burst into Flames

1 ACTIVATE Look at the headlines. Match each definition to one of the underlined words in the headlines.

1 to frighten _____
2 to make an agreement by discussion _____
3 to earnestly persuade someone to do something _____
4 to criticize _____
5 to take a hold of suddenly and forcefully _____
6 to appear as a vague form, especially one that is large or threatening _____
7 to run away from a place or situation of danger _____
8 to work in an organized way toward a goal _____

2 BUILD Complete each sentence with a word from Exercise 1.

1 The police _____ the stolen electronics in the raid on the warehouse.
2 I plan to _____ for better local government.
3 As graduation _____, we need to start looking for jobs.
4 My boss always _____ my ideas but compliments Kevin on his.
5 The wildfire forced hundreds to _____ their homes.
6 My parents _____ me to go to college.
7 Employees can _____ for better pay and benefits.
8 Do bad weather reports sometimes _____ you?

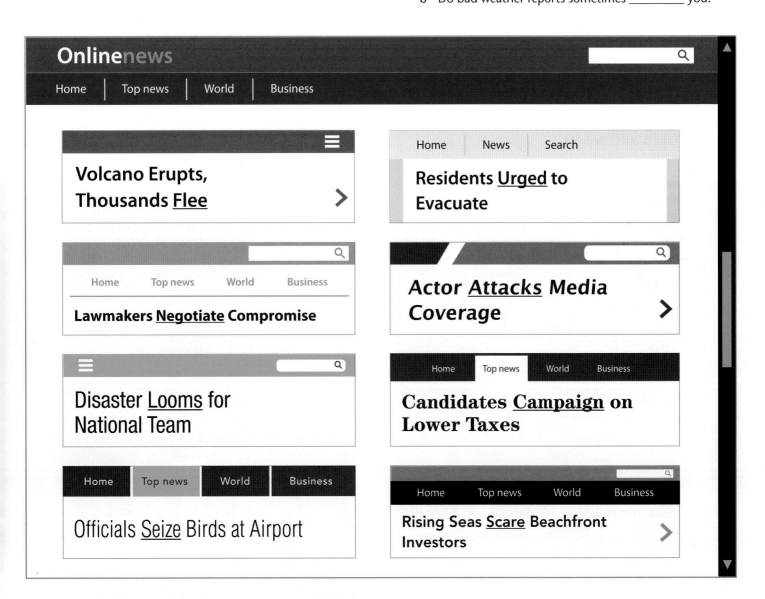

117

3 WHAT'S YOUR ANGLE? Answer the questions. Then discuss your answers with a partner.

1 How do you attack a problem? Do you criticize the source or focus on solutions?

2 What qualities do people need when they negotiate?

3 Are you a careful planner or do you seize opportunities quickly?

4 Have you ever campaigned for a cause, for example, to protect the environment? What was the cause?

5 What kind of news scares you the most?

4 🔊 **IDENTIFY** Listen to the news report. Choose the best headline. Discuss with a partner.

___ Oil Truck Overturns, Closes Highway

___ Driver Injured When Truck Overturns

___ Careless Driver Flees Scene of Accident

5 🔊 **ASSESS** Answer the questions. Compare answers with a partner. Listen again if needed.

1 Who was the driver of the truck?

2 What happened?

3 Where did it happen?

4 When did it happen?

5 Why did it happen?

6 How did it affect people?

6 INTEGRATE Identify the true statements. Rewrite the false statements to make them true.

1 The truck was carrying oil.

2 Traffic backed up for 14 miles.

3 Someone was fatally injured.

4 It wasn't the truck driver's fault.

5 The highway was cleared and reopened quickly.

6 Miguel Garcia was the driver of the Toyota.

> ### GRAMMAR IN CONTEXT Discourse markers
>
> Discourse markers help us organize and connect what we say so that it is easier for our readers to follow and participate. We use discourse markers to help us link ideas together, show our attitude to what we are saying, or indicate what we're going to say next.
>
> Link ideas—*because of*:
>
> *According to witnesses, Hodge lost control of his truck because of another driver's erratic driving.*
>
> Show attitude—*fortunately*:
>
> *Fortunately, no one besides the truck driver was injured.*
>
> Contrast—*however*:
>
> *However, some of the stranded motorists did not share this rosy view.*
>
> Order—*finally*:
>
> *Finally, at 7 p.m., the road reopened.*

See Grammar focus page 168.

7 IDENTIFY Read the sentences. What is the relationship between the ideas as signaled by the discourse marker?

1 The two sides signed a peace treaty. <u>However</u>, the peace did not last long.
    a contrast   b reason   c order
2 The workers were trapped in the mine for two months. <u>Finally</u>, on May 12, they were rescued.
    a contrast   b purpose   c order
3 <u>In order</u> to shelter all the people fleeing the situation, the organization is seeking $12 million in donations.
    a purpose   b reason   c similarity
4 Government spending is expected to increase. <u>Likewise</u>, taxes will rise.
    a result   b contrast   c similarity
5 Warmer temperatures are changing animal habitats. <u>Consequently</u>, some species are struggling to survive.
    a purpose   b result   c reason

8 ASSESS Match the sentences.

1 Ten people went to the hospital with injuries. ___
2 The driver tried to avoid hitting the other car. ___
3 The cleanup was a long process. ___
4 The police sent out a description of the missing driver. ___
5 They arrested her briefly. ___

a However, he couldn't turn in time and they collided.
b As a result, she was located a mile away.
c Naturally, she was upset.
d Fortunately, no one was seriously injured.
e Finally, the road reopened and traffic flowed again.

WRITING SKILL Using discourse markers

Use discourse markers to help your readers follow your ideas and understand your point of view. Remember to signal relationships such as contrast, similarity, reason, purpose, result, and order. Writers use discourse markers to make connections between sentences and between paragraphs in longer text. Even difficult or lengthy text can be made more comprehensible with discourse markers.

---

9 EXPAND Complete the sentences with your own ideas. Discuss with a partner.

1 Our community has a traffic problem. Unfortunately,…
2 Crime has been rising lately. However,…
3 The last few years have been the warmest on record. Consequently,…
4 Some positive things have happened recently. First,…
5 My neighborhood is not perfect. To be honest,…

10 WHAT'S YOUR ANGLE? Answer the questions. Discuss your ideas with a partner.

1 What newsworthy events have happened recently in your community?
2 Why do you think they are newsworthy?
3 Which is the most interesting to you? Why?

11 PREPARE Choose one of the events from Exercise 10. Then answer the following questions.

1 What happened?

_____

2 Who was involved?

_____

3 Where did it happen?

_____

4 When did it happen?

_____

5 Why did it happen?

_____

6 How did it affect people?

_____

12 WRITE Write a news report about the event. Use your answers to Exercise 11 and the news report in Exercise 4 as models.

13 IMPROVE Read your news report. Check that it follows these guidelines.

☐ Is it newsworthy? Will it interest the reader?
☐ Does it provide this information: who, what, when, where, why, how?
☐ Does it use discourse markers to help readers follow the connections between ideas?
☐ Does it use verbs that tell the reader what happened?

14 SHARE Exchange news reports with a partner. Check each other's work with respect to the guidelines in Exercise 13.

15 IMPROVE Rewrite the news report to incorporate your partner's feedback.

10.4 I'm Not Really Sure

1 ACTIVATE Which of the following would you feel comfortable talking about with someone you're not very close to?

- You won the prize for the contest you both entered.
- You got a promotion at work that you both wanted.
- Only you got accepted to the university you both applied to.
- You both submitted ideas for a project, and only yours was accepted.

2 ▶ IDENTIFY Watch the video and find out what happened.

1 What did Cathy tell Sam?   2 What was the reason?   3 What did Cathy tell Andy?

3 ASSESS Do you ever avoid talking about certain things because you don't want to make someone feel bad? Why or why not?

REAL-WORLD ENGLISH Evading

People usually evade answering delicate questions because they want to avoid embarrassment to themselves or the listener.

When evading a question, you can stall or offer a soft denial.

A: Amir just told me I didn't get the promotion. I saw you talking to him, too. What did you talk about?

B: Um…nothing. It wasn't important.

If you are confronted, it's best to answer gently and honestly so that you are not perceived as misleading.

A: I bet he offered you the promotion, didn't he?

B: Uh…well…actually…yes, he did.

Ask a question in return to redirect the focus.

B: Now that this is over, are you going to take some time off from work?

A: I'm really not sure what I'm going to do next.

Offer reassurance by giving a compliment.

B: Hey, you always come up with creative ideas. Just because this didn't happen for you now, doesn't mean they won't take notice down the line.

Using a transitioning device will signal the end of the conversation.

B: Oh wow, it's almost lunchtime. Why don't we check out that new restaurant together?

When evading questions, move through these tactics with mindfulness.

4 ▶ **IDENTIFY** Watch the video again. What question is Andy evading and why?

5 **ANALYZE** Work with a partner. Decide which tactics (a–e) Andy uses when evading Jenna's question.

a   Confronted so answering gently and honestly
b   Transitioning to signal the end of the conversation
c   Offer reassurance by giving a compliment
d   Redirect focus by asking a question
e   Stalling/offering soft denial

Sam: What about your meeting with Cathy?

___ 1   Andy: Well…nothing really.
        Jenna: I think she offered you the paid internship position!

___ 2   Andy: Um, actually…Yes, she did.
        Jenna: Wow! I knew she might do that today.
        Sam: Congratulations, Andy! You deserve it!

___ 3   Andy: Thanks, Sam. I really appreciate that. Are you going to stay on here?
        Sam: I'm not really sure. Maybe I'm not meant to be a lawyer.

___ 4   Jenna: Don't give up! You might be disappointed now…but anything can happen!

___ 5   Andy: Hey…it's nice outside and I think we're all due for a break. Coffee is on me.

6 **EXPAND** In which part of the conversation in Exercise 5 do you think Andy could have offered Sam reassurance with a compliment?

7 **BUILD** Your supervisor and your co-worker have known each other for a few years and hang out together after work often. You have only worked at this office for less than a year, and you are not very close with either of them. Also, your co-worker feels like you are vying for the same promotion he or she is. One day, your supervisor invites you out to lunch while your co-worker isn't around. You accept. Later, your co-worker sees you get off the elevator with your supervisor. You are both carrying identical take-out containers. You don't want your co-worker to feel left out, so how would you evade the topic if he or she asks you a question?

Co-worker: Hey, I saw you two get off the elevator together?
You: (Stall) _____

Co-worker: Really? It looks like you got lunch together.
You: (Answer the question honestly and gently)

_____

Co-worker: Oh, well that sounds nice.
You: (redirect the focus) _____

_____

Co-worker: Not yet. I really love that restaurant though.
You: (offer reassurance) _____

_____

Co-worker: Yeah, you're probably right.
You: (transition to end the conversation) _____

_____

8 **INTERACT** With a partner, role-play the following situations.

1   You went to the party of the season hosted by someone you both know. Only one of you was invited.
2   You both applied to be paid teaching assistants for your favorite professor. Only one of you was selected.
3   Someone you know well has an extra ticket to the biggest sporting event of the year. Only one of you got it.

GO ONLINE
to create your own version
of the English For Real video.

10.5 I'm Sorry to Say

1 ACTIVATE Look at the photos. Answer the questions. Discuss with a partner.

1 What kind of news do people give and receive in these situations?

2 How do the roles of the people affect the way they give news?

 2 WHAT'S YOUR ANGLE? Have you received news in the kinds of situations from Exercise 1? What was it? Discuss with a partner.

3 IDENTIFY Listen to a conversation between Ellen and Marie. They talk about good and bad news. Answer the questions.

1 What is the relationship between Marie and Ellen?

2 How do you know?

3 What is Ellen's good news?

4 What bad news does Marie deliver?

5 Does Marie do a good job of giving the news? Why or why not?

4 ASSESS Listen to the conversation again. What examples do you hear of responses to good and bad news?

_____

_____

_____

_____

_____

_____

SPEAKING
Expressing certainty, probability, and doubt

Use these expressions to convey degrees of certainty.

When you think something is probable:

It's likely that…
It's probable that…

When you think something is possible:

There's a remote / slight / definite / distinct possibility (or chance) that…
I suppose that…

When you doubt something or think it unlikely:

It's unlikely that…
I doubt that…
There's some doubt that…
I have my doubts that…

When you have limited knowledge:

As far as I know…
To the best of my knowledge…

5 PREPARE Listen to the excerpts and write the expressions of certainty, probability, and doubt you hear.

PRONUNCIATION SKILL Hesitating with hedging

Speakers often hesitate when they use hedging. Hesitation gives the speaker time to think about how to soften language, and it also signals to the listener that the speaker may use hedging. The speaker may pause or use fillers, such as *uh, you know, basically, actually,* and *what I'm trying to say is.*

When we say these words or phrases, we may draw the vowel sound out for longer than normal, and we would apply a flat intonation pattern to communicate the fact that our pause does not mark the end of our speech.

Basically, what I'm trying to say is, it looks like your position may be eliminated.

6 NOTICE Listen to the excerpt. Where do you hear a speaker pause? Compare your answers with a partner. Notice the intonation used with the phrases.

7 IDENTIFY Mark the places where you might hesitate with hedging. Work with a partner. Take turns reading the sentences and noticing the pauses.

1 I hate to say this, but you didn't get the promotion.

2 Actually, I can't make it to your party. I'm really sorry.

3 You know, this is hard to say, but I don't want to work with you on the project.

4 What I'm trying to say is that we hired someone else.

5 I hate to have to say this, but, uh, the class was canceled. Basically, there were too many complaints.

8 INTERACT Work with a partner. Brainstorm three situations involving good news and three involving bad news. Choose one to role-play with a partner. Use hedging and expressions of certainty and doubt.

Now go to page 156 for the Unit 10 Review.

11 Communication

How does hierarchy affect communication?

Is a shared language necessary for good communication?

Who is a better communicator: a good talker or a good listener?

BEHIND THE PHOTO

REAL-WORLD GOAL

Learn about body language gestures in an unfamiliar culture.

Work with a partner. Identify four different forms of communication and the benefits and drawbacks of each.

Communication	Benefit	Drawback
Texting	Very fast to send	Easy to make mistakes in texting

11.1 Talking to the Animals

1 ACTIVATE How do species other than humans communicate? Check all that apply. Discuss with a partner.

___ speech   ___ gestures   ___ facial expressions

___ noises   ___ smells   ___ visual cues

___ other: _____

VOCABULARY DEVELOPMENT Phrasal verbs

Phrasal verbs are phrases that consist of a verb and one or more prepositions. Prepositions in phrasal verbs are sometimes called particles because they behave differently from stand-alone prepositions. A phrasal verb has a different meaning from the usual meaning of the verb and preposition.

I can bring up the package when it arrives. (usual meaning of verb and preposition combination)

I can bring up the issue at our staff meeting. (*bring up* is a phrasal verb here, meaning "to introduce a topic for discussion")

---

2 BUILD Read the sentences. Choose the correct meaning for the phrasal verb in bold.

1 The results of the study **bear** that **out**.
   a support or confirm something
   b carry something away

2 Our findings **cast doubt** on the theory that only people can use language.
   a call into question
   b reinforce

3 Everyone **chipped in** with suggestions.
   a broke into pieces
   b contributed

4 We've **narrowed down** our options to just two.
   a reduced
   b made less wide

5 I don't want to see that movie. We can **rule** it **out**.
   a follow guidelines
   b exclude as a possibility

6 Smart phone technology is changing so fast that I can't **keep track of** all the things phones can do.
   a stay fully informed about
   b make a list of

7 Some issues **cut across** political parties.
   a to affect two or more different groups
   b use a sharp instrument

8 The large size of their brains **accounts for** the gorillas' intelligence.
   a provides an explanation for
   b makes a record of

 Oxford 5000™

3 USE Choose the correct phrasal verbs to complete the paragraph.

Language is a universal—it [1] *cuts across / rules out* all cultures and peoples. Linguists believe that our brains are hardwired for language. This may [2] *keep track of / account for* the fact that even people who can't hear will try to communicate their ideas through signs and gestures. However, unless we are exposed to language at a young age, we can't become fluent. Research with children raised in the wild [3] *bears this out / rules this out*. They never learn to speak much at all. And if we don't hear certain sounds as babies, we lose the ability to make those sounds. That's why pronunciation in a foreign language can be so difficult. The wide range of possible sounds [4] *chips in / narrows down* to just those found in our native language during the first two years of life.

4 WHAT'S YOUR ANGLE? Which of the following do you agree with? Discuss your answers with a partner.

1 Humans are the only species capable of language.
2 Only species with large brains can communicate.
3 Humans should try to communicate with other species.
4 We will never figure out how other creatures communicate.

LISTENING SKILL Understanding the use of thinking and reporting verbs

Speakers often use verbs that talk about what they or others are thinking (thinking verbs). They also use verbs that refer to putting thoughts into words, called *reporting verbs*.

Listen for verbs that refer to thinking or perceiving:

think	*remember*	*understand*	*know*
believe	*notice*	*observe*	

Listen for verbs that refer to thoughts that have been communicated to others:

say / tell	*suggest*	*recommend*	*report*
argue	*advise*	*report*	

---

5 IDENTIFY Listen to the sentences. Write the words you hear.

1 I _____ that other creatures communicate in a variety of ways.

2 Researchers _____ that dogs are especially attentive to people.

3 A recent study _____ that elephants signal to each other.

4 Some people _____ exactly, word for word, what they hear.

5 Some people don't _____ the role human activity plays in global warming.

6 I _____ that animals have their own body language.

6 🔊 **ASSESS** Listen to the podcast. Check the main ideas.

☐ 1 Many animals, including dogs and apes, can communicate with humans.

☐ 2 Dogs have adapted to life with humans.

☐ 3 Sign language is easy to learn.

☐ 4 Chimps use gestures and body language to communicate with each other.

☐ 5 Birds like parrots are as smart as chimps.

☐ 6 Animals communicate in different ways.

7 🔊 **EXPAND** Listen again. Complete the sentences.

1 _____ can follow a pointed finger.

2 Because dogs have lived with people for a long time, they _____ what we do and say.

3 One way chimps and gorillas can learn to communicate is through _____.

4 Some species of songbirds _____.

5 _____ leave a glowing trail to communicate with each other.

6 Stink bugs _____ to communicate.

GRAMMAR IN CONTEXT
Verb patterns in reported speech

When we use reporting verbs, we follow several patterns.

1. Reporting verb + (*that*) + clause

say	*report*	*confirm*	*explain*
insist	*suggest*	*claim*	*argue*

Scientists say that they are one of the few species that can follow a pointed finger.

2. Reporting verb + direct object + (*that*) + clause

tell	*assure*	*convince*

Does your research tell us that great apes communicate with each other?

3. Reporting verb + to infinitive

agree	*ask*	*claim*	*offer*
promise	*propose*	*refuse*	

This promises to be an interesting discussion.

4. Reporting verb + direct object + to infinitive

ask	*encourage*	*instruct*	*tell*	*urge*

I'd encourage your listeners to pay attention to other animals.

See Grammar focus page 169.

8 🔊 **INTEGRATE** Put the words in the correct order to make sentences with reporting verbs. Then listen and check your answers.

1 climate control / work / on / the politicians / agreed / to

2 outside of class / encouraged / our teacher / practice / to / us

3 animals / in many ways / communicate / us / tells / recent research / that

4 wild birds / the study / learn / can / that / confirmed / speech

5 to record / offered / the interview / the journalist

9 **APPLY** Choose the correct pattern to complete each sentence.

1 The research assistant asked the chimp *that it use / to use* a sign for "grape."

2 The trainer *claimed that the dog / instructed the dog* could follow complicated commands.

3 The report explained *animals to communicate / that animals communicate* in different ways.

4 This article suggests *that we pay / us to pay* more attention to animals.

10 **WHAT'S YOUR ANGLE?** Look at the photo. Complete the sentences with your ideas. Then discuss your answers with a partner.

1 In the photo the trainer is instructing _____.

2 A good trainer encourages _____.

3 If an animal refuses _____, then _____.

4 This photo convinces _____.

11.2 A Nod Means No?

1 ACTIVATE Look at the illustration. Answer the questions with a partner.

1 When and where do you think this is? Why do you think so?

2 What kind of rules are these people following?

3 How do you think people communicated with each other in the past?

4 What has changed?

2 VOCABULARY Read the sentences. Choose the word that is the most similar in meaning to the bold word.

attack	declare	description	failure
help	honest	look	self-control

1 Being polite will **promote** good relationships with other people. _____

2 The linguistics expert **asserted** that language is universal. _____

3 The coach offered **commentary** on the video of the game. _____

4 We were only in Japan for a couple of days, but it was enough to get a **glimpse** of the culture. _____

5 My sister is very affectionate and outgoing, but I usually show more **restraint**. _____

6 Although both sides hoped to reach an agreement, there was a complete **breakdown** in negotiations. _____

7 **Straightforward** people are often perceived as impolite, but I think that's unfair. _____

8 Staring and growling are signs of **aggression** in dogs. _____

🔲+ Oxford 5000™

3 USE Complete each sentence with the correct bold word from Exercise 2.

1 Americans are often talkative and opinionated in business meetings, whereas the Japanese show more _____.

2 When you _____ something in an essay, you should support it with evidence.

3 Did you read the _____ about the election in the newspaper this morning?

4 I heard about the _____ in the peace talks last week. What went wrong?

5 Although chimpanzees are less violent than humans, there has been a recent increase in _____.

6 Understanding the other people involved can _____ cooperation.

7 My interaction with the taxi driver gave me a _____ into the difficulties of his profession.

8 The email was very _____ and showed exactly how he felt and why.

4 WHAT'S YOUR ANGLE? Read the statements. Which do you agree with? Discuss with a partner.

1 Most cultures use body language and gestures in a similar way.

2 Using the wrong gestures can cause more communication breakdowns than not knowing the language.

3 Nonverbal communication patterns remain stable over time.

4 It's more important to be straightforward than to show restraint.

5 Books written in another time can give us a glimpse of the society at that period in history.

5 ASSESS Read the blog post. Which sentences in Exercise 4 would the writer of the blog post agree with?

6 IDENTIFY Reread the blog post. Choose the true statements. Then rewrite the false statements to make them true.

1 *Cassell's Household Guide* describes society in the United States during World War II.

2 In parts of Bulgaria, Turkey, and Greece, nodding the head means no.

3 Looking someone in the eye signals you are being straightforward in Asian and African cultures.

4 People in the United States stand closer together than people in Latin America.

5 If a Japanese person smiles, it may mean "I don't understand."

6 In Victorian England, a strong handshake was considered polite.

Getting Along Today

Body Language and Gestures

In the age of globalization, communicating effectively is more important than ever. And much of this communication is nonverbal. Even if you don't speak the language, understanding body language and gestures will promote better relationships. While some nonverbal communication seems to be universal, it's important to keep a couple of things in mind.

Nonverbal Cues Can Change Over Time

In Victorian England, people in polite society observed strict rules. These were described in *Cassell's Household Guide*, which offered commentary on a wide range of topics, from the care of animals to the use of tools to the proper dress for children.

The guide asserted that, when going into the city, ladies should look in the opposite direction from someone approaching. This practice of avoiding someone's gaze "is not to be confused with cutting, the most ill-mannered act possible to commit in society. A person can only be cut by coolly staring him in the face without any sign of recognition." Today, most people give a quick glimpse of recognition when about ten feet away from someone approaching and then look away.

In addition, *Cassell's* recommended that gentlemen raise their hats as a form of greeting, usually with the hand farthest from the acquaintance. Nowadays, men rarely wear hats unless it's cold outside, and they almost never raise them in greeting.

And at Victorian-era concerts, the guide insisted that ladies not be too demonstrative. They could show their appreciation for the music only through "the rustling of programmes and tapping of fans." In contrast, today's concert goers show much less restraint, engaging in vigorous clapping and even calling out.

Body Language and Gestures Are Culturally Determined.

In most countries, nodding the head up and down means yes. But this isn't always true. In parts of Bulgaria, Turkey, and Greece, nodding indicates no. In other parts of Turkey and the Middle East, "tutting" means no, but the same noise communicates disgust in other regions of the world. If you interact with people from other cultures, you need to be aware of the body language they use, or you could have a complete breakdown in communication.

Eye contact: In Arab cultures, Spain, and Greece, looking someone in the eye signals that you are straightforward. In some Asian and African cultures, it shows respect when you avoid eye contact.

Proximity: In the U.S., people usually stand two to three feet away from someone in conversation. In Latin American cultures, people may stand closer together and occasionally touch each other as they talk.

Facial expressions: Although most people interpret a smile positively, it doesn't always mean someone is happy. For example, in Japan, a smile may mean yes or even "I don't understand."

Handshakes: In Victorian England, people often greeted each other with a slight bow or curtsy. A handshake was really just a "gentle pressure and very slight movement of the wrist." In many cultures, people still greet this way. In some East Asian cultures a bow is preferred; whereas in Middle Eastern cultures, people prefer a soft handshake. A strong handshake can be seen as a sign of aggression.

Even within cultures, body language can reveal status or background. Cultures are not monolithic. People from the same country may use different nonverbal cues and gestures.

Wealthy people may seem less engaged. In a study conducted by researchers at the University of California, Berkeley, people from a higher socioeconomic status were more likely to fidget and be less engaged than people from a less-privileged background. Those with lower socioeconomic status were more likely to nod, smile, and maintain eye contact.

Ethnic origin still influences behavior. In one of the early studies of body language, Paul Ekman observed that New Yorkers with an Italian background used bigger gestures than Jewish New Yorkers. This shouldn't be surprising, as Italians in Italy use more than 250 gestures.

The Takeaway?

If you're doing business with someone from another culture, I suggest that you should do research first.

Pay attention to others. They may know more than you do.

READING SKILL Reading from the perspective of a historical or cultural context

Reading involves an interaction between the reader and the text. Every text is written within a historical and cultural context, and readers bring their own historical and cultural contexts with them when they engage with the text. The meaning of a text is constructed by history, politics, and culture. As you read, ask yourself questions:

What are the writer's intentions?

What is the historical background?

What sociocultural context is the writer coming from?

What texts is the writer familiar with?

7 IDENTIFY Read the quotes below. Guess or look up which speaker said each quote. Use historical and cultural cues. Discuss and check your answers with a partner.

1 It is wise to apply the oil of refined politeness to the mechanism of friendship. ___

2 An insolent reply from a polite person is a bad sign. ___

3 Promises and pie crust are made to be broken. ___

4 Man alone amongst the animals speaks and has gestures and expressions, which we call rational, because he alone has reason in him. ___

5 By nature men are alike. Through practice they have become far apart. ___

6 Good breeding consists in concealing how much we think of ourselves and how little we think of the other person. ___

a Confucius, Chinese philosopher

b Mark Twain, 1835–1910, American writer and humorist

c Hippocrates, 460–367 BCE, Greek physician

d Colette, 1873–1954, French novelist

e Jonathan Swift, 1667–1745, Irish poet and satirist

f Dante Alighieri, 1265–1321, Italian poet, philosopher and political thinker

8 APPLY Reread the section in the blog post called *Nonverbal Cues Can Change Over Time*. With a group, discuss the following questions.

1 How has the role of women in British society changed over the last 150 years?

2 What can you tell about British fashion in the Victorian era? How did fashion reflect cultural norms?

3 What did people value in Victorian England? How do you know? What was going on historically?

> **GRAMMAR IN CONTEXT Subjunctive and *should***
>
> The present subjunctive is used in reported speech to talk about a demand or proposal in the present or past.
>
> The subjunctive uses the base form of the verb (*she go, we be*, etc.) and is quite formal.
>
> verb + (*that*) + object + subjunctive with: *ask, demand, insist, recommend, request, suggest*
>
> Cassell's *recommended that gentlemen raise their hats as a form of greeting.*
> Cassell's *requested a lady be polite with older people.*
>
> Note that *do* is not used in the negative.
>
> *The guide insisted that ladies not be too demonstrative.*
>
> Note that *should* + infinitive is less formal than the subjunctive and more commonly used. There is little or no difference in meaning.
>
> *I suggest that you should do research first.*

See Grammar focus page 169.

9 IDENTIFY Complete each sentence with the correct form of a verb from the box. You may need to use a negative.

applaud	be	eat	order	take

1 The group facilitator asked that we all _____ respectful of each other.

2 I had to insist that he _____ first. After all, he arrived at the restaurant before I did.

3 The doctor recommended that I _____ red meat. Too much is bad for my health.

4 Her supervisor suggested that she _____ a management course.

5 The announcer requested that we _____ until everyone had received their awards. Clapping for each person slows the program down.

10 🔊 **ASSESS** Listen and check your answers to Exercise 9.

11 INTEGRATE Decide if the sentences are grammatically correct (C) or incorrect (I). Rewrite the incorrect sentences with the correct form.

1 The royal court demanded that all subjects knelt before the king or queen.

2 His host requested that he removes his shoes upon entering the house.

3 Is it too much to ask that you be on time?

4 I suggest that you not ask too many questions.

5 It is recommended that guests should bring a hostess gift.

12 EXPAND Look at the illustration on page 126 again. What recommendations or suggestions would a writer in Victorian England make? Discuss your ideas with a partner.

13 WHAT'S YOUR ANGLE? Complete the sentences with your own ideas. Then discuss with a partner.

1 In my interactions with people, I insist that _____.

2 I don't like it when others demand _____.

3 My parents always asked _____.

4 When someone requests that _____, it makes me uncomfortable.

5 When you travel to my country, I suggest that _____.

11.3 Context Is Everything

1 ACTIVATE Work with a partner. Discuss the best way to communicate in the situations below: text, call, email, face-to-face, or other. Support with reasons.

1 Arrange a meeting
2 Apologize for a mistake
3 Ask a big favor
4 Report to co-workers on sales figures
5 Say you'll be late

🔊 PRONUNCIATION SKILL Elision

Elision is the omission of one or more vowels, consonants, or syllables. We do this frequently to connect many words in English. This helps speakers sound fluent and not choppy. For example, speakers frequently elide the /t/ and /d/ sounds in past tense reporting verbs when they are followed by *that*. Listeners will not hear the /t/ or /d/ sound before the /ð/ sound of *that*.

Sam thought that the other driver was insulting him.
Whether you text or email, experts recommend that you follow up to make sure your message was understood correctly.

---

2 IDENTIFY Read the sentences. Predict where elision will occur.

1 One expert said that teenagers need to learn interpersonal skills.
2 The article asserted that body language and gestures provide context.
3 I suggested that you should show respect for other people.
4 Who recommended that we read the article first?
5 The study reported that six billion text messages are sent every day.

3 🔊 ASSESS Listen and check your answers to Exercise 2. Then listen again and repeat.

4 IDENTIFY Read the problem–solution essay. Find the thesis statement, which is the sentence that tells what the essay is going to be about.

| Home | About | | Search 🔍 | ▲ |

Taken Out of Context

Have you heard the anecdote about the two drivers? The first driver, Sam, was approaching the top of a hill. Suddenly, another car hurtled over the top of the hill coming from the other direction. The second car was swerving all over the road and almost struck Sam's car. The narrow escape had Sam's heart racing. He looked over as the second driver yelled, "Donkey!" Sam thought that the other driver was insulting him. Still shaken and puzzled by the driver's anger, he continued up and over the hill more slowly. As he started down the other side, there, in the middle of the road, stood a donkey. The lesson? Context in communication is everything. Modern communication often lacks such context, which creates problems we need to solve.

Technology promotes rapid communication and the exchange of ideas, but it also can remove necessary context. This lack of context is particularly noticeable in texting. When people engage in face-to-face interaction, they have much more than words to go on. They use body language, gestures, and facial expressions, as well as intonation, to convey information. Even phone conversations provide auditory cues that help us decipher the other person's message.

However, many people today conduct a lot of their "conversations" through texts. According to a recent survey, more than two-thirds of people aged 18–29 reported that they'd sent and received text messages a lot the previous day. About half of the survey participants said that they talked on a cell phone a lot or used email. The problem is that without context misunderstandings happen. For example, the response *no way* could mean either "I don't believe you" or "I refuse." In addition, many researchers report that texting prevents young people from learning essential interpersonal skills. It's easier to do something difficult, such as apologizing or refusing an invitation, through a text. However, dealing with difficult interpersonal situations helps develop empathy.

Although texting is useful, convenient, and nearly impossible to avoid, there are ways to combat its negative effects. First, you can provide context. Many people use emoji to convey the texter's emotions and attitude to provide missing visual cues. You can also expand on the message in your text. Shorter is not always better. Whether you text or email, experts recommend that you follow up to make sure your message was understood correctly.

Second, you can improve your interpersonal skills overall. If you practice empathy, for example, by imagining how the person on the other end of your text or email feels, you will be a better communicator. Careful use of language shows respect for the other person, so psychologists suggest you reread your texts or emails before hitting *send*.

Technology has transformed our lives in many ways, including how we communicate. As technology allows us to send messages more easily and rapidly, it may strip away some of the context that enables effective communication. We may perceive an insult where none was intended or miss an important warning. Providing more context and practicing interpersonal skills, including empathy, clarification, and the careful expression of ideas, can minimize negative effects.

5 INTEGRATE Complete the outline with information from the essay.

I. Introduction

Hook: (Something that grabs your reader's attention in the introduction)

___ quote   ___ rhetorical question

___ anecdote   ___ interesting fact

___ simile or metaphor

Thesis: _____

II. Body Paragraph 1

Topic sentence: _____

Problem 1: Lack of context can cause

_____

III. Body Paragraph 2

Problem 2: Young people don't learn

_____

IV. Body Paragraphs 3 & 4

Topic sentence: _____

A. Solution 1: _____

B. Solution 2: _____

V. Conclusion (check all that are present)

___ restatement of thesis   ___ summary of main points

___ tie back to intro

6 EXPAND Answer the questions with a partner.

1 Why does the writer begin the essay with the anecdote about Sam?

2 How is the information we get different in these three communication situations: texting, phone calls, face-to-face interactions?

3 What kind of information does the writer include to describe the problem? Why?

4 What details does the writer use to support the proposed solutions?

WRITING SKILL Using appropriate register

Register refers to the variety of language in a particular setting and/or for a specific purpose. In writing, we usually use one of three registers.

Familiar: used with family or friends, often spelling and grammar are not important

No way!

Informal: conversational in tone, usually uses correct grammar but may use colloquial language

He looked over as the second driver yelled, "Donkey!"

Formal: more academic, grammatically correct, higher-level vocabulary

Providing more context and practicing interpersonal skills, including empathy, clarification, and the careful expression, of ideas can minimize negative effects.

---

7 IDENTIFY Read the sentences. Choose the most appropriate setting to use the sentence in.

1 "Can't make it. Sorry!"

   a text

   b email to co-worker

   c academic paper

2 "Research indicates that teenagers and young adults are the early adopters of new technology."

   a text

   b email to co-worker

   c academic paper

3 "We're behind schedule this month and will need to make up time."

   a text

   b email to co-worker

   c academic paper

4 "Not only did subjects in the control group perform more poorly on indicators of empathy, but they also retained less information.

   a text

   b email to co-worker

   c academic paper

5 "Don't know. Can u?"

   a text

   b email to co-worker

   c academic paper

8 ASSESS Think about appropriate register, and choose the correct words to complete the email.

> Hi Manny,
> I just wanted to ¹ *let you know / provide the information* that our first meeting on Monday has been rescheduled. It ² *transpires / turns out* that Jack Saunders had a previous commitment ³ *of which his assistant was unaware / that his assistant didn't know about*. We still have our lunch with the sales ⁴ *delegation / team* at noon and will ⁵ *convene / meet* with Jack at three. That will ⁶ *leave us some time / afford us the opportunity* to strategize our approach with Jack.
> –Jordyn

9 WHAT'S YOUR ANGLE? Work in a group. Which of the following do you consider problems? Explain your position and suggest possible solutions.

1 Texting's impact on grammar and spelling

2 The effect of smart phones on family and social life

3 The effect of social media on self-esteem

4 The possibility of hacking

10 **PREPARE** Choose one of the topics in Exercise 9 or your own idea. Create an outline.

I. Introduction

Hook: (check what you will use)

___ quote   ___ rhetorical question

___ anecdote   ___ interesting fact

___ simile or metaphor

Thesis:_____

II. Body Paragraph 1

Topic sentence: _____

A. Problem 1: _____

B. Problem 2: _____

III. Body Paragraph 2

Topic sentence: _____

A. Solution 1: _____

B. Solution 2: _____

IV. Conclusion (include all)

___ restatement of thesis   ___ summary of main points

___ tie back to intro

11 **WRITE** Write an essay about a problem in modern communication, and propose solutions. Use your outline in Exercise 10 and the essay in Exercise 4 as models.

12 **DEVELOP** Read your essay. Does it follow these guidelines?

☐ Is there a thesis?

☐ Does it grab the reader's attention in the introduction?

☐ Does it describe one or more problems related to modern communication?

☐ Does it propose one or more solutions to each problem?

☐ Does the conclusion restate the thesis and summarize the main points?

☐ Does it use appropriate register?

13 **SHARE** Exchange essays with a partner. Check each other's work with respect to the guidelines in Exercise 12.

14 **IMPROVE** Rewrite your essay to incorporate feedback.

Teenagers in Swaziland

11.4 All Clear

1 ACTIVATE If you have a disagreement with someone you know well that ends on a bad note, do you let it go, or do you try to resolve it? What about with someone you aren't that close to?

2 ▶ IDENTIFY Watch the video, and find out what happened.

1 Did Kevin and Max end their first conversation on a high note?

2 Does Max have his discussion with Kevin in front of Andy at their apartment?

3 Was it only Kevin who had the misunderstanding?

3 ASSESS Discuss your answers to the following questions with a partner.

1 What was the problem between Kevin and Max?

2 Why do you think Kevin felt he needed to talk to Max?

3 Would it have been better for Max and Kevin to have their discussion in front of Andy?

REAL-WORLD ENGLISH Clearing up a misunderstanding

Knowing *when* to clear up a misunderstanding is just as important as knowing *how*. First, think about the nature of the disagreement, and consider whether you need to have a conversation to clear the air. If you decide that such a conversation is useful, **ask to speak to the person in private and begin by apologizing for the miscommunication.**

I'm sorry about the other day when we were talking about selfies and selfie sticks.

State what you think you did wrong and accept responsibility for any confusion.

What I said came out wrong. When I said I think selfie sticks and people taking selfies are dumb, I didn't mean that I think you're superficial when you take them.

If the other person explains their side of the story, **paraphrase what they've said back to them to show you've understood their feelings and words.**

A: It hurt my feelings because I thought you were calling me superficial for all the likes I get on my Instagram. I was really excited about some of my photos because they were being re-tweeted.

B: I didn't realize how harsh I sounded. I was crabby about someone stepping on my foot the other day because they backed up into me to take a selfie. Then they yelled at me and accused me of trying to photobomb their perfect shot.

If there is anything you misunderstood in the previous conversation, be sure to get it off your chest. You may be able to simply and quickly clear up a misunderstanding, but take your time and don't rush. It's worth taking the time to smooth everything over with someone.

ENGLISH FOR REAL

4 ▶ **ANALYZE** Watch the video again. What strategies do Kevin and Max use to communicate with each other?

1 Kevin: Uh, I um...could I talk to you for a second?
_____

2 Kevin: I just wanted to apologize for what I said earlier. I didn't mean to be so harsh.
_____

3 Max: It just felt like you were putting down the U.K.! And you know how much I love my home, too.
_____

4 Kevin: Sorry. I didn't even consider how negative that sounded. You're right. It could be a great opportunity for Andy.
_____

5 **ASSESS** When do you think Kevin determined he needed to clear the air with Max?

6 **ANALYZE** When do you feel it's worthwhile to clear up a misunderstanding?

Not worth it ⊢————————— Not super urgent —————————⊣ It would really bother me not to

1 Your mother thinks you don't like the dinner she made for you the other night.
2 Your colleague of a few months keeps calling you by the wrong name.
3 Your sick friend gets on your nerves after they say, "What are you, my mother," when you recommend he or she see a doctor, drink more water, and take some medicine.
4 At a meeting, you embarrass your co-worker because he or she says something that makes you laugh. You think it's a joke when it is actually something serious.

7 **EXPAND** How would you clear up the misunderstandings in the following situations?

Your classmate of a few months asked to borrow your lecture notes from a day he or she missed class. The person misunderstood that he or she should make a copy of your notes and bring them back to you the next day because you need to study for the midterm exam next week. Instead, your classmate returns the notes after the exam.

You and your colleague of a year are having lunch at a restaurant. Last week, you paid the tab and politely told your colleague to get you lunch next time, but he or she misunderstood your gesture and only brought enough money to pay for his or her own meal today.

Your boss or professor asks you to come to his or her office at 2:15. You have a doctor's appointment at 3:00 and you are really busy with other work, but you move your schedule around anyway. When you arrive at your boss or professor's office, they are not there. You wait for a while, and they eventually show up at 2:50.

8 **BUILD** With your partner, prepare a role play for one of the situations in Exercise 7.

9 **SHARE** Role-play your conversation for the class.

GO ONLINE to create your own version of the English For Real video.

11.5 Hypothetically Speaking

1 ACTIVATE What does *negotiation* mean? Do you have any negotiating experience? Explain and discuss your ideas with a partner.

2 🔊 ⬛ **IDENTIFY** Listen to the conversation. Answer the questions. Then discuss with a partner.

1 What do you think is the relationship between the speakers? How do you know?
2 What is the woman doing?
3 How does her assignment relate to their conversation?
4 Do they reach an agreement? If so, what is it?
5 What does each person want?

—adapted from *The Oxford Companion to American Law*, by Kermit L. Hall

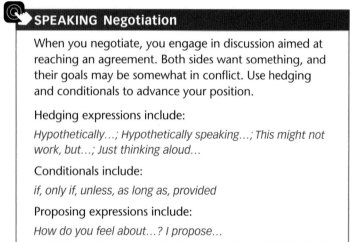

SPEAKING Negotiation

When you negotiate, you engage in discussion aimed at reaching an agreement. Both sides want something, and their goals may be somewhat in conflict. Use hedging and conditionals to advance your position.

Hedging expressions include:

Hypothetically…; Hypothetically speaking…; This might not work, but…; Just thinking aloud…

Conditionals include:

if, only if, unless, as long as, provided

Proposing expressions include:

How do you feel about…? I propose…

3 🔊 **IDENTIFY** Listen to the excerpt. Put the phrases in the order they're used in the conversation.

___ as long as   ___ that might be difficult
___ hypothetically speaking   ___ might consider
___ if   ___ this might not work

GRAMMAR IN CONTEXT
Causatives with *have* and *get*

We use *have* and *get* in various structures to talk about arranging something or causing something to happen.

Subject + *have / get* + sth/sb + past participle:
We got the house painted last week.

Subject + *get* + sb/sth + *to* infinitive:
Can I get you to pick up the kids today instead?

Subject + *have* + sb + infinitive without *to* + (sth):
I could probably have Han reschedule our basketball practices.

Subject + *got* + sb/sth + -*ing* form (sth):
It's on negotiation, and it's got my head spinning.

See Grammar focus page 169.

4 INTEGRATE Work with partner to complete the conversations. Then practice them. Switch roles and practice again.

A: I've got a commitment tomorrow at ten. I need to
   1 _____ someone meet with the clients.
   Are you available?
B: 2 _____ they arrive on time, it should
   be no problem. However, I'll need to leave for an
   appointment at two.
A: Hmm. I'd have to 3 _____ someone to
   take over for you if I'm still out of the office.
   4 _____, could you reschedule your
   appointment if I let you take tomorrow off? Not sure
   yet if we can make that happen.
B: I don't know. The report is due tomorrow.
   5 _____ I can reschedule today's
   appointment, I might be able to do that. But
   6 _____ I can 7 _____ the
   report done today, it won't work.

5 PREPARE Discuss the following situations with a partner. For each situation, should you text or call? Why?

You're going to be late to an event.
You misunderstood a conversation.
You need to negotiate responsibilities on a project.

6 DEVELOP Work with a partner. Create a conversation about one of the topics in Exercise 5. Imagine that the choice you made to text or call caused a problem. Negotiate a solution to the problem.

7 WHAT'S YOUR ANGLE? Read the situations below. Which ones have you participated in? Discuss with a partner.

- A business negotiation
- Bargaining at a market
- Agreeing to household chores or obligations
- A legal disagreement

Now go to page 157 for the Unit 11 Review.

12 Impressions

▼ Why do clothes matter to people?

▼ When are first impressions important?

▼ What makes a good impression on you?

BEHIND THE PHOTO

1 Have everyone in class write their names on the top of a piece of paper in capital letters. Put the papers on the desks, and walk around. Write your first impression of each person on his or her paper anonymously.

■ I thought she was very quiet.

■ I loved his laugh as soon as I heard it.

■ She looks very smart.

■ Read the first impressions about you. Share with your class what surprised you.

2 Read the first impressions about you. Share with your class what surprised you.

REAL-WORLD GOAL

Introduce yourself to someone you don't know but have wanted to meet

12.1 To Avoid Getting Fired

1 ACTIVATE Look at the pictures. Who would you hire and why? Discuss with a partner.

2 VOCABULARY Write the words or phrases next to the definitions.

association	be laid off	brush up on
networking	professional	counselor

1 _____: improve one's existing knowledge or skill in a given area

2 _____: a group of people organized for a joint purpose

3 _____: relating to or belonging to a profession

4 _____: a person who gives advice on a specified subject

5 _____: interacting with others to exchange information and develop professional or social contacts

6 _____: told by one's employer to leave the job, usually because there is no work

⁺ Oxford 5000™

3 BUILD Complete the paragraph using words from Exercise 2.

I ¹_____ last week. Now I have to look for a new job. Fortunately, I like to stay informed about my field, so I read ²_____ journals. I also belong to a(n) ³_____ for small businesses. It helps members with ⁴_____ and provides resources. These things will help me in my job search. Before I interview, I think I need to ⁵_____ my Spanish. I've forgotten a lot of it. I have an appointment with a career ⁶_____ next week, and that should help me, as well…

GRAMMAR IN CONTEXT Cleft sentences

We use cleft sentences to create emphasis. *Cleft* means "divided into two parts." The part that we want to emphasize comes after the verb *be*. We can form cleft sentences with *if, what,* and *all.*

It was the interviewer who was late. (The interviewer was late.)

All they could think about was getting fired. (They thought about getting fired.)

What I talk about is attire. (I talk about attire.)

In sentences with *what*, the word order can be reversed.

Attire is what I talk about.

See Grammar focus on page 170.

4 INTEGRATE Rewrite the sentences to avoid the cleft structure.

1 All I wanted was to go to sleep.

_____

2 It was then that she remembered.

_____

3 What she advises is that you know your skills.

_____

4 All I can think about is that I might get fired.

_____

5 What it promotes is good health.

_____

5 EXPAND Rewrite the sentences to use a cleft sentence beginning with the word in parentheses.

1 I don't understand the application form. (*what*)

_____

2 You think about appearance. (*all*)

_____

3 The schedule was difficult. (*it*)

_____

4 I tell applicants to focus on their skills. (*what*)

_____

Speakers often use cleft sentences to emphasize certain information in a sentence. Listen for the information that comes after the verb *be* in a cleft sentence.

What I talk about is their attire. (what you wear to work)

6 🔊 **IDENTIFY** Listen to the sentences. What is the speaker emphasizing in each one?

1 a thinking
   b saving
   c retiring

2 a selling
   b caring
   c products

3 a getting fooled
   b the packaging
   c us

4 a the client's name
   b making things worse
   c he forgot

5 a what you can do
   b the best
   c hope

7 **ASSESS** In the video, you will hear about a career coach. Check the things you think a career coach does.

___ 1 Practices interview questions
___ 2 Gives advice on what to wear
___ 3 Administers skill surveys
___ 4 Sets up interviews
___ 5 Writes cover letters and resumes
___ 6 Provides references

8 ▶ **INTEGRATE** Watch the video. Identify the things in Exercise 2 that Satya mentions she does.

9 **ASSESS** Choose the statements that are true according to the information in the video. Rewrite the false statements to make them true.

1 Satya helps people find and keep jobs.
2 How you dress is very important.
3 You shouldn't ask for a raise but should wait to be offered one.
4 Only managers need to read professional journals.
5 If your pay is cut, you should ask for other things in exchange.
6 Benefits are less important than salary.

10 ▶ **EXPAND** Watch the excerpt. Complete the cleft sentences with the words you hear.

What I [1]_____ who are in this situation is [2]_____ on your job search skills, your networking skills, and [3]_____ outside of work with people in your industry—attend [4]_____, join [5]_____ in your field.

11 **APPLY** Complete the outline of the video lecture.

I   Questions at intake: educ., past work exp.,
    _____

II To get ahead
    A Build _____ with _____
    B Attire – dress _____
    C _____ – building rel. – lunch

III To get a raise
    A research _____
    B ask for _____

IV Worried about getting fired
    A Skills – _____
    B Relationships outside _____ – prof.
       _____ and _____ in field

V   To avoid getting fired
    A show up _____
    B produce _____
    C ask for _____

VI If paycut
    A _____
    B _____

VII Benefits
    A maternity and paternity leave
    B _____

VIII Prep. for interview
    A need to know: past exp., _____, accomp.
    B 1st Q:

12 **WHAT'S YOUR ANGLE?** Discuss the questions with a partner.

1 Do you think it's difficult to find a good job? Why or why not?
2 Do you agree with Satya's advice about what to wear?
3 What advice do you think is the best?
4 Do you disagree with anything Satya said? If so, what?
5 What skills do you need to brush up on?
6 Do you belong to any professional organizations?
7 Do you think it's a good idea to see a career counselor? Why or why not?

12.2 Capture the Market

1 ACTIVATE Look at the photo. What could it be advertising? How might this be an effective way to advertise something?

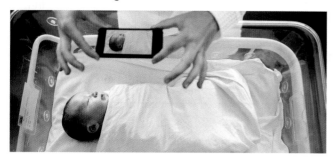

2 VOCABULARY Read the sentences. Use the words from the box to complete the sentences.

capture	differentiate	endorsements
gear	imagery	maximize
strategic	**targets**	

👫+ Oxford 5000™

1 Companies often seek out successful athletes to provide product _____, especially for shoes or equipment.

2 An effective advertisement uses visual _____ like photos or graphics.

3 Many cereal companies _____ their ads towards young children.

4 We're hoping to _____ the market in athletic shoes.

5 The campaign _____ consumers of the latest electronics.

6 To boost smart phone sales by younger customers, their _____ marketing plan will focus on pop culture.

7 To _____ an ad's effectiveness, place it where the most customers will see it.

8 Companies also use ads to clearly _____ their product from other brands.

3 BUILD Match the sentence halves.

1 We can maximize our ___
2 That video game is targeted at ___
3 These shoes are geared ___
4 They've captured the ___
5 They adopted a strategic ___

a marketing plan that focuses on recent retirees.
b market in fashionable low-cost eyeglasses.
c effectiveness by working with an outside marketing team.
d consumers under 30.
e toward the weekend runner rather than the marathoner.

4 WHAT'S YOUR ANGLE? Look at the list of ways to create interest in products or services. With a partner, discuss how effective you think each method is.

logos in sports arenas	poster or billboard	newspaper ad
TV commercial	jingles	endorsements
word of mouth	social media	blog posts
online ads		

5 IDENTIFY Read the article. Which of the methods from Exercise 4 are mentioned? How should entrepreneurs advertise themselves today?

Branding yourself

You know what advertising is, right? Paying to communicate a message, especially to sell something, with text and/or images. For instance, a brand logo in an arena or on a sport team's shirts, an image paid for by Amnesty International, a giant poster in a field beside the highway, or a jingle on the radio are all examples of advertisements. Advertising can appear in various media: newspapers and magazines, radio and television, and on the Internet.

Before the late nineteenth century, advertising mainly involved flyers and newspaper inserts, largely in text, calling attention to products, sometimes with <u>product</u> endorsements from members of the upper class. Beginning in the 1870s, *not only did advertising begin* to use more emotion-laden terms, but it also employed more <u>visual</u> imagery. Newspapers and magazines became filled with more advertising around 1900 as part of the conversion to a true mass press. Soon, radio and other outlets provided new means of advertising, as well. Early techniques started to spread globally.

As they were in the eighteenth and nineteenth centuries, newspapers and magazines remain a <u>crucial component</u> of advertising, targeting <u>consumers</u> in various markets. However, changing technologies and modes of transportation continue to allow advertisements new outlets: billboards and bumper stickers, posters on subways, and animated advertisements that are geared specifically <u>toward</u> Internet users.

Brand names continue to thrive as the key way to differentiate between sometimes indistinguishable products. *No sooner does a popular brand-name* product come out with a high-profile product than it moves to capture the market. Like clothing, few are the products that lack a brand name or logo prominently emblazoned upon them. Advertisers also have capitalized on the integrity of <u>word-of-mouth endorsements</u> from friends by using "viral marketing," an approach that compensates otherwise ordinary consumers for promoting brands via conversations, clothing, or other signals.

6 ASSESS Choose the true statements. Rewrite the false statements to make them true.

1 In the nineteenth century, advertising was mostly on billboards and in magazines.

2 With changes in transportation, new forms of advertising, including bumper stickers and subway posters, appeared.

3 One way to tell similar products apart is through the use of brand names.

4 Strategic marketing compensates ordinary consumers for promoting products by word of mouth.

5 If you want to start your own business, you should build your personal brand through an online presence.

Advertising expenditures constitute a significant component of the cost of branded products, and advertising now pervades (and to varying degrees, defines) popular culture. *So pervasive is advertising that authors, artists, and advocacy groups* have considered the potentially damaging impact of advertising on quality of life and on children. *Seldom do these critics examine the ways they, too, use advertising to promote their own causes.*

Today's artists and wannabe entrepreneurs may not be able to afford to pay for advertising in the classic sense. However, the changing landscape of communication and technology means that they may be able to do some of their own strategic <u>marketing</u>. As an entrepreneur with a fledgling company, one of your main products is yourself. Never in recent memory have there been so many start-up companies or people going out on their own. Fortunately, the Internet and social media allow you to attract the attention of potential investors and customers with minimal expense and manageable effort.

So, how can you <u>create a favorable</u> impression? Start by building your personal brand through your online presence. Use social media to network. Produce a blog with content to attract attention in much the same way companies sponsored programs in the early days of television. When you build an audience for your content, they may buy your product or service. In addition, you are making important contacts and building your reputation. Increasing your visibility while demonstrating value without being too boastful can be a challenge, but a low-key approach at the beginning may help. If you also promote others in your social network, they will be more likely to help you. Creating an extensive supportive network will allow you to maximize <u>the effectiveness</u> of your message.

—adapted from *Oxford Encyclopedia of the Modern World*, edited by Peter N. Stearns

7 INTEGRATE Complete the sentences with information from the reading.

1 One kind of advertising is a _____ on the radio.

2 Early advertising often including an endorsement by a member of _____.

3 _____ are geared toward consumers on the Internet.

4 People sometimes criticize advertising's effect on _____.

5 For some entrepreneurs, one product they need to sell is _____.

READING SKILL
Understanding complex sentences

Many articles and texts include complex sentences, especially those geared toward a particular field such as business or marketing, rather than a general-interest publication. Complex sentences include an independent clause with one or more dependent clauses.

To understand a complex sentence, identify the core idea conveyed in the independent (main) clause. Then identify the subordinating connectors to understand the connection between the ideas in the clauses.

Dependent clauses include:

- Adverb clauses, introduced by subordinators such as *before, as, since, unless, although,* and *while.*

  (dependent) <u>*As they were in the eighteenth and nineteenth centuries,*</u> (independent) *newspapers and magazines remain a crucial component of advertising, targeting consumers in various markets.*

- Noun and adjective clauses, introduced by pronouns such as *that, who, what, if,* and *whether.*

  (dependent) *If there is an opportunity,* (independent) *advertisers will use product placement to their advantage.*

---

8 ASSESS Read the excerpts below. Answer the questions about each.

> However, changing technologies and modes of transportation continue to allow advertisements new inroads, including billboards and bumper stickers, posters on subways, and animated advertisements that are **geared** specifically toward Internet users.

1 What is the subject of the independent clause?

2 What are examples of the new inroads of advertisements?

3 What is the dependent clause, and what does it do?

> Advertisers also have capitalized on the integrity of word-of-mouth endorsements between friends by using viral marketing, an approach that compensates otherwise ordinary consumers for promoting brands via conversations, clothing, or other signals.

4 How many clauses are there in this sentence?
5 Which is the independent clause?
6 Which noun phrase does the dependent clause give more information about?
7 Which of the following is the best summary of the sentence?

   a Advertisers use word-of-mouth endorsements between friends.

   b Through viral marketing, advertisers maximize the effect of word-of-mouth endorsements.

   c One approach that advertisers use is to compensate ordinary consumers for brand promotion.

9 IDENTIFY In each sentence below, identify the independent clause.

1 Even though I like that product, it's too expensive.
2 Unless we capture the market of consumers between 35 and 54, we won't be successful.
3 I've been successful in business because I stay informed.
4 Products that appeal to a certain segment of the market may do better than others.
5 Impressions are important even if they are superficial.
6 Studies show that people make accurate judgments after only 30 seconds.

GRAMMAR IN CONTEXT Inversion

Some emphatic structures require the normal sentence word order to be changed by inverting the order of the subject and the auxiliary. This inversion is most common in more formal writing and speech, such as in literary and academic contexts.

Words and expressions that are negative or restrictive are followed by inverted structures when they begin a sentence or clause. After these words and phrases the auxiliary or modal verb comes before the subject.

Beginning in the 1870s, <u>not only did advertising begin</u> to use more emotion-laden terms, but it also employed more visual imagery.

If there is no auxiliary or modal verb, *do* + subject + infinitive is used, instead.

Seldom do these critics examine the ways they too use advertising to promote their own causes.

We can use *so* + adjective/adverb…*that.*

So pervasive is advertising that authors, artists, and advocacy groups have considered the potentially damaging impact of advertising on quality of life and on children.

See Grammar focus on page 170.

10 INTEGRATE Complete the sentences, which all use inversion.

1 Not only _____ advertising entertain us, but it also persuades us to buy products.
2 So convincing _____ advertisements for junk food that we buy what we know is bad for us.
3 Never _____ I think that I would have a blog.
4 Rarely _____ people analyze the impact of advertising on their purchasing behavior.
5 In no way _____ I responsible for that message.

11 EXPAND Combine each pair of sentences using inversion. Begin with the word or phrase in parentheses.

1 I'm excited about this position. I also think I'm a good candidate. (*not only*)
2 I've got the experience in multiple fields. Employers seldom see this. (*seldom*)
3 I never expected to get a job. That job is so amazing! (*never*)
4 Her résumé was so impressive. We didn't interview anyone else. (*so*)

12 WHAT'S YOUR ANGLE? Complete the sentences with your own ideas about the topic. Then discuss them with a partner.

1 Never did I think… (something in the article that surprised you)
2 Not only do ads… (two characteristics of ads that appeal to you)
3 Rarely do I… (a way to use social media that you don't take advantage of)
4 So important is… (something you would include as part of your personal brand)

12.3 Involuntarily Separated?

1 ACTIVATE Do you know someone who has been fired from a job? Have you ever had to apply for a job?

> **VOCABULARY DEVELOPMENT Euphemisms**
>
> Euphemisms are inoffensive words or phrases we use as substitutions for those that are considered unpleasant or rude. For example, we might say *pass away* instead of *die* to soften the impact. Very often, euphemisms are longer or more formal sounding than the words they replace.

2 BUILD Match the euphemism to what it really means.

1 well-off _____
2 **economically disadvantaged** _____
3 **administrative assistant** _____
4 **involuntarily separated** _____
5 **depressed socioeconomic environment** _____
6 **a lack of adequate financial backing** _____
7 a courtesy call _____
8 **undergo a restructuring** _____

a sales call
b bad neighborhood
c poor
d rich
e fired / lost job
f secretary
g no money
h changing things in the company because of problems

3 USE Complete each sentence with a euphemism from Exercise 2.

1 The company has to _____ after recent losses in the market.
2 We couldn't produce the play because of _____.
3 I'm currently a(n) _____, but I hope to take on more responsibility soon.
4 Schools in _____ neighborhoods often have higher test scores than those in _____ neighborhoods.
5 Jake hasn't had a job since he was _____ from his previous position.
6 In my last job, I had to make _____. I could work from home, and all I needed was a phone.
7 He came from a(n) _____ but overcame those challenges to get a scholarship to a very good university.

4 IDENTIFY Read the cover letter. Why is the writer looking for a job?

To: recruitmentofficer@amail.com

Cc:

Subject: Vacancy for Arts Program Coordinator

Attachment: cduncanresume.doc

Dear Sir or Madam,

Re: Vacancy for Arts Program Coordinator

1 I am writing in reply to your listing for the position of Arts Program Coordinator, which was posted on GoodJobsHere on May 20, 2017. Please see the attached résumé.

2 As you will see from my résumé, I have an undergraduate degree in Marketing with a minor in Visual Art. Furthermore, I have two years' experience as an administrative assistant with an organization that assisted the economically disadvantaged. Working in a depressed socioeconomic environment taught me the importance of the arts and cultural enrichment for all communities. In my position, I acquired critical interpersonal, motivational, and communication skills that will serve me well in any work environment. I'm eager to apply these skills in arts education, and very much look forward to doing so.

3 Unfortunately, a lack of adequate financial backing forced the organization I was working for to undergo a restructuring, and I was involuntarily separated. Since then, I have been taking graduate-level classes in nonprofit management at the university. Not many people in my program of study have also worked in nonprofits, but I have. I believe this gives me an advantage. In addition, I am familiar with Microsoft Office and Adobe Creative Suite. As a child, my family lived abroad for several years. What this taught me is an appreciation for people of all backgrounds. Not only am I fluent in Spanish, but I am also proficient in French.

4 I feel that as an arts program coordinator, I can make a real difference to the lives of the children and families in the area you serve. I would also welcome working for an organization that is as passionate about arts education and working with **underserved populations** as I am. I would be available to start working on April 1. I look forward to hearing from you in the near future.

Sincerely,
Claire Duncan

5 ASSESS Answer the questions. Then discuss with a partner.

1 What position is the writer applying for?

_____

2 What did she study in college?

_____

3 What was her previous job?

_____

4 How long did she work in that capacity?

_____

5 Why doesn't she work there anymore?

_____

6 What skills does she have?

_____

7 Why does she want this job?

_____

6 IDENTIFY Write the number of the paragraph next to the description.

1 Closing paragraph ___
2 Position applied for ___
3 Reason you want the job ___
4 Current situation ___

7 WHAT'S YOUR ANGLE? Answer the questions. Then discuss with a partner.

1 What are the writer's positive qualities?
2 What might be some negative aspects to her background?
3 Would you interview her for this position? Why or why not?

GRAMMAR IN CONTEXT
Using auxiliaries to avoid repetition

We often replace verbs and verb phrases with an auxiliary verb to avoid repeating a verb or verb phrase that has already been used.

Not many people in my program of study have also worked in nonprofits, but I have.

We can also use a form of _have_ or _do_ + _so_. This is usually in more formal contexts and only when referring to a topic that was previously mentioned.

I'm eager to apply these skills in arts education and very much look forward to doing so.

See Grammar focus on page 170.

8 INTEGRATE Combine each pair of sentences. Use auxiliaries to avoid repetition.

1 The company didn't want to take chances. I wanted to take chances. (_but_)

_____

2 The office relocated to another state. I couldn't relocate to another state. (_but_)

_____

3 I've always wanted to work for a publishing company. I look forward to working for a publishing company. (_and_)

_____

4 Not many people have experience working in both education and business. I have experience working in both. (_although_)

_____

WRITING SKILL
Using inversion and cleft sentences for emphasis

Writers often use inversion and cleft sentences for emphasis and sentence variety. Complex sentences make your writing more interesting.

In a cleft sentence, the information after the verb *be* is emphasized.

What this taught me is an appreciation for people of all backgrounds.

You can use inversion to make your sentence sound more surprising or unusual.

Not only am I fluent in Spanish, I am also proficient in French.

9 EXPAND Rewrite the sentences as inversions or cleft sentences.

1 I can play the piano. I can also sing.
   Not only _____.

2 I never expected to be the head of a company at 26.
   Never _____.

3 I have rarely enjoyed a job so much.
   Rarely _____.

4 It changed his life. He didn't know it would.
   Little did he know _____.

5 I will be able to contribute only in this way.
   Only in this way _____.

10 PREPARE Imagine you are looking for a job. Complete the outline for a cover letter responding to an ad for the position you want. Be sure to include these sections:

I.   Position you are applying for:
II. Background
     A. Relevant work experience and/or education
     B. Skills
III. Current situation
IV. Reason you want the job / feel you would be a good fit

11 WRITE Write a cover letter for a position you want. Use the cover letter in Exercise 4 and your outline in Exercise 10 as models.

12 IMPROVE Read your cover letter. Does it follow these guidelines?

☐ Does it clearly state the position sought and how you heard about it?

☐ Does it state relevant experience, education, and skills?

☐ Do you explain why you want this job and how you would be good for the company or organization?

☐ Does your letter use cleft sentences or inversions for emphasis?

☐ Do you use appropriate euphemisms when necessary?

☐ Do you use auxiliaries as needed to avoid repetition?

13 SHARE Exchange cover letters with a partner. Check each other's work with respect to the guidelines in Exercise 12.

14 IMPROVE Rewrite your essay to incorporate feedback.

A vintage typography machine

143

12.4 Been There, Done That

ENGLISH FOR REAL

1 ACTIVATE Do any of the following interest you, but you haven't done them because you are afraid or unsure?

- Skydiving
- Performing in front of a group of people
- Speaking in public to a crowd of people
- Quitting your job
- Moving away from home
- Trying new food

2 ▶ IDENTIFY Watch the video and find out what happened.

1   What was the phone call about?
2   What does Andy encourage Kevin to do?
3   Why is Max happy at the end of the conversation?

3 SHARE Which sentences do you think are true? Discuss your answers with a partner.

1   Andy doesn't really want to go to Minnesota.
2   Kevin does want to go to Minnesota, which is why he's so interested in Andy's decision.
3   Andy is sarcastic when he suggests Kevin go to Minnesota instead.
4   Max cares about Andy's career plans.

4 ASSESS How do you think Andy made his choice?

REAL-WORLD ENGLISH Persuading

When we persuade people, we are encouraging them to accept a view point and/or perform an action. How you persuade is just as important as what you are convincing someone to do. When you wish to persuade someone, you don't always have to state the suggested action directly. Instead, you could:

Give a recommendation or advice.

Even though it's expensive, you should take this vacation to Machu Picchu right now while you have the time.

Pitch your idea by emphasizing certain words as you speak.

Apparently, they give these <u>amazing</u> tours that are <u>like nothing else</u>. The views are <u>incredible</u>. Seeing a picture <u>does not compare</u> to seeing it in person.

Focus on the future to help the other person establish confidence in moving forward with a decision.

A trip like this is definitely something you can cross off your bucket list. I'm pretty sure you'll have a lot of great stories to tell!

Make it clear that this opportunity may never come again.

I hear they are going to close many of the sites in order to preserve them from potential damage because of tourism.

5 ▶ **ANALYZE** Watch the video again. Andy uses the following functions in his attempt to persuade Kevin. What words does he use for each?

1 Gives recommendation or advice

_____

2 Pitches idea with powerful words

_____

3 Focuses on the future

_____

4 Explains opportunity is finite

_____

6 **EXPAND** Why do you think Andy took the time to persuade Kevin?

7 **IDENTIFY** What is the difference between these two statements?

1 Going to that school will broaden your horizons.
2 You're parents will be really let down if you don't go to that school.

8 **ASSESS** How much influence do any of the following have on your big or small decisions?

your family	money	your close friends
opportunity	advertising	appearance
people you've just met	ease	difficulty

Not at all	A bit	I would consider	Very influential

1 How much money you spend on a new car
2 Where you go on vacation
3 Taking a new job
4 Which movie you are going to see
5 Which school to attend
6 Which clothes you wear
7 How you spend your free time
8 Trying a new hobby

9 **INTEGRATE** Work with a partner, and discuss how you would persuade someone in the following situations.

1 Your friend would like to get a second job to supplement his or her income, but he or she won't have a social life for a while.
2 Your friend is given an opportunity to give a speech to a large audience, but he or she is shy about speaking in public.
3 Your friend won a ticket to travel around the world next summer, which would mean having to put all other plans and responsibilities on hold for a few months.

10 **BUILD** With your partner, prepare a role play for one of the situations in Exercise 9.

11 **SHARE** Role-play your conversation for the class.

GO ONLINE
to create your own version
of the English For Real video.

145

12.5 Making a Good Impression

1 ACTIVATE Look at the photo. Who do you see? What is the relationship between the people? How do they feel?

2 🔊 IDENTIFY Listen to the conversation. Then discuss the following questions with a partner.

1 What is the interview for?
2 Why is someone thinking about moving?
3 Why is someone wearing a suit?
4 What are some good points about the new apartment?
5 What advice does the roommate give?

3 🔊 ASSESS Complete the conversation with appropriate structures and expressions. Then listen and check.

above all	actually	had I known	not only
do I speak	really	strongly	what

A: I see on your résumé that you lived in Japan for a while. Do you speak Japanese?

B: ¹_____ ²_____ Japanese, but I've also tutored students in the language lab at school.

A: That's ³_____ impressive. We're ⁴_____ looking for someone who is fluent in Japanese.

B: ⁵_____ you were looking for proficiency in Japanese, I would have included my test results. I'd be happy to send them to you.

A: That would be great. ⁶_____ we need is someone who's a self-starter. ⁷_____, the successful candidate would need to be a team player.

B: In my work in the language lab, I set up my own tutoring curriculum. I also had to coordinate with the other tutors. I ⁸_____ believe that I have the background necessary to do the job.

4 INTEGRATE Read the sentences. Predict where the speakers will pause.

1 All he wanted was to make a good impression on them.
2 What I hope to do is meet some new people.
3 Little did we know that they were actually lost.
4 Not only do I speak Spanish, but I also understand German and Arabic.
5 Had I researched the company first, I would have answered the question better.

5 🔊 NOTICE Listen and check your answers to Exercise 4.

6 WHAT'S YOUR ANGLE? Answer the questions with your ideas. Discuss your answers with a partner.

1 What is the best way to make a good impression on employers or new friends?
2 Does your strategy change in different situations? Why or why not?
3 Do you think first impressions are accurate? Why?

7 INTERACT Work with a partner. Have a conversation about how to make a good impression in different contexts.

Now go to page 158 for the Unit 12 Review.

Unit Reviews

Unit 1

VOCABULARY

1 Use the words in the box to complete the text.

composition	medium	enthusiast	vibrant
master	sacred	backdrop	

Many art ¹ _____ are excited about this painting because the artist was a ² _____ of disguising ³ _____ objects in his work. This ⁴ _____ took two years to create using the artist's preferred ⁵ _____. The colors in this painting are particularly ⁶ _____. What I like about this image is the contrast between the boat and the ⁷ _____ of the water.

2 Identify the kind of music each person heard with a two-word collocation.

1 "Their deep voices together nearly raised the roof."
2 "75,000 fans waving flags and singing the official song of their country was very moving."
3 "Wow! I can't get that song out of my head."
4 "I learned so much about the culture through watching the dancers perform to traditional music. Fantastic!"

3 Use the correct suffix with the word in parentheses to complete each sentence.

1 By the time the political situation had (stability) _____stable_____, she was already an accomplished artist.
2 The photographer (simple) _____simply_____ his compositions, which led to his increased popularity.
3 The acrobats always double-check and (tight) _____tighten_____ their safety ropes.
4 The dates for the festival are perfect, so (time) _____Anytime_____ there's no issue with my schedule.

 GO ONLINE to play the VOCABULARY GAME

GRAMMAR

4 Correct the text using the most appropriate present form of each word in italics.

I ¹ *notice* noticed the number of younger museum members ² *increase* increased lately. I'm pleased to see that more young people ³ *come* came to enjoy the art here. But, I wish they'd leave their cell phones at home. They always ⁴ *take* selfies next to the paintings, which ⁵ *make* makes everything crowded!

5 Choose the correct word or phrase to complete the text.

1 I stopped doing my photography project that evening because ~~I'd had~~ / I had a headache.
2 I started studying fine arts after I'd *been living* / *been lived* in Paris for two years.
3 We went to several exhibitions *when I was staying* / *when I had stayed* with my cousin in Sydney.
4 *He performed* / *He's been performing* since 1998.
5 When I was small, I *used to* / *would* love designing houses and objects.

6 Complete each sentence with the appropriate form of the verb in parentheses.

1 I can't find my theatre ticket. I think I forgot _____ (put) it in my bag.
2 The painter went on _____ (stretch) a new canvas after he finished the painting.
3 The band stopped _____ (sign) autographs so they could give an interview.
4 I quit _____ (study) in my teens. I regret _____ (give) it up.

 GO ONLINE to play the GRAMMAR GAME

DISCUSSION POINT

7 Read the quote. Do you agree with it? Share your ideas with the class.

 "The more you reason, the less you create."
—Raymond Chandler, selected from *Oxford Essential Quotations*, 5ᵗʰ ed., edited by Susan Ratcliffe

 **GO ONLINE and listen to a podcast. Then add your comments to the discussion board.**

ZOOM IN

8 What about you?

Task 1 Work with a partner. Talk about the kind of art you appreciate and why.

Task 2 Write a short opinion essay about how education should aid creativity in learners.

Task 3 Find a picture of a piece of art that you have not seen but would like to see in person.

9 How did you do in the tasks? Complete the prompts.

I found Task ___ easy because…

I found Task ___ difficult because…

I need to improve… To do this, I'm going to…

Unit 2

VOCABULARY

1 What is an appropriate simile for each photo?

2 For each item, choose the word that does not mean something similar to the first adjective.

1 poignant: *heartfelt* / *sincere* / *mild*
2 intriguing: *curiosity* / *boring* / *attracting*
3 appealing: *repulsive* / *attractive* / *pleasing*
4 credible: *believable* / *unlikely* / *trustworthy*
5 accessible: *understandable* / *available* / *difficult*
6 compelling: *fascinating* / *optional* / *interesting*
7 elaborate: *simple* / *ornate* / *complicated*

 GO ONLINE to play the VOCABULARY GAME

GRAMMAR

3 Identify the correct narrative tense.

Our public library is closed now, but it [1] *has been* / *had been* there for 75 years. When the council explained the library [2] *is going to close* / *was going* to close, residents [3] *were* / *had been* furious. After all, some of the locals [4] *had been going* / *were going* there since they were children. People [5] *signed* / *were signing* a petition and promised they [6] *will take* / *would take* the matter further. Nothing [7] *had worked* / *worked*. After we [8] *had been sending* / *had sent* about 300 letters, we received the final decision from the city council. The library [9] *is* / *was* to close. The news came on the day of the Town Festival when, confident of a positive result, we [10] *were celebrating* / *celebrated* our anticipated success. What a disappointing day that was!

4 Reword each sentence using the words in italics and perfect tenses.

1 "Thank you, Aunt Lucy. Your homemade cake was wonderful." *The girl thanked…*
2 "I'm so sorry I missed the earlier bus and made you all late." *James apologized…*
3 "My plan is to write another novel by this September." *I intend…*
4 "At school, I chose not to continue with Latin, which is a shame." *The professor regretted…*
5 "My intention was to text my neighbor this morning, but I forgot!" *Martha meant…*
6 "Next Friday's my deadline for finishing the project." *I hope…*
7 "I finally passed the literature exam." *It was a relief…*

 GO ONLINE to play the GRAMMAR GAME

DISCUSSION POINT

5 Read the quote. Is the original book better than the film adaptation? Share your ideas in a small group.

 "Never judge a book by its movie."
—J.W. Eagan, selected from *Oxford Essential Quotations*, 5th ed., edited by Susan Ratcliffe

 GO ONLINE to listen to a podcast. Then add your comments to the discussion board.

ZOOM IN

6 What about you?

Task 1 Work with a partner. Choose a short story in English that you can both read. Then discuss it.
Task 2 Write an online review of a book that you have recently read.
Task 3 Find a paper or online book (fiction or non-fiction) that has an attractive image on the cover. Bring in a photo, and talk about its relationship to the book.

7 How did you do in the tasks? Complete the prompts.

I found Task ___ easy because…
I found Task ___ difficult because…
I need to improve… To do this, I'm going to…

Unit 3

VOCABULARY

1 Using the correct prefixes, write the opposites of each adjective.

1 organized _Disorganized_

2 mature _immature_

3 qualified _unqualified_

4 flexible _inflexible_

5 patient _inpatient_

6 logical _illogical_

7 experienced _inexperienced_

2 Match the types of decisions with their meanings.

1 mutual decision ___

2 straightforward decision ___

3 conscious decision ___

4 costly decision ___

5 disastrous decision ___

6 rational decision ___

4 a it is very expensive

5 b it can end very badly

1 c it is shared, so the decision-makers agree

6 d it is based on reason rather than emotions

2 e it is easy to make

3 f it is made on purpose, having considered all the facts

 GO ONLINE to play the VOCABULARY GAME

GRAMMAR

3 Correct the errors.

1 In the photos, each people are outside.

2 Every of the people are doing something.

3 The first photo does not have as much people as the second photo.

4 Also, the crowd in the second picture is twice large as the first picture.

5 In other words, there are much less people in the first picture.

6 A great deal people are sitting down in the first picture.

7 Either way, the people in the first picture appear to be every bit relaxed as in the second.

4 Complete the paragraph using a, the, or zero a

I was born and raised in [1] _○_ Chicago and have never left [2] _∅_ United States. I've decided to take [3] _a_ trip around [4] _the_ world which will last [5] _a_ few months. Before booking [6] _the_ trip, I need to apply for [7] _a_ passport. My first stop will be [8] _○_ UAE because I'd like to experience how [9] _the_ people there live, and I've always wanted to see [10] _the_ Burj Khalifa. It's [11] _the_ tallest building in the world! This is all I've planned so far. I'm going to buy [12] _a_ open around [13] _the_ world ticket, so I can decide where I want to go and when I want to leave. There is more to [14] _the_ life than staying in my hometown, and I am excited to discover as much as I can!

 GO ONLINE to play the GRAMMAR GAME

DISCUSSION POINT

5 Read the two proverbs. Do they mean the same thing? Share your ideas with the class.

 "First thoughts are best."
"He who hesitates is lost."
—selected from *Oxford Dictionary of Proverbs*, 6th ed., edited by Jennifer Speake

 GO ONLINE and listen to a podcast. Then add your comments to the discussion board.

ZOOM IN

6 What about you?

Task 1 Work with a partner. Talk about a bad decision that someone you know has recently made.

Task 2 Write a real or imaginary blog post about a new course, role, or job you have just started.

Task 3 Think about a historical decision that had a big impact on society. Find a photo that represents it, and then share your opinion about it.

7 How did you you do in the tasks? Complete the prompts.

I found Task ___ easy because…

I found Task ___ difficult because…

I need to improve… To do this, I'm going to…

Unit 4

VOCABULARY

1 Complete the paragraph using the words from the box.

combat	survival	expose	clarity
sensations	damage	accelerates	chronic
supply	acute	collapse	

Stress is actually a kind of ¹_____ tactic. It seems that ²_____ stress, which is sudden and short-term, can be beneficial. A small amount of stress actually improves your ³_____ of mind, so it is useful before exams, for example. But, if you're not careful, ⁴_____ stress can wear the body down. When stressed, different people will feel similar ⁵_____ in different parts of the body, such as sweaty hands. One's heart rate ⁶_____ and the blood ⁷_____ increases. It can ⁸_____ your body to risks, making it weaker when trying to ⁹_____ disease. Stress can seriously ¹⁰_____ your health, and some sufferers may even ¹¹_____ under pressure.

2 Complete each sentence about the toy robot with the correct phrase.

1 When I was eight *or more* / *or so*, my grandpa gave me a toy robot.

2 I named it *Ronnie* because it was very *human-like* / *humanish*.

3 He was *greyish* / *grey-like* blue, with a *boy-like* / *boyish* face.

4 He was powered by a battery that lasted *or thereabouts* / *somewhere in the region of* 12 hours.

5 Ronnie had a vocabulary of 350 words, *give or take* / *somewhere between* a few.

 GO ONLINE to play the VOCABULARY GAME

GRAMMAR

3 Complete each sentence using the verb given. Use the future perfect simple or future perfect continuous or the future continuous.

1 Can I ask what time you _____ (come back) this evening?

2 We _____ (visit) the robot exhibition on Friday, so I can tell you what it's like.

3 By the end of the week, I _____ (buy) myself a new robotic vacuum for the house!

4 We _____ (use) AI in our factories for ten years this autumn.

5 So, if you don't mind me asking, where _____ (stay) next week?

6 By the time I'm middle-aged, robots _____ (replace) people in numerous fields, including education.

7 By the end of this year, I _____ (study) philosophy, ethics, and AI for 12 months.

4 Identify the noun phrase in each sentence.

1 One of the biggest questions people ask is what cars will look like in the future.

2 Many people speculate that cars of the future will likely be driverless.

3 If a car is driverless, will there still be a need for a steering wheel?

4 With technological advances, cars will be able to make ethical life-and-death decisions.

5 It is believed that there will be fewer car accidents because of a decrease in human error.

6 Even so, there is a concern that driverless cars are vulnerable to hacking.

 GO ONLINE to play the GRAMMAR GAME

DISCUSSION POINT

5 Read the quote. Do you agree? Share your ideas.

 "The illiterate of the 21st century will not be those who cannot read and write, but those who cannot learn, unlearn, and relearn."
—Alvin Toffler, selected from *Oxford Essential Quotations*, 5th ed., edited by Susan Ratcliffe

 GO ONLINE and listen to a podcast. Then add your comments to the discussion board.

 ZOOM IN

6 What about you?

Task 1 Work with a partner. Talk about whether people are naturally kind or not.

Task 2 Write about your views on the future: Are they positive or negative, and why?

Task 3 Find a photo that reflects the consequences of a major recent event. Describe its significance in a small group.

7 How did you do in the tasks? Complete the prompts.

I found Task ___ easy because…

I found Task ___ difficult because…

I need to improve… To do this, I'm going to…

Unit 5

VOCABULARY

1 Identify the item in italics that does *not* fit with the meaning of the sentence as a whole.

1   *Blouses* and *sportswear* tend to be a little stretchy and are often made of material from synthetic fibers, like Lycra.

2   The quality of *cotton blouses* and *sheets* is often measured by the number of threads woven together per square inch, called the "thread count."

3   Breathable fabric that has a soft texture is generally selected for *suits* and *pajamas*.

4   Fabrics such as *polyester* and *silk* are made from natural fibers that can be spun into thread.

2 Complete each sentence by changing the verb to a noun form.

1   After the _____ (disturb) this morning at around 3 a.m., I couldn't get back to sleep.

2   We made a few _____ (adjust) to the schedule, and it looks better now.

3   This project showed that _____ (collaborate) between many several different countries and continents is possible.

4   _____ (consider) of the needs of the elderly is one of the main reasons for 3-D food printing.

5   My parents gave me a monthly_____ (allow) of $20 to buy my own clothes when I was 16.

 GO ONLINE to play the VOCABULARY GAME

GRAMMAR

3 Add in the missing relative clauses in the description of cotton production below.

a   which   c   where
b   that   d   Ø

 The cotton plant produces seedpods, [1] A known as *cotton bolls*. Seed fibers grow from the skin of the seedpod, [2] b bursts open. The longest fibers are grown in the Nile Delta of Egypt, in Brazil, on the Sea Islands (off South Carolina's coast), and in Texas, [3] c these cottons are relatively limited in production and are used for fine-quality fabrics. The medium-length cottons [4] b are used for good quality fabrics and are the most common. Short cottons are mainly grown in India, and they are used for coarse-quality goods. (Although India also makes cottons [5] b are actually of the finest quality.)

—adapted from *The Oxford Encyclopedia of Economic History*, edited by Joel Mokyr

4 Correct the words in italics.

1   There's Thai or Lebanese food here. You can have *wherever* you want.

2   You're welcome to come without a reservation *however* you like, but you may end up waiting a while.

3   Do you want your potatoes soft or crunchy? *Whoever*.

4   *Whichever* chooses the restaurant needs to consider all our preferences.

5   You can have *whenever* you want from the list of dishes as long as it costs under $15.

5 Change the sentences using the present, past, or perfect participle. Make other minor changes as needed.

1   The students learned how 3-D printing could be used to make body parts, such as ears, and they were fascinated.

2   Often 3-D printing is used in cake decoration and can produce incredibly detailed designs.

3   If you farm in a remote area, you can save a lot of time and money with access to a 3-D printer.

4   She was asked to explain about 3-D printing but didn't know what to say.

5   They were shown how the process worked, and they were amazed.

 GO ONLINE to play the GRAMMAR GAME

DISCUSSION POINT

6 Read the quote. How does this relate to innovation? Discuss in a small group.

 "Failure is not fatal, but failure to change might be."
—John Wooden, selected from *Oxford Dictionary of Quotations*, 8th ed., edited by Elizabeth Knowles

 GO ONLINE and listen to a podcast. Then add your comments to the discussion board.

 ## ZOOM IN

7 What about you?

Task 1 Work with a partner. Talk about one other use of 3-D printing that you find interesting.

Task 2 Write a detailed review of an app that you have acquired recently.

Task 3 Find a photo of something that you find useful and revolutionary. Describe it to your partner.

8 How did you do in the tasks? Complete the prompts.

I found Task ___ easy because…

I found Task ___ difficult because…

I need to improve… To do this, I'm going to…

Unit 6

VOCABULARY

1 Find the word in italics that does *not* fit in the sentence.

1 The police brought a *warning* / *search* / *arrest* warrant.
2 They found the three people who had *carried out* / *committed* / *made* the crime.
3 Some *stolen* / *corrupt* / *illegal* goods were found in the couple's garage.
4 The police were *armed* / *unarmed* / *weaponed*.
5 They *investigated* / *inspected* / *searched* the vehicle thoroughly.
6 After his arrest, the man was charged with committing a dangerous *driving* / *criminal* / *stealing* offense.
7 We were stopped at the *police* / *legal* / *army* checkpoint for several minutes.

2 Complete each sentence with the correct word.

prosecuted	recover	was heard
assaulted	bugged	under surveillance

1 The store manager who was Assaulted during the robbery could not identify thief.
2 The police put nine suspects under surveillance for a week.
3 Police followed the nine people and _____ their phones and were eventually able to make an arrest.
4 While _____, the suspect _____ leading the police to _____ the stolen items from the store.
5 The suspect was quickly _____ and the court case _____ the following week.

 GO ONLINE to play the VOCABULARY GAME

GRAMMAR

3 Rewrite each sentence using the clue provided so that it means the same thing.

1 In Denmark, it is *obligatory* for parents to choose their children's names from a list of about 7,000.
2 In Singapore, you are *not allowed* to chew gum in a public place.
3 In Singapore, if you are caught littering, you *have to* do community work.
4 In the UK, you are *prohibited* from importing potatoes if you think they might be Polish.
5 In Sweden, it's *advisable* to drive with your headlights on all the time.

4 Complete the description of the famous Boston art gallery theft. Choose the correct option in each case.

Almost 30 years ago, $500 million worth of paintings by Rembrandt, Vermeer, Monet, and Degas were stolen just after midnight at the Isabella Stewart Gardner Museum in Boston. Police first suspected the security guard who opened the door for two men dressed as police officers [1] *might have been* / *couldn't have been* involved. The FBI believes the theft [2] *should have been* / *must have been* committed by a criminal organization. Experts fear that after so many years, the works [3] *could have been* / *can't have been* destroyed and that some of the criminals involved [4] *can have* / *may have* died. Some experts think the art [5] *may never have been* / *may never be* found. The criminals clearly [6] *can't have* / *may not have* been tempted by the museum's $10 million reward. Certainly after so much publicity, the artworks [7] *might* / *must* have been practically impossible to sell. Meanwhile, huge empty frames still hang on the walls of the Boston museum. For visitors, this [8] *must* / *can't* be a very sad.

 GO ONLINE to play the GRAMMAR GAME

DISCUSSION POINT

5 Read the proverb. In what ways is this a pessimistic view in terms of crime and criminals?

 "The leopard does not change his spots."
—selected from *Oxford Dictionary of Proverbs*, 6th ed., edited by Jennifer Speake

 GO ONLINE and listen to a podcast. Then add your comments to the discussion board.

ZOOM IN

6 What about you?

Task 1 Work with a partner. Talk about a recent international, national, or local crime.
Task 2 Write up an exclusive interview you have with one of the Hatton Garden burglars.
Task 3 Find a photo of a famous object that was/has been stolen or a famous thief. Tell your partner(s) about it/them.

7 How did you do in the tasks? Complete the prompts.

I found Task ___ easy because…
I found Task ___ difficult because…
I need to improve… To do this, I'm going to…

Unit 7

VOCABULARY

1 Look at the photos of people throughout the book. Use the phrases in the box to describe the people. What else can you say about them?

This person has
- a sense of optimism
- a tolerant attitude
- a healthy self-esteem

This person is usually
- ahead of the curve
- ahead of the pack

2 Choose the best word or phrase to complete each sentence.

1 Creative people are almost always *ahead of the curve / in uncharted territory.*

2 People who are often inspired have *competitiveness / a sense of optimism.*

3 I think filmmakers, especially in science fiction, need *an active imagination / a healthy self-esteem* to think about other worlds.

4 Not everyone needs to be inspired or creative. Sometimes *competence / imagination*, or just being able to get something done, is more important.

5 When you try something you've never done before, you are *cut from a different cloth / in uncharted territory.*

3 Work with a partner. Think of a person who has inspired you. Describe the person using vocabulary for personal qualities and figurative language. Say why you find him or her inspirational.

 GO ONLINE to play the VOCABULARY GAME.

GRAMMAR

4 Choose the correct words to complete the text.

What is the best way to become inspired? That may depend on the person. [1] *Assuming / Unless* you work all the time, you [2] *got / might get* inspiration on vacation. Other people use their emotions to become more creative. [3] *Suppose / Provided* you were angry or upset about something at work—you [4] *could have used / could use* that negative feeling to think about things in a new way. What have you got to lose in that situation? According to research, [5] *unless / if* you are open to new experiences, you [6] *wouldn't be / won't be* inspired. I wish I [7] *knew / had known* that when I was younger.

5 Complete the sentences with your ideas. Remember to use conditionals and related expressions.

If I need to be creative, I go on a long walk to come up with ideas.

If I need to be creative, I _____.

I don't feel inspired unless _____.

If I had _____, I wouldn't have _____.

Anyone can become more creative provided that _____.

I wish _____.

 GO ONLINE to play the GRAMMAR GAME.

DISCUSSION POINT

6 Read the quote. Do you agree with Max Weber? How might inspiration be different in different fields?

 "Inspiration plays no less a role in science than it does in the realm of art."
—Max Weber, selected from *Oxford Dictionary of Scientific Quotations*, edited by W.F. Bynum and Roy Porter

 GO ONLINE and listen to a podcast. Then add your comments to the discussion board.

 ZOOM IN

7 What about you?

Task 1 Work with a partner. Talk about three new ideas or strategies you will use to find more inspiration in your daily life.

Task 2 Think about a piece of art, writing, or music, or a building that inspires you. Write a paragraph to describe it, and explain why it inspires you.

Task 3 Find an image you think is inspiring. Describe it to the class.

8 How did you do in the tasks? Complete the prompts.

I found Task ___ easy because…

I found Task ___ difficult because…

I need to improve… To do this, I'm going to…

Unit 8

VOCABULARY

1 Choose the best word to complete each sentence. You will not use two.

frustration	eager	guilt
embarrassment	hopeful	triumph

1 His _____ is obvious. He's been trying to fix his computer for hours, and he's not succeeding.
2 The team celebrated their _____ with a parade.
3 I felt a lot of _____ after the accident. It was all my fault.
4 She's _____ to start her new job. It's what she's always wanted to do.
5 When I spilled my coffee on my new boss, I was overcome with _____. I'm sure my face was red.
6 I'm _____ about my test results. I studied hard and understood the material.

2 Choose the correct word or phrase to complete the text.

It is easier for most people to express ¹ *delight / guilt* because we don't like to share negative feelings as much as positive ones. Therefore, a story about a situation that made you feel ² *embarrassment / appreciation* is easier to tell than one that ³ *you thought was torture / thrilled you to bits*. And who wouldn't rather hear about when someone was ⁴ *walking on air / filled with frustration*? When you hear a sad story, you rarely feel ⁵ *tickled pink / music to one's ears*.

 GO ONLINE to play the VOCABULARY GAME.

GRAMMAR

3 Choose the best word or phrase to complete the sentences that use ellipsis.

1 You have trouble expressing negative feelings, but I *can't / don't*.
2 There are several moral theories, but utilitarianism is one of the *most popular / popular*.
3 Although most emoji are fun, the faces are the *ones / one* I like best.
4 I can't attend the opening at the art gallery, even though I really want *to attend / to*.
5 Many people have difficulty expressing themselves in emails, but I don't understand *why / where*.

4 Complete the sentences with your own ideas. Use ellipsis.

1 I think it's hard to express my feelings sometimes, but _____.
2 It's important to show empathy to others, especially _____.
3 Do you want to live a happy life? If _____, _____.

 GO ONLINE to play the GRAMMAR GAME.

DISCUSSION POINT

5 Read the quote. Do you agree with it? Share your ideas with the class.

 "Happiness is not a goal, it is a by-product."
—Eleanor Roosevelt, selected from *Oxford Dictionary of Quotations*, 8ᵗʰ ed., edited by Elizabeth Knowles

 **GO ONLINE and listen to a podcast. Then add your comments to the discussion board.**

ZOOM IN

6 What about you?

Task 1: Work with a partner. Talk about how you will express feelings, even difficult ones, in the future.

Task 2: Think about a poem, story, or movie that made you feel deeply. Write a paragraph to describe what it was about and how you felt.

Task 3: Find an image that makes you feel a strong emotion. Describe it to the class.

7 How did you do in the tasks? Complete the prompts.

I found Task ___ easy because…
I found Task ___ difficult because…
I need to improve… To do this, I'm going to…

Unit 9

VOCABULARY

1 Choose the best word to complete each sentence.

1 I need to *modify / evolve* my reservation. I will arrive at 2 p.m., not 6 p.m.

2 You can *amend / transform* yourself by coming to our amazing self-help seminar.

3 The company's marketing approach continues to *evolve / modify* as they open new markets.

4 We need to *transform / amend* the contract to add a schedule.

5 Lana has to *undergo / adjust* surgery for her broken hand.

2 Choose the correct words to complete the text. You will not use two.

| apparatus | devise | enhance | facititate |
| function | interventions | on the horizon | specialized |

Getting Enough Sleep

Research shows that we all ¹ _____ better with enough sleep. However, for many of us, this is hard to do. Some people sleep poorly because they have breathing problems. They can use ² _____ equipment, including a breathing ³ _____ called a *CPAP*. Most of us don't need such complicated ⁴ _____. We can ⁵ _____ simpler solutions such as making our rooms darker and quieter. Also, we can ⁶ _____ our sleep quality if we put away our laptops and phones a couple of hours before we go to bed.

 GO ONLINE to play the VOCABULARY GAME.

GRAMMAR

3 Complete the questions with the correct tag.

1 You took the test, _____?

2 He hasn't had surgery, _____?

3 I can't become an expert at my age, _____?

4 There's an article that explains this, _____?

5 They'd need special equipment, _____?

4 Rewrite the sentences in the passive.

1 Someone needs to completely transform the curriculum.

_____

2 We have modified our methods of production.

_____

3 Someone had described the retreat center as life changing.

_____

4 I've adjusted my expectations since I read the latest reviews online.

_____

5 Technology has radically changed everyday life.

_____

 GO ONLINE to play the GRAMMAR GAME.

DISCUSSION POINT

5 Read the quote. Do you agree with Nicholas Murray Butler? Share your ideas with the class.

 "An expert is one who knows more and more about less and less."
—Nicholas Murray Butler, selected from *Oxford Dictionary of Modern Quotations*, 3ʳᵈ ed., edited by Elizabeth Knowles

 GO ONLINE and listen to a podcast. Then add your comments to the discussion board.

 **ZOOM IN**

6 What about you?

Task 1: Work with a partner. Talk about inventions that have transformed society and how they affected you personally.

Task 2: Think about a recent negative experience with a product or service. Write an email to a company or organization to complain.

Task 3: Find an image that shows how something has developed. Describe it to the class.

7 How did you do in the tasks? Complete the prompts.

I found Task ___ easy because…

I found Task ___ difficult because…

I need to improve… To do this, I'm going to…

Unit 10

VOCABULARY

1 Answer the questions.

1. What kind of news do you monitor?
2. How do you know if it's trustworthy?
3. Do you ever verify the details?
4. How do you know if the writer is neutral?
5. What kinds of stories do you exclude from your newsfeed?

2 Complete the expressions for giving estimates.

1. Off _____, I'd say a half million people attended the event.
2. We're _____ winds of maybe 40 to 50 miles per hour.
3. It's _____ say, but I think maybe 30 whales washed ashore.
4. If I _____, I'd say a dozen cars were involved in the accident.
5. How much did it cost? Somewhere in _____ of a million dollars.

3 Complete the paragraph with the correct form of the word. You will not use two of the words.

attack	campaign	flee	loom
negotiate	scare	seize	urge

News stories fall into different categories. One popular category is politics. When an election ¹_____, candidates ²_____ actively. Sometimes, it can get heated, and one candidate will ³_____ the others. This tactic can backfire with the voters. Too much negativity can ⁴_____ them away, discouraging them from voting. Candidates almost always ⁵_____ their supporters to show up on election day since even a few votes can make a difference. Because almost any media coverage helps, most candidates ⁶_____ any opportunity they can to make the news.

 GO ONLINE to play the VOCABULARY GAME.

GRAMMAR

4 Rewrite each sentence using the words in parentheses.

1. I worked on this unit, but it was difficult to understand. (*hard, extremely*)
2. I think political news articles are boring. (*very, to be honest*)
3. I believe fake news articles. (*sometimes, surprisingly*)
4. I got caught in a frightening storm. (*really, unfortunately*)
5. I read news to understand the world. (*very, carefully, every day*)
6. Someone will give me bad news. (*very, hopefully, directly*)

5 Use the prompts to write complete sentences with your own ideas about the news. Discuss them with a partner.

1. It's possible that…
2. It's unbelievable that…
3. It's been difficult for…
4. It's time to…
5. There are several ways to verify a news story. First,…
6. As a result of social media, the news has become…

 GO ONLINE to play the GRAMMAR GAME.

DISCUSSION POINT

6 Read the quote. Do you agree with Arthur Miller? Share your ideas with the class.

"A good newspaper…is a nation talking to itself."
—Arthur Miller, selected from *The Oxford Dictionary of American Quotations*, 2ⁿᵈ ed., edited by Hugh Rawson and Margaret Miner

 GO ONLINE and listen to a podcast. Then add your comments to the discussion board.

ZOOM IN

7 What about you?

Task 1: Work with a partner. Talk about a news story that personally affected you.

Task 2: Think about a recent event in world news. Write a report to describe what happened.

Task 3: Find an image that shows something newsworthy (e.g., a photo) or that comments on the news (e.g., a cartoon). Describe it to the class and explain why it is news.

8 How did you do in the tasks? Complete the prompts.

I found Task ___ easy because…
I found Task ___ difficult because…
I need to improve… To do this, I'm going to…

Unit 11

VOCABULARY

1 Rewrite the sentences to be less formal. Use phrasal verbs.

1 We can eliminate the third option.

_____

2 Can you offer a satisfactory explanation for your behavior?

_____

3 I need to stay more fully informed about my assignments.

_____

4 Do you have any good ideas to contribute?

_____

5 There are many good candidates for the position, but we have reduced the options to two.

_____

2 Complete the paragraph with the correct form of a word from the box. You will not need to use all the words.

aggression	assert	breakdown	commentary
facilitate	glimpse	restraint	straightforward

In the ¹ _____ that accompanies the documentary, the researchers describe their methods. They sat long hours in the forest trying to get a
² _____ of the gorillas. It was difficult to practice ³ _____ sometimes, but in the beginning, the animals showed signs of
⁴ _____ when they saw people. The researchers' patience was finally rewarded. The gorillas became comfortable with their presence, and this
⁵ _____ the research. After months of observation, the scientists were able to
⁶ _____ that gorillas have sophisticated communication systems.

 GO ONLINE to play the VOCABULARY GAME.

GRAMMAR

3 Put the words in the correct order to make sentences.

1 call 911 / to / I / him / told him
2 that / technology / communication / has changed / the writer / asserts
3 we / to meet / the clients / earlier / offered
4 text / reported / than they email / the researchers / that / young people / more

4 Match the sentence halves.

1 Our teacher insists ___
2 The announcement told everyone to ___
3 We agreed ___
4 The guidelines suggested ___
5 You've almost convinced ___
6 They had ___

a to reschedule the presentation.
b me to go back to school.
c we be on time.
d exit immediately.
e that women should curtsy.
f their flight rescheduled.

 GO ONLINE to play the GRAMMAR GAME.

DISCUSSION POINT

5 Read the quote. Do you agree with the quote? Share your ideas with the class.

"Every journey into the past is complicated by delusions, false memories, false namings of real events."
—Adrienne Rich, selected from _The Oxford Dictionary of American Quotations_, 2ⁿᵈ ed., edited by Hugh Rawson and Margaret Miner

 GO ONLINE and listen to a podcast. Then add your comments to the discussion board.

 **ZOOM IN**

6 What about you?

Task 1: Work with a partner. Give advice about communicating with people from another culture.

Task 2: Think about a problem related to communication. Write a description of the problem and propose solutions.

Task 3: Find an image that reflects what you know about communication. Describe it to the class.

7 How did you do in the tasks? Complete the prompts.

I found Task ___ easy because…

I found Task ___ difficult because…

I need to improve… To do this, I'm going to…

Unit 12

VOCABULARY

1 Complete the conversation with euphemisms.

Brad: Jon! It's so good to see you. What have you been up to?

Jon: Hey, Brad. Not too much, sadly. I was
¹ _____ last month from my company. I'm looking for work.

Brad: I'm sorry to hear that. It's a tough time. Right now, our company ² _____, too. I'm not sure of my own job.

Jon: Good luck. I had an interview for a job where I can work at home. I'd make ³ _____. I hate talking on the phone, though.

Brad: That doesn't sound like a good job for you. You're so good with people who are ⁴ _____. Why don't you look into social services?

Jon: I've thought about it. I might not make as much money, but I feel it's important to help those who live in a ⁵ _____.

2 Choose the correct word to complete the text.

capture	endorsement	gear
imagery	maximize	strategic

Large sporting goods companies often use ¹ _____ marketing to attract more consumers. They ² _____ their marketing toward a wide range of customers, including serious athletes, the weekend exerciser, and kids at all levels. In order to ³ _____ the greatest share of the market, they have to use different approaches. One way to ⁴ _____ sales to multiple groups is to have mini stores within a larger store, for example, one area devoted to yoga. Another strategy is to get ⁵ _____ from famous athletes. One group every company wants to reach is those aged 18 to 19 years old. They respond to emotional TV ads, multimedia, and exciting ⁶ _____.

3 Answer the questions with your own information. Discuss with a partner.

1   Have you ever been laid off?
2   What skills should you brush up on?
3   What professional associations do you belong to?

 GO ONLINE to play the VOCABULARY GAME.

GRAMMAR

4 Rewrite each sentence as a cleft sentence or inversion.

1   You don't like conflict.
2   I've never seen such a mess.
3   She only cares about money.
4   The course was so interesting that she signed up for another one.
5   The interviewer rescheduled.

5 Complete the sentences with your own ideas.

1   What I really notice about someone I meet is _____.
2   All most people notice is _____.
3   Never did I expect to learn _____.
4   Most of the people I know have _____, but I haven't.

 GO ONLINE to play the Unit GRAMMAR GAME.

DISCUSSION POINT

6 Read the quote. Do you agree with this proverb? Why or why not? Share your ideas with the class.

 "First impressions are the most lasting."
—selected from *Oxford Dictionary of Proverbs*, 6ᵗʰ ed., edited by Jennifer Speake

 GO ONLINE and listen to a podcast. Then add your comments to the discussion board.

ZOOM IN

7 What about you?

Task 1: Work with a partner. Talk about a time when your first impression of someone was inaccurate.

Task 2: Think about a job you've had. Write a description of what you did and the skills you acquired.

Task 3: Choose an image that reflects what you know about making an impression. Describe it to your classmates, and explain the kind of impression it makes.

8 How did you do in the tasks? Complete the prompts.

I found Task ___ easy because…

I found Task ___ difficult because…

I need to improve… To do this, I'm going to…

Grammar focus

Unit 1

Present tenses

SIMPLE PRESENT AND CONTINUOUS

We often use time words or phrases such as *always*, *rarely*, *often*, *whenever*, *from time to time*, etc. with the simple present. We use the simple present: to talk about general truths, habits, or permanent states or situations; to talk about fixed or scheduled events in the future; to talk about the future after time phrases, after some relative pronouns, and in clauses that begin with *as*, *than* and *whether*; in newspaper headlines, reviews, or summaries of books and movies and live commentaries; and to tell the main events of a joke or anecdote.

We often use time words or phrases such as *still*, *right now*, *at the moment*, *at present*, *this week*, *today*, etc. with the present continuous. We use the present continuous to talk about temporary actions, events, or situations that are in progress now or around now; future arrangements; and changing or developing situations. We use it with *always*, *constantly*, or *continually* for situations that the speaker finds annoying, strange, or funny; and for giving background to jokes and anecdotes.

PRESENT PERFECT AND CONTINUOUS

We use the present perfect to talk about: actions that happened at an unspecified point in the past or where the result of the action is more important than when the action happened; actions or states that began in the past and continue up to the present; an experience with *ever*, *never*, *already*, *just*, or *yet*; and finished actions in the future after time phrases.

We use the present perfect continuous to talk about situations or actions that began in the past and are still in progress; an action that has happened repeatedly in the past and is still happening now; and an action or situation which has just stopped, but which has a result that can still be seen.

Constructions with *-ing* or with *to* infinitive

-ING FORM

We use the *-ing* form of the verb after certain verbs; like a noun, as the subject or object of a sentence; after most prepositions and some adjective/noun + preposition constructions; after time conjunctions when the subject is the same in both clauses; and after *for*, to describe the purpose of a thing.

INFINITIVE

We use the *to* infinitive after certain verbs; after some verb + object combinations; after certain adjectives or nouns, *too* + adjective and *something / nothing / anything / anywhere / nowhere, time*; and after some nouns + *be*.

We use the infinitive without *to* after *make* and *let* + object.

We use the infinitive with or without *to* after *help* + object.

-ING FORM OR *TO* INFINITIVE?

We can use either the *-ing* form or the *to* infinitive after some verbs, with little change in meaning.

Some verbs are followed by *-ing* or the infinitive with *to* with a change of meaning.

Past forms

SIMPLE PAST AND CONTINUOUS

We use the simple past to talk about completed past actions, sequences of actions in the past, past states, and habits.

We use the past continuous to talk about: events in progress at a time in the past; and longer actions that happened at the same time as a shorter action. We also use the past continuous for background descriptions in stories and anecdotes.

We use the past continuous of *was / were going to* + infinitive to talk about plans, intentions, or predictions in the immediate future.

We can use the past continuous with adverbs of frequency like *always* or *constantly* to express irritating or strange habits.

PAST PERFECT

We use the past perfect to talk about completed actions or events that happened before another action or event in the past, often with time expressions such as *by the time*, *when*, *before*, *after*, and *until*.

We use the past perfect continuous to talk about ongoing or repeated actions or situations leading up to another past event, or to give background information about an event or story.

We can use *would* or *used to* to talk about past habits or repeated actions. They always describe a habit or repeated action in the past that no longer happens now.

We can also use *used to*, but not *would* to talk about past states that are no longer the case.

 GO ONLINE for the complete grammar reference.

Unit 2

Narrative tenses

SIMPLE PAST AND PAST CONTINUOUS

We generally use the simple past to talk about the main event or a sequence of actions or events. We also use it to talk about habits.

We generally use the past continuous to talk about background descriptions or actions in progress at the time of the main event(s). We often use it to talk about longer actions that happened at the same time as a shorter action, or longer actions interrupted by a shorter action.

PAST PERFECT AND CONTINUOUS

We use the past perfect to talk about actions or events that happened before another past action or event in the narrative.
We use the past perfect continuous to talk about ongoing activities leading up to a more recent past event, and to give background information about an event.

FUTURE IN THE PAST

Sometimes in a narrative about the past, we want to refer to things which were in the future at that time. We can do this by using a number of forms to express the future from a past perspective.

Was / were to can be used to talk about events in the future that did take place or also about ones that were expected to happen but didn't.

Perfect infinitives and perfect *-ing* forms

FORM

We form the perfect infinitive with *to have* + past participle.
We form the perfect *-ing* form with *having* + past participle.

USE

We use the infinitive after certain verbs, adjectives, and nouns. We use the perfect infinitive instead of a simple infinitive when we talk about actions or events that happened earlier or that will be completed at some point in the future.

We use the *-ing* form after certain verbs (or verbs + prepositions) and in clauses of time, reason, and result. We use the perfect *-ing* form (e.g., *having done*) to express or to emphasize that something is in the past.

Verb patterns after verbs of the senses

USE

We often use verbs of senses + object + infinitive without to to talk about a whole action or completed event.

We often use verb + object + *-ing* form to show a snapshot of a moment that we saw or heard, or to express that we have seen part of an incomplete or repeated activity.

We often use *can / could* with verbs of senses (e.g., *feel, see, hear, watch*) when we are speaking at the time of the experience.)

We use *see* + object + (*being*) + past participle as a form of reduced passive when we watch something happening to someone or something else.

We can use *look, feel, smell, sound, taste + like* to talk about similarities.

We can use *look, feel, smell, sound, taste* + adjective to give opinions.

 GO ONLINE for the complete grammar reference.

160

Unit 3

Quantifiers

ALL

We use *all* before numbers and plural nouns. We also use *all of the* or *all the* + plural and uncountable nouns.

We use subject pronoun + *all* or *all of* + object pronoun.

EITHER / NEITHER

We use *either / neither* + singular noun + singular verb.

We use *either of the* and *neither of the* + plural noun + singular verb. We also use *either of* and *neither of* + object pronoun. After *either of the* and *neither of the* we can also use a plural verb. This is more common in informal English.

We use *neither ... nor* and *either ... or* to talk about two possibilities.

EVERY AND EACH

We use *every* and *each* + singular noun + singular verb. *Every* and *each* are often interchangeable.

However, we tend to use *each* to distinguish individual differences. Also, we do not use *every* to talk about just two items.

We can say *each / every one of* and also *each of*.

MUCH, MANY, A LOT OF / LOTS OF / PLENTY OF, A LITTLE, A FEW

We use *many* and *a few* with countable nouns and *much* and *a little* with uncountable nouns. We can use *a lot of / lots of / loads of / plenty of* with both countable and uncountable nouns.

We generally use *much* and *many* in negative sentences and questions and we generally use *a lot of / lots of / loads of / plenty of* in affirmative sentences.

Much and *many* are common in affirmative sentences in a formal style.

Comparative sayings

USE

We can use various words and structures to express the degree of difference between things we are comparing. Some of the most common and useful words and structures include:

- *nowhere near / nothing like / (not) nearly / not / not quite / almost / just / every bit / twice / three times* + *as* (adjective/adverb) *as*
- *much / far / a lot / a great deal / considerably / significantly / 10% / five hours / a little / a (little) bit / slightly / no* + comparative adjective or comparative adverb
- *much / many / far / a great deal / a lot / a little / a bit* + *more / fewer / less* + noun
- *as much / many* + noun *as*
- *the more ..., the more ...*

We can use this structure when one situation automatically results in another situation. We use *the ..., the ...* with the comparative forms of adjectives/adverbs, verb clauses and nouns.

We can use *more and more, fewer and fewer, less and less* + noun and *bigger and bigger, longer and longer*, etc. to give emphasis and to show the difference is increasing.

Articles

A / AN (THE INDEFINITE ARTICLE)

The basic use of *a / an* is when we are talking about something specific, but we don't know or don't specify the exact thing. For example, when we first mention something.

We use *a / an* when we are talking in general about one example of a class (but not about the whole class).

We use *a / an* in phrases such as *once a week, twice a year*.

We use *a / an* when we introduce new information.

We use *a / an* for a member of a group or profession.

We use *a / an* to express *one*.

THE (THE DEFINITE ARTICLE)

The basic use of *the* is when both the speaker and the listener know the specific thing being talked about. For example, because it has previously been mentioned or when it is the only one.

We use *the* with a singular countable noun to talk in general about a whole class.

We use *the* with a plural or uncountable noun + *of* + phrase to generalize.

We use *the* with superlative adjectives.

We use *the* with adjectives that describe groups.

We use *the* with nationality adjectives and some countries.

We use *the* with adjectives to refer to general abstract ideas.

We use *the* with the physical environment.

We use *the* with unique items and famous organizations.

We use *the* in prepositional phrases with an uncountable noun + *of*.

NO ARTICLE (OR THE ZERO ARTICLE)

The basic use of no article is with uncountable or plural nouns when we are talking about people or things in general.

We use no article in some common expressions with *work, school, university, college, church, prison,* and *bed* when we talk about the activity that usually happens there.

We use no article after phrases like *amount of, number of, kind of, sort of*.

We use no article with abstract nouns, languages, or nationalities.

We use no article with proper nouns and most countries.

We use no article with some common fixed expressions.

 GO ONLINE for the complete grammar reference.

Unit 4

Talking about the future

BE GOING TO

We use *be going to* + infinitive to talk about intentions and plans, and to make predictions based on direct evidence.

WILL

We use *will* and *won't* + infinitive to talk about

- predictions or future facts that we are certain about or predictions we are less certain about (often with *probably*),
- predictions based on personal opinion,
- promises and hopes for the future, and
- things we decide to do at the moment of speaking, including spontaneous decisions, offers, requests, and promises.

PRESENT TENSES

We use the present continuous to talk about personal arrangements which are arranged, agreed, or finalized for a future time or date.

We use the simple present to talk about future events that are fixed because they are based on a schedule, calendar, or timetable.

FUTURE CONTINUOUS AND FUTURE PERFECT

We use the future continuous with a future time expression to talk about actions that will be in progress at a definite time in the future.

We also use the future continuous to describe a future action that is fixed or decided. A time expression is not always necessary. Note that the meaning here is not continuous.

We use the future perfect to talk about actions or events that will be completed before a definite time in the future.

We also use the future perfect continuous to talk about actions that will continue up to a definite time in the future.

OTHER EXPRESSIONS FOR TALKING ABOUT THE FUTURE

We use *be (just) about to* + infinitive and *be on the verge / point of* + *-ing* to describe something that will or may happen very soon.

We use *aim to / plan to / hope to / expect to* + infinitive to express future plans, expectations, and hopes.

We can use *be to / be set to / be due to* + infinitive to talk about formal or officially arranged events. This is common in news reports or other official documents.

Noun phrases

FORM

A noun phrase consists of a main noun (the head noun), the parts which come before the main noun (pre-modification), and the parts which come after the main noun (post-modification).

USE

Pre-modification can consist of:

- determiners — *a, the, some, several, every, this / that, these / those*
- numbers and ordinals — *six, thousands of, first,* etc.
- possessives — *my, their, the organization's*
- adjectives and adverbs + adjectives — *unusual, biggest, really incredible*
- nouns — *TV, government, family*

Post-modification can consist of:

- prepositional phrases — *about his childhood, for students*
- participle clauses — *selling chocolate, made from glass*
- relative clauses — *which everyone knows, who I'm talking about*

We often use various types of pre- and post-modification in the same sentence.

We can also use adverb phrases such as *next door*.

We commonly use phrases that begin with prepositions (*of, in, to,* etc.) to post-modify a noun. Common patterns of post-modification include a noun followed by:

- preposition + noun phrase or pronoun
- preposition + *-ing* form
- preposition + question word/*whether* + clause
- preposition + question word/*whether* + *to* infinitive
- *to* infinitive
- *for* + object + to infinitive

 GO ONLINE for the complete grammar reference.

Unit 5

Relative clauses

USE

We can describe relative clauses as defining and non-defining. We use defining relative clauses to identify who or what we are talking about. We use non-defining relative clauses to give additional information about a person or thing.

We often use relative clauses to avoid repeating words or to combine two clauses.

We usually use *whom* instead of *who* in formal situations when we are referring to the object of the clause. In correct formal and written language *whom* should always be used after a preposition, but in everyday speech we usually do not follow this rule.

DEFINING RELATIVE CLAUSES

In defining relative clauses we can leave out the relative pronoun when it identifies the object of the verb.

When a relative pronoun is followed by the verb *be* we can leave out *be* and the relative pronoun. Sometimes we call this a reduced relative clause.

We can use the relative adverbs *when* and *that* (for time), *why* (for reasons), and *where* (for places). We usually leave out *why* after the reason, *when* after some time phrases, and *where* after *somewhere*, *everywhere*, *anywhere*, and *nowhere*.

In very formal language, we can separate a preposition from the verb/adjective/noun that it combines with.

NON-DEFINING RELATIVE CLAUSES

A non-defining relative clause can appear in the middle or at the end of a sentence.

We cannot leave out the relative pronoun in non-defining relative clauses.

We often use quantifiers such as *all*, *both*, *either*, *neither*, *much*, and *many* + *of* before *whom* or *which*, but not other relative pronouns, in non-defining relative clauses.

Whoever, whatever, whichever, whenever, wherever, and however

USE

We can use *whatever*, *whichever*, and *whoever* to mean "it doesn't matter what/which/who." They can be used as the subject or the object of the clause. (*Whomever* is also possible but is rarely used in contemporary English, and sounds very formal.)

They can be used as the subject of the clause.

They can also be used as the object of the clause.

We use *whenever*, *wherever*, and *however* at the beginning of an adverbial clause with the meaning "it doesn't matter when/where/how."

We also use *however* before an adjective or adverb.

Whenever can also have a similar meaning to "every time."

We can use *whichever*, *whoever*, *whenever*, *wherever*, and *whatever* to finish an open-ended list. The meaning is similar to "etc." or "and so on."

We can often use *whatever* or *whichever* instead of *whoever*, *whenever*, and *wherever*.

When the phrases are used as two words they show surprise or difficulty in understanding something. We can also use *why ever* in this way. For example, *Whoever came up with this idea is a genius!*

Whatever can be used alone as a rather rude reply, meaning "I don't care" or "I'm not interested in what you're saying."

Whatsoever is used after a negative phrase, for emphasis. It has a similar meaning to "at all."

We can use *whatever*, *whichever*, *wherever*, *whenever*, *whoever*, and *however* as short answers on their own to mean "anything," "anywhere," "at any time," "anyone," or "in any way."

Participle phrases and clauses

FORM

There are three main participles:

- the present participle — *asking, standing, speaking*
- the past participle — *asked, stood, spoken*
- the perfect participle — *having asked, having spoken*

Note that we often use the past participle to express passive meaning. We can also use the other participles in the passive voice, such as *being asked, having been asked*.

To form the negative, we put *not* before the participle: *not speaking, not being asked*.

A participle clause is formed when a participle is followed by an object, a complement, or an adverbial phrase.

USE

Participle clauses often, but not always, enable us to be more efficient with the language and use fewer words. In particular, they can be used in place of subject clauses with conjunctions. Participle clauses generally sound quite formal and are used more in writing than in speech. We use them to express reason, result and condition; to show the sequence of events; and after certain prepositions and conjunctions.

 GO ONLINE for the complete grammar reference.

Unit 6

Expressing obligation, prohibition, and advice

OBLIGATION

We use *must* and *have to* to express obligation. We use *had to* as the past tense of both *must* and *have to*. We use *can't* as the negative of *must*.

We can also use *need to* to express obligation and necessity. In more formal contexts, we can also use phrases such as *be compulsory* and *be obligatory*.

We also use *be supposed to*, but this can suggest that people sometimes may not comply.

LACK OF OBLIGATION

We use *don't have to* to express a lack of obligation, in other words to say that someone is not obliged to do something.

We can also use *don't need to*.

We can also use the phrase *be not necessary*.

PROHIBITION

We use *can't*, *couldn't*, and *not be able to* to express prohibition.

We can also use *be not allowed to*.

We also use *be not supposed to*, but this can suggest that people sometimes may not comply.

ADVICE OR SUGGESTION

We use *should(n't)* and *must* to give advice and make strong suggestions.

We can also use *had better (not)* to express what we think is the correct or best thing to do.

Retrospection

ADVICE OR SUGGESTION

We use *ought (not) to* to give advice and make strong suggestions. We generally do not use *ought to* in direct questions and negatives.

RETROSPECTION

We use *ought to have* to criticize things we or other people did or didn't do in the past and to suggest a better alternative.

Modals of speculation

USE

We can express probability, likelihood, supposition, and speculation by using modal verbs (e.g., *might*, *could*). We use them to say how certain we are about something based on evidence or our experience.

When speculating about the present or future, modal verbs are followed by an infinitive without to.

When speculating about the past, they are followed by a perfect infinitive without to. The verb form can be simple (*must have done*), continuous (*must have been doing*) or passive (*must have been done*).

SPECULATION ABOUT THE PRESENT AND FUTURE

We use *must* and *have to* to say we are certain that something is true at the moment of speaking.

We use *can't* to say we are certain that something is not true at the moment of speaking.

We use *can* to say that something is often, but not always, true.

We use *will / won't* to predict what we think is or is not true.

We use *may (not) / might (not)* or *could* (but not *could not*) to say that it is possible something is or is not true, but we do not know for sure. *Might* and *could* are weaker than *may*.

We use *should (not)* to say we expect that something is or will be true. *Ought to* has the same meaning, but it is less commonly used.

SPECULATION ABOUT THE PAST

We use *must* to say we are certain that something happened.

We use *can't / couldn't* (but not *mustn't*) to say we are certain that something did not happen.

We use *may (not) / might (not)* or *could* (but not *could not*) to say that it is possible something did or did not happen, but we do not know for sure.

We use *will / won't* to say it is likely that something did or did not happen.

 GO ONLINE for the complete grammar reference.

Unit 7

Conditionals

ZERO CONDITIONAL

We use the zero conditional when one situation automatically results from another. This is normally used with present tenses, but can also be used with real situations in the past.

FIRST CONDITIONAL

We use the first conditional to talk about a present or future situation that is possible or probable.

SECOND CONDITIONAL

We use the second conditional to talk about a present or future situation that is unreal because it is imaginary or hypothetical.

THIRD CONDITIONAL

We use the third conditional to talk about a hypothetical situation in the past with a past consequence/outcome. It is formed with a past perfect tense in the if clause and *would* (or other modal verbs, such as *may*, *might*, *could,* or *should*) in the result clause, followed by the perfect infinitive.

MIXED CONDITIONALS

We can mix conditionals when the time reference in the if clause is different from the time reference in the main clause.
For a hypothetical situation in the past with a present consequence/outcome, we use past perfect + *would / might / could / should*.
For a hypothetical situation in the present with a past consequence/outcome, we use simple past/continuous + *would / might / could / should have.*

Structures for unreal situations

USE

We use *wish / if only* and other structures to talk about things that we would like to change now or in the future and to express regret about past actions or events.
We use *wish / if only* + simple past for regrets about a present situation or state.
We use *wish / if only* + past perfect for regrets about the past.
Wish and *if only* have the same meaning, but *if only* is more emphatic. We often explain our wishes and regrets by adding a clause before or after the *wish / if only* clause.
We use *wish* + subject + *would* + infinitive without to to complain about what someone does or doesn't do, or to show we are annoyed or frustrated by an action or habit. The subjects in the the *wish*-clause and *would*-clause need to be different.
We use *wish / if only* + subject + *could* + infinitive without to to talk about ability or permission in the present.

Similarly, we use *wish / if only* + subject + *could* + *have* + past participle to talk about ability or permission in the past.
We can also use *would rather / sooner* to talk about wishes and preferences, but *would rather* is more common. If the alternative to our preference is not clear from the context we use *than* + infinitive to explain.
When the subject and object of the wish is the same we use *would rather / sooner* + infinitive without to to talk about present wishes or preferences.
We can also use *would rather / sooner* to talk about past wishes or preferences. When the subject of *would rather / sooner* and of the *wish*-clause are the same, we use *have* + past participle.

They'd rather have spoken to you in person than by phone.

When the subject of *would rather / sooner* and of the *wish*-clause are different, we use a past tense to talk about present or future situations.
To talk about past situations when the subject of *would rather / sooner* and of the *wish*-clause are different, we use the past perfect, simple past, or past continuous.
We use the phrase *It's (high / about) time* + subject + simple past/continuous to talk about things we want to happen now or in the immediate future.
We can use the subjunctive in the structures shown below. This is considered more formal or old-fashioned by some people.

Alternatives to *if*

USE

In sentences with auxiliary verbs *should* or *were* (second conditionals) or *had* (third conditionals) we can reverse the auxiliaries and their subjects and leave out *if*. This is more common in formal English.
Some words and expressions can be used in all conditionals with a similar meaning to *if*, for example: *provided that*, *as long as,* and *on condition that.*
No matter how / who / what / where is used to say that the outcome will be the same regardless of the circumstances.
Whether or not also means that the outcome will be the same regardless of the circumstances.
Unless is used with a positive verb and has the same meaning as *if* with a negative verb. *Unless* cannot be used in third conditional sentences.
We can use *imagine*, *suppose*, *supposing,* and *assuming* as alternatives to *if.*

 GO ONLINE for the complete grammar reference.

Unit 8

Ellipsis with nouns

USE

We use ellipsis when we want to leave out words in a sentence to avoid repeating the same words or ideas. We often leave out several words in a sentence because we want to be more efficient with our language, and we know the person we are speaking to already understands the context or the ideas we are talking about. However, we can only leave out words to avoid repetition if the meaning is clear without them.

The following words can be left out to avoid repetition if the meaning is clear without them:

- words after the auxiliaries *be, do,* and *have*
- words after modal verbs
- infinitives in a *to* infinitive clause
- words in *if* clauses
- nouns after a number, a quantifier (such as *any, some, loads*), a superlative adjective, or *this / that / these / those.*

Ellipsis in clauses

USE

The following words can be left out to avoid repetition if the meaning is clear without them:

- clauses after question words (such as *how, where, who*).
- main verbs when there are two clauses with the same structure and the same verb. If there is an auxiliary verb this is also left out.

 GO ONLINE for the complete grammar reference.

Unit 9

Passive voice

FORM

We form the passive with *be* + past participle. We can use the passive in all tenses, with modal verbs, and in the infinitive.

PASSIVE WITH VERBS WITH TWO OBJECTS

Some verbs can have a direct object and an indirect object. In passive sentences, either of these objects can be the subject. When the indirect object comes after the passive verb, we put either *to* or *for*.

> *People in the camp were offered temporary shelter.*
> *Temporary shelter was offered to people in the camp.*

USE

We use the passive for various reasons:

- to allow the main focus (usually the existing topic) to come at the beginning of the sentence or clause; if we say who or what does the action (the agent), we use *by*
- to keep the focus on the action by not mentioning the agent, usually because the agent is not known, is not important, or is obvious
- to create a more impersonal or objective style, for example in official, business, or academic contexts
- to report information in an impersonal way, using verbs like *believe, claim, estimate, expect, hope, report, say, think, reckon, rumor,* and *understand*

Tag questions

USE

We use tag questions to check information or to find out if someone agrees with us. We use falling intonation if we are fairly sure about the information and are asking someone to confirm it or agree. We use rising intonation if we are not sure about the information.

We use tag questions to show that we are paying attention to what someone is saying and to encourage further conversation.

We can soften imperatives with tag questions using *will / would / could*. The tag question is always positive, even when the main part of the sentence is negative.

With verb forms that use an auxiliary or a modal verb, we use the modal or auxiliary verb, not the main verb, in the tag question.

When we use negative words such as *no, no one, hardly, nothing, never, nobody,* the main verb and the tag question are both positive.

When the subject is *everyone, no one, someone,* etc. we use a plural verb in the tag question.

We can use positive statement + positive tag question when we make a guess and then ask to see if our guess is correct, often to show surprise or to challenge an idea.

Use of the passive in impersonal reporting

FORM

We can use reporting verbs in the passive after *it* or other subjects.

It + *be* + past participle of reporting verb + (*that*) …

> *It is reported that around half a million people joined the protests.*

Subject + *be* + past participle of reporting verb + *to* infinitive …

> *The medicine is claimed to have cured most occurrences of the disease.*

USE

We use reporting verbs such as *believe, claim, consider, know, report, say,* and *think* in the passive to talk about general beliefs and ideas. We often use passive structures in news reports and formal written English to make a text or report more impersonal. We use passive reporting verbs when we don't know or don't want to say who the information came from.

 GO ONLINE for the complete grammar reference.

Unit 10

It as introductory subject

USE

We often start a sentence with *it* as an introductory or "empty" subject, followed by the verb *be*. Using *it* in this way makes a statement more objective. The most common structures are:

- *It* + adjective/noun + infinitive
- *It* + adjective + *for / of* + object + infinitive
- *It* + adjective + *that* clause
- We use *it's time* + infinitive to indicate that an action is needed. We can add *for* + object to say who should do it.
- We use *it's high time / about time* + pronoun/noun + simple past to express a present wish that sth be done very soon.
- *It's the first / second / third time* + present perfect

Sometimes *it* is not followed by an infinitive or *that* clause. We use this structure to say that something is or is not desirable:

- *It's* + adjective + question word
- *It's* + *no good / (not) worth / not much use* + *-ing* form

Adverbs

POSITION OF ADVERBIALS

Single-word adverbs generally go in the middle of a clause. Longer adverbial phrases generally go at the beginning or at the end.

Adverbs of frequency (*often*, *usually*, *occasionally*) generally go before a simple verb, after the (first) auxiliary verb, or after the verb *be*, and can be at the beginning or end of a clause.

Adverbs of relative time (*already*, *just*) generally go before the verb, after the (first) auxiliary verb, or after the verb *be*.

Adverbs of degree (*very*, *really*, *so*, *extremely*, *quite*, *really*) generally go directly before the word they modify. They generally go before the main verb when there is an auxiliary.

Adverbs of manner (*slowly*, *rapidly*, *suddenly*) generally go after the verb and its object. Some can also go before the verb, especially if the object is long.

Adverbs and adverbials of place (*on the coast*) and time (*on the weekend*, *yesterday*) generally go after the verb and its object. They can also go at the beginning of a sentence or clause.

Adverbs that comment on or express attitude towards a whole clause or sentence generally go before the clause or sentence, but can possibly go after.

ADVERB COLLOCATIONS

Examples of common verb + adverb collocations are *clearly remember*, *desperately need*, and *eagerly await*. Examples of common adverb + adjective collocations are *perfectly clear*, *blatantly obvious*, and *bitterly disappointed*.

ADVERBS WITH TWO FORMS

Some adverbs have two spelling forms: with and without the *-ly* ending. These adverbs have different meanings and can be easily confused. Some common adverbs with two forms are: *easy / easily*, *free / freely*, *hard / hardly*, *high / highly*, *late / lately*, *most / mostly*, *sure / surely*, *wide / widely*.

Discourse markers

USE

We use discourse markers to make it easier for our listeners and readers to follow and participate.

We can use discourse markers in speaking and writing. They can be formal or informal, and they can be a single word such as an adverb or a whole phrase. They can come anywhere in a sentence depending on our message. We use discourse markers to:

Show how ideas link together

- for contrast — *although*, *but*, *despite*, *however*, *in spite of*, *nevertheless*, *on the one / other hand*, *on the contrary*
- order — *first*, *firstly*, *first of all*, *next*, *afterwards*, *secondly*, *finally*, *last of all*, *lastly*
- purpose — *to*, *in order to*, *so as to*, *in case*
- reason — *because*, *as*, *since*, *due to*, *hence*, *owing to*, *thus*
- result — *as a result*, *consequently*, *otherwise*, *so*, *therefore*
- similarity — *similarly*, *likewise*, *equally*

Add to previous ideas

- less formal — *also*, *additionally*, *alternatively*
- formal — *moreover*, *furthermore*, *in addition*, *indeed*, *further*
- speaking only — *besides*, *too*, *what's more*

Give examples — *for example*, *for instance*, *that's to say*

Generalize — *broadly speaking*, *on the whole*, *generally*, *in general*, *to a certain extent*

Clarify — *after all*, *in other words*, *in a sense*, *I mean*

Show our attitude toward what we are saying — *fortunately*, *frankly*, *obviously*, *of course*, *naturally*, *sadly*, *to be honest*

To Introduce an unwelcome idea — *I'm afraid*, *I regret*, *I'm sorry but...*, *unfortunately*

Draw attention to what we are about to say — *actually*, *basically*, *right*, *so*, *well*, *you know*

Change direction in a conversation — *anyway*, *as I was saying*, *by the way*, *in any case*, *incidentally*, *regarding*, *speaking of*

Show we are finishing what we have to say

- formal writing or speaking — *to conclude*, *to sum up*
- informal speaking — *anyway*, *OK*

 GO ONLINE for the complete grammar reference.

Unit 11

Verb patterns in reported speech

USE

We use the following verb patterns in reported speech:

- verb + (*that*) clause with *acknowledge, admit, agree, assert, claim, complain, confirm, deny, emphasize, explain, insist, promise, recommend, repeat, reveal, say, suggest, think*, or *warn*
- verb + object + (*that*) clause with *assure, convince, inform, promise, reassure, remind, tell*, or *warn*
- verb + *to* infinitive with *agree, ask, claim, demand, offer, promise*, or *refuse*
- verb + object + *to* infinitive with *advise, ask, beg, encourage, invite, order, persuade, remind, tell, urge*, or *warn*

To report a negative statement we use verb + object + *not* + *to* infinitive. Structures include:

- verb + *to* + perfect infinitive with *claim*
- verb + *-ing* form with *admit, deny, recommend*, or *suggest*
- verb + preposition + *-ing* form/object with *apologize for, complain about, insist on, object to*, or *reflect on*
- verb + object + preposition + *-ing* form/object with *accuse … of, compliment … on, congratulate … on, praise … for, remind … about, talk … into, thank … for*, or *warn … against / about*
- verb + (object) + *if / whether* with *ask (someone), inquire, want to know*, or *wonder*
- verb + (object) + question word with *ask (someone), describe, inquire, explain, suggest, want to know*, or *wonder*

Subjunctive and *should*

SUBJUNCTIVE AND *SHOULD*

The present subjunctive is used in reported speech to talk about a demand or proposal in the present or past.

The subjunctive uses the base form of the verb (*she go, we be*) and is quite formal. The form would be verb + (*that*) + object + subjunctive with *ask, demand, insist, recommend, request*, or *suggest*:

> *The Environment Agency insisted (that) businesses take action on reducing carbon emissions.*

Note that *do* is not used in the negative.

> *We ask (that) the minister not ignore the protests.*

Also note that *should* + infinitive is less formal than a subjunctive and more commonly used. There is little or no difference in meaning.

> *They suggest (that) households should try to reduce the amount of water they use.*

Causatives with *have* and *get*

CAUSATIVE SENTENCES

We use the following structures in causative sentences:

Subject + *have* / *get* + sth/sb + past participle
Subject + *get* + sb/sth + *to* infinitive
Subject + *have* + sb + infinitive without *to* + (sth)
Subject + *have* + sb/sth + *-ing* form (sth)

SIMILAR STRUCTURES

We use the following structures in sentences where something is experienced:

Subject + *have* / *get* + sth/sb + past participle
Subject + *have* / *get* + sb/sth + infinitive without *to* / *-ing* form
Subject + *not have* + sb/sth + *-ing* form + (sth)

CAUSATIVE SENTENCES

We use *have* and *get* in various structures to talk about arranging something or causing something to happen. These include:

- *have* / *get* + something/someone + past participle, for various arrangements, often when we use a service. *Get* is generally used in more informal contexts.
- *have* + someone + infinitive without *to*, when we arrange for someone to do something for us, or we make them do it.
- *have* + someone + *-ing*, to show or emphasize activity or duration.

SIMILAR STRUCTURES

We use a few structures with *have* or *get* to talk about things that happen to us. These include:

- *have* / *get* + something/someone + infinitive without *to* or *-ing* form to describe something we experience or have
- *have* / *get* + something + past participle, used when something unwelcome or unpleasant happens to somebody/something
- *won't have* + someone + *-ing* or infinitive without *to*, used to say we will not tolerate something or we object to something

 GO ONLINE for the complete grammar reference.

Unit 12

Cleft sentences

FORM

We can form cleft sentences with *it*, *what*, and *all*.

It + *be* + noun phrase + relative clause

It	*be*	**noun** phrase	**relative clause**
It	is	the noise of the traffic	that keeps me awake.
It	was	my brother	who left the keys in the front door.

What + clause + *be* + phrase

What	clause	*be*	phrase
What	keeps me awake	is	the noise of the traffic.
What	would really help	is	if you could clean up before people arrive.

USE

We use cleft sentences to create emphasis. "Cleft" means divided into two parts. The part that we want to emphasize comes after *be*. For example, look at this sentence:

They didn't like the steep steps up to the front door.

We can use a cleft sentence structure to emphasize one part of the sentence:

It was the steep steps up to the front door that they didn't like.

What they didn't like was the steep steps up to the front door.

The verb *be* is usually singular after a *What* clause, but it can be singular or plural if it is followed by a plural noun phrase.

We can emphasize an action, or even an adverbial, with a cleft sentence. We can also use phrases like "The person who/that …," "The thing which/that …," "The place where…," "The day when…," and "The reason why…."

Inversion

INVERSION

Some emphatic structures require the normal sentence word order to be changed by inverting the order of the subject and the auxiliary. This inversion is most common in more formal writing and speech, in literary and academic contexts, for example.

Words and expressions that are negative or restrictive are followed by inverted structures when they begin a sentence or clause. These include time phrases, such as *never* (*before*), *no sooner … than*, *at no time*, *not since / until*, *only when* and *hardly … when*, as well as words and phrases, such as *by no means*, *little*, *not only*, *on no account*, *rarely*, *scarcely*, *seldom*, and *under no circumstances*.

After inverted words and phrases the auxiliary or modal verb comes before the subject.

If there is no auxiliary or modal verb, *do* + subject + infinitive is used instead.

INVERSION WITH *SO* AND *SUCH*

We can use *so* + adjective/adverb… *that*:

So important is the history of navigation that there are museums devoted to the topic.

We can use *such* …+ noun … *that*:

Such was the wealth created by the discovery of new lands that European cities grew rapidly.

Using auxiliaries to avoid repetition

AUXILIARIES

We often replace verbs and verb phrases with an auxiliary verb to avoid repeating a verb or verb phrase that has already been mentioned.

I don't drive, but a few of my colleagues do. (do = drive)

They arrived a few minutes before I did. (did = arrived)

We can also use a form of *have* or *do* + *so*. This is usually in more formal contexts and only when referring to the same topic as previously mentioned. We do not usually use *do* + *so* in short replies.

We should all try to do some physical activity each day. The benefits of doing so are obvious.

We also use auxiliary verbs in short replies with *so / neither / nor*.

I don't think it's a good idea and neither does Mary Jones.

ONE / ONES

We can use *one* or *ones* to avoid repeating a noun or noun phrase that has already been mentioned.

We use *one* to substitute singular nouns and *ones* to substitute plural nouns.

We do not use *one(s)* for uncountable nouns.

I prefer fresh vegetables to canned ones.

We can leave out *one(s)* after a superlative adjective, *this*, *that*, *these*, and *those*, and some determiners such as *either* and *neither*.

That ship is the biggest (one) that's ever been built.

 GO ONLINE for the complete grammar reference.